Gandhian Approach to Development and Social Work

About the Author

Prof. K.D. Gangrade (*b.* 1926), Vice-Chairman of Gandhi Smriti and Darshan Samiti, New Delhi, has been a former Pro-Vice-Chancellor, Dean, Faculty of Social Sciences, and Head, Department of Social Work, University of Delhi. He has also taught at the University of Manchester, U.K. and Tata Institute of Social Sciences, Mumbai. He has served the United Nations as well in various capacities. Prof. Gangrade has 12 books to his credit. He is recipient of Samaj Gaurav (1988) from the Bhartiya Sangthan, Rashtra Ratna (1998) from Viswa Jagriti Mission, and Radha Raman Award (2000) for outstanding contribution to education.

Gandhian Approach to Development and Social Work

K. D. Gangrade
Gandhi Smriti and Darshan Samiti
Gandhi Darshan, Rajghat, New Delhi

Published for

Gandhi Smriti and Darshan Samiti, New Delhi

By

CONCEPT PUBLISHING COMPANY PVT. LTD.
NEW DELHI-110059

ISBN : 978-81-8069-177-5

Edition 2022

Published and Printed by

Concept
Since 1974

Concept Publishing Company Pvt. Ltd.
A/15-16, Commercial Block, Mohan Garden,
New Delhi-110059 (INDIA)
T : +91 11 41101460
E : publishing@conceptpub.com, *W* : www.conceptpub.com

Cataloging in Publication Data--Courtesy: D.K. Agencies (P) Ltd. <docinfo@dkagencies.com>

Gangrade, K. D. (Kesharichand Dasharathasa), 1926-
Gandhian approach to development and social work / K.D. Gangrade.
p. cm
Includes bibliographical references.
Includes index.
ISBN 9788180691775

1. Gandhi, Mahatma, 1869-1948.—Political and social views. 2. Social service—India
I. Title.

DDC 361.309.54 21

Preface

Mahatma Gandhi said, "I want to write many "new things" but they must all be written on the Indian slate. I would gladly borrow from the west when I can return the amount with decent interest". (Gandhi M.K. 1924, Young India, June 26, p.209) This basic philosophy has neither been followed by the Indian educationists nor by the professional Social Work Educators.

An important Social Work Educator, from the Philippines had once said that although Indians were very proud of their nationalism what they taught in their courses of Social Work was just stinking American material. Recently, an eminent American Social Work Educator of the same hue had found that the Schools of Social Work in India were very conservative in their approach and subservient to the establishment. The Deans in the U.S.A had in 1982 issued a stern warning to the Reagan administration for its education policy. Can our Deans, Directors or Heads of Department of Social Work do that?

While Indian Schools (Department or Institutes) serve unabashedly American and western material, they make only a peripheral grafting of the thought of the great social reformers and activists of the Indian nation. The graft naturally becomes very artificial. It indeed hangs loose from the rest of the material and can be treated merely as a ritual that could well be discarded as something alien to the hardcore of the syllabi one teaches. The materials are in no way related to the profession per se, much less to its method.

Most of the Indian teachers dismiss Gandhi as totally irrelevant to the teaching and practice of social work as an Australian educator found them to do so. Gandhi was a great Social Activist but our social work practitioners do not find any material of relevance in Gandhi that would enrich the methods of the profession. Whereas Gandhi was quoted exhaustively by Prof.Aliniky, to draw sanctions for his theory and methods, his dismissal seems to be ironical. Is it akin to the exile of Marx from Germany?

The profession shows great deal of impertinence and immaturity when we find that it has refused to draw from Gandhi on methods of individual and group help as well as social action to build its own infrastructure of theories or methods. The situation looks equally dismal when we find that social workers of stable societies fail to compile materials for building infrastructure of theories from the society itself which though impoverished in goods, so rich in relationship of therapeutic value.

The situation becomes worse confounded when we find that we are trying in vain, to cling to types of professionalism and dogmas borrowed from the U.S.A, which interesting enough the thinking elite of the West have now given up. The latter's emphasis is on development social action, nonviolence, conflictiology and development of social networks as a universal agency, that might replace the outmoded bunch of classical institutions - provides pointers to the direction of dynamic experiment in the midst of which the Western civilization finds itself today. On development Gandhi said: "I will give you a talisman. Whenever you are in doubt or when the self becomes too much with you, apply the following test. Recall the face of the poorest and the weakest man whom you may have seen and ask yourself if the step you contemplate is going to be of any use to him. Will he gain anything by it? Will it restore him to a control over his own life and destiny? In other words, will it lead to Swaraj for the hungry and spiritually starving millions? Then you will find your doubts and yourself melting away."

This is the best cardinal principle which all workers should follow who intend or work with people. For a development worker it provides a best guide and direction.

Gandhi insisted on purity of means to achieve ends. The ideal Gandhian way of thinking about the matter is to do away with the distinction between means and ends altogether. Gandhi saw the relationship between these two not in the mechanical cause-and-effeet way that we usually do; instead he saw the relationship as hydraulic, with one flowing naturally from the other. He also employed a biological metaphor, describing the connection between the means and the ends as that between a seed and the tree that emerges naturally from it(See also, Juergensmeyer Mark, Fighting with Gandhi, Harper & Row Publishers, San Francisco, London, 1984, p.41).

The book will remove many cob-webs which are existing in our minds. It will help us to understand and develop intimate relationship between Gandhian Approach to Development and Social Work. The chapter on NGOs was originally written jointly with Dr. R.Sooryamoorthy of Loyola College, Trivandrum.

I am extremely thankful to Dr.Savita Singh, Director of Gandhi Smriti and Darshan Samiti, New Delhi, to provide a congenial environment to complete this volume.

Thanks are also due to Dr. Sita Ojha who assisted me at several steps in my task. My thanks are also due to my staff: Mr.Ramesh who compared the computer print out from the manuscript; Mr.Rizwan shared the main burden getting several computer prints out and ultimately giving it a final shape; Mrs. Seema also put out some chapters from computer and Mrs. Samiksha Mudgal also did one of the chapters of the book.

Gandhi Darshan, Rajghat,
New Delhi

—K.D.Gangrade

Contents

1

Gandhian Approach to Development and Social Work

ABSTRACT

The concept of Gandhian social work or constructive programmes is far wider than we understand it. It is not only philosophical and theoretical but also experimental in life.

Gandhiji's dream of building a society with the active participation of people still remains a distant goal. The concept of development has been looked at from a different angle than merely as the gross national product to improve the economic condition of the people. Development should not lead to tensions and inequalities. People have been disenchanted with the development workers who have changed from innovative missionary workers to workers for the maintenance of the status quo *and creators of institutions as designed by aid-giving agencies. The professional social workers have also not given a good account of themselves in enlisting and encouraging people's participation in the planned development of the country.*

II
GANDHIJI'S DREAMS AND IDEALS

Gandhiji said: "I shall work for an India in which the poorest shall feel that it is their country, in whose making they have an effective voice, and an India in which all communities will live in perfect harmony. There can be no room in such an India for the curse of untouchability, for the curse of intoxicating drugs or drinks. Women will enjoy the same rights as men.

Gandhian idealism had nothing to do with the awakening of class consciousness. His scheme of socialism has, as its core the "equality of all individuals", despite diversities in respect of functions they perform in society. *Sarvodaya* or 'Welfare for all' embraces the development of all individuals instead of the welfare of a section of the community at the expense of the rest.

The basic error, according to Gandhiji, consists in an attempt to modernize faster than the conditions of the economy permit. He emphasized the acceptance of the *Swadeshi* approach rather than following western models since many of their approaches, concepts, beliefs, ways of life are in crisis even in their countries of origin.

III
CONCEPT OF DEVELOPMENT

The concept of development refers to the kind of society one is aiming to build. Development policies which concentrate on relieving 'absolute poverty' or on meeting 'basic needs' can properly be adopted as a matter of first priority. However, they should not be seen as policy goals in themselves. Moreover, the satisfaction of basic human needs would be permanently achievable only with structural changes at local, national and international level that would enable those concerned to identify their own needs, mobilize their own resources and shape their future in their own terms.

Development should be understood as a process designed progressively to create conditions in which every person can enjoy, exercise and utilise, under the Rule of Law, all his human rights—whether economic, social, cultural, civil or political. Every person has the right to participate in, and benefit from development in the sense of a progressive improvement in the standards and quality of life. The right to development is to be implemented not only by development aid but by removing the asymmetry in economic relations.

The contrast between the enormous growth in production and productivity in the world in the last decades, and the reality of destitution for so many people, has been due to certain myths which govern the policies of development and the relation between states and peoples' that growth will solve the problem of poverty and that the western style of modernization is development.

Development without people's participation is not genuine development. Assistance will lead to true development only if there is a "political will" obtained by consensus, for its proper utilization. In most cases the people are far removed from policy making and implementation, with the result that aid has often been channelled for personal gain or for repression.

IV
PEOPLE'S PARTICIPATION

People's participation is a necessary precondition for the successful implementation of any programme. This is based on the assumption that the process of people's development is not likely to strike very deep unless the target group themselves are part of it. Participation is a means of reducing power difference and is, therefore, contributory to equalization and social justice.

It should be noted that decentralisation does not increase participation or create new opportunities if the people remain unorganized, and if the government retains the power of decision. There is a deeply rooted belief held by many educated officials and professionals that the poor and illiterate are incapable of improving themselves and must have their decision made for them. This is absolutely incorrect.

V
VOLUNTARY ACTION AND PEOPLE'S PARTICIPATION

Indians have responded in men, money and material to any noble cause. The call to collect funds for Kasturba Gandhi Memorial Trust became a national campaign. The bagmen contributed as eagerly as the rag-men, and donations ranging from rupees three lakhs to rupees 0.25 were offered. The collection exceeded the target of Rs.7.5 million by as much as Rs.13.1 million. In the issue of *Harijan* dated 21st July, 1946 writing about the Kasturba Fund, Gandhiji said that it was necessary to proceed with caution.

In his lifetime Gandhiji promoted various types of constructive programmes. Over the years he added to it, one item after another. But there was an underlying unity in all his endeavours which made the different items of the constructive programmes constitute a single whole. What gave unity to all his activities was Gandhiji's view of the good society, a society which would be in tune with the spirit of India and relevant to its people.

The society envisaged by Gandhiji was to be self-initiated and nonviolent. In it, the individual would have maximum freedom for himself and yet he would be linked to a larger community until, ultimately, all became part of the larger world community. All his actions were governed by his passion for the good society he envisaged.

The leadership of these organizations have not yet passed in the hands of the local people or the so-called beneficiaries or participants. They are considered as subjects to be served. They are organized to utilize the services provided to them. The leadership is in the hands of elderly persons and exhibits a combination of authoritarian and democratic leadership. The comparatively young leaders are found to be more democratic than the elderly leaders. In a number of organizations the office of President and Secretary are inter-locking as these revolve around a few persons.

Three facts about voluntary organizations: (i) There is a countless number of organizations in the country; (ii) There is a large number of people who have no membership either in any association or organization; (iii) There exists in any association or organization, an active minority and an inactive majority among the members. Though these organizations are subject to democratic control, it appears that the actual formulation of policy is in the hands of a few interested individuals. Associations and organizations abound in cities and towns. On the other hand, none or few organisations are found in rural India.

VI
TYPOLOGY, PHASES, STEPS AND ORIENTATION OF WORK

Typology of work is dependent on the characteristics of the people with whom the workers intend to work. The people in any society are stratified according to various parameters. The economic criterion is the easiest and most acceptable. In India, caste also plays an important role in ranking people in different categories. On the economic criterion, the people can be classified into three broad groups: (i) The rich; (ii) The middle class, and (iii) The poor. Chart I on the next page graphically gives the characteristics of the people.

Chart I : Characteristics of the People

R	Knowledge	
	Skill	Strong
I	High Resource Manipulation	Organisational
	Capability	Sinews
C	High Risk Taking Ability	
	Universalistic/World-wide	
H	Exploit Development	
	Perspective	Fully
M	Partial knowledge	
I	Inadequate skill	Weak
D	Low Resource Manipulation	Organisational
D	Low Risk Taking Ability	Capability
L	Universalistic/World-wide	Partial
E	Perspective	Exploitation of
		Development
P	Ignorance	Organisational
O	Very little or No skill	Capacity very
O	Resource Manipulation Capacity	weak or nil
	Minimal	
R	Risk Taking Ability Minimal/	Inability to
	Absent, Narrow World Perspective	exploit
	[focused on survival]	Development

The rich, the middle class and the poor vary considerably as regards the following factors :

1. Availability of economic resources.
2. Ability to mobilize resources.
3. Knowledge and skills or accessibility to knowledge and skills.
4. Organisational ability.
5. Contact with people in power.
6. Membership in social organisations.
7. Aspirations and awareness.

The rich are at the positive end of the continuum, the poor at the negative end and the middle class are somehow in the middle. It is unfortunate that, despite efforts made by government agencies, Gandhian Institutions, voluntary organisations, industrial organisations and professional bodies, the condition of the poor has not changed. Development, with the full participation of the poor, may be the answer to the situation.

The typology of work may be considered as having five phases, fifteen steps and five orientations. Chart II shows the phases, steps and orientations with respect to work with people.

The following flow chart gives the Phases, Steps and Orientation work and Action :

Chart II : Phases, Steps and Orientation of Voluntary Action

Phases	Steps	Orientation
Initiation	Establishing Rapport / Generating confidence / Getting Acceptance programmes	Missionary (worker)
Execution	Identification of needs or problems and planning of activities Generating Resources Implementing / Providing services / Action projects	Executive (Programmes)
Expansion	Evaluating Effectiveness Development of Infrastructure (specialization) Increase of work load	Career (Expansion)
Consolidation	Stabilising operations / Enforcing Rules / Inserving organizational entity	Institutional (Stability)
Decline / Decay/ Renewal / Rebirth	Subjecting people to Rules Emphasising Institutional survival Alienating organization from people Decay / Rebirth	Survival (Maintenance)

VII
COMMUNITY DEVELOPMENT

In the first phase of initiation, or conception, the primary orientation of the workers is missionary. He is inspired by an ideal or a goal dear to his heart. This phase is people-centric, as without their active involvement and participation, nothing can be done. He as an outsider, does not impose his values and programmes on the people. Three steps that are essential in this phase are: (a) Establishing rapport, (b) Generating confidence, and (c) Getting acceptance. These steps will be discussed in detail in the following paragraphs.

There can be various points of entry into a known or an unknown community. But the worker's task will become relatively easy if the organisation which he is representing has credibility in these little communities. If the image is good it would greatly facilitate the work and also help in establishing rapport with the people. The work of the social worker involves building relationships, whether with individuals, groups, communities, representatives, organizations, institutions or the whole community. In any work, a bond must be established between the worker and the people. If that feeling of confidence cannot be inspired, the relationship is not likely to be meaningful enough to cause any change.

The major handicap the worker may face is that he is a stranger to the people. He has no knowledge of the men, their problems and their interpersonal relations. Nor does he know the men of influence. All this information may be gradually obtained and studied. The Gandhian Constructive Workers did not face much difficulty in finding entry to the villages, winning their confidence and acceptance as Gandhiji's name and programmes had already travelled into all the villages from Kashmir to Kanyakumari. On the other hand, professional social workers, or other workers, may have to find their way first to enter into the villages or other communities and win their confidence and get their acceptance.

The methods which may be primarily used during this phase are face to face communication, inter-group meetings, home visits, recreational and cultural activities. The worker has to live a lifestyle which is in conformity to rural norms and customs.

Motivation is a complex phenomenon and involves both altruism and self-interest. However, the danger arises when the worker is so busy creating a situation which will satisfy his own needs that he is unable to respond to the needs of the villagers. When this happens his help may actually be a hindrance, or cease to be conducive to the growth of democratic institutions and the development of local leaders of the villages.

It is important that a worker should undertake an honest self-examination or evaluation. He needs to explain to himself why he wants to help others. This question should also help clarify what are the rewards he seeks for himself—money, prestige, professional advancement, political leadership or research data. The rewards must be examined in terms of what the village needs. They may accept those workers who practice without utilizing much material assistance. They are willing to take risks. They want only know-how or technical help.

The worker, in his visits, finds that the rich people generally respond quickly to his new ideas. The middle group of people listen patiently and take to new innovations after testing and evaluation. They want the worker to obtain material assistance and help for them from external resources in addition to know-how. The poor very rarely respond to his ideas and often fail to express their own needs. They may give lip sympathy to the worker. They may even show that apparently they are interested in their own development.

The worker must bring all these three groups together. This he does by working through the leaders of the various factions and groups present in the village. It is not possible for a worker to work with each and every member of a village community. He works with the formal and informal leaders of the village community. He should not take sides or patronize anyone faction or individual in the village.

The worker, who has developed good rapport with people, seeks to increase the amount of satisfaction in interpersonal relations and co-operative work among different people groups. With his skilful handling of the situations, he so organizes his meetings with the people that they feel comfortable and free to verbalise. In the beginning, the worker is the cementing force between the various factions and groups in the village. He is often the only link and the influence that brings these factions to work together. If the worker is accepted, liked and trusted, villagers identify with him and express their needs and problems. But the worker must safeguard against making people permanently dependent on him. He must gradually and slowly pass this responsibility on the people as the community develops the skill to carry on by itself.

The second phase, is concerned with the execution and its primary orientation is the programme. In this phase, the worker takes the role of an executive. The worker should become an excellent executive. His method of accomplishing the task should be such as not to lose the missionary zeal. He should continue to prepare the people so that they take his place as early as possible. The three steps important in this phase are: (i) Identification of needs or problems and planning of programmes/activities; (ii) Generating resources; and (iii) Implementing the plan, creating or providing services or improving the existing services.

The role of the worker consists in helping people to become aware of their needs, to assess their resources more realistically, to organize themselves and their resources in such a way to satisfy some of their needs through action projects and in doing so, acquire technique and experience necessary for repeating the process again on their own initiative. It is a process in the sense that it is a dynamic sequence, which being set in motion, supplies its own efforts to move steadily towards the goal of self-improvement. The approach will not allow the worker to degenerate into an executive only interested in programmes, but a builder of society ready to withdraw at the earliest opportunity rather than to have a vested interest in the perpetuation of his role.

The successful completion of the project or projects spreads the message in the area. There is a demand for the worker to take up work with the help of additional workers. The work now does not remain only at the level of education or social awakening. He wants to create the necessary infrastructure to provide specialized services to the people. The worker also begins to take the role of being a liaison. He enables the people to take advantage of various programmes and schemes launched by the government and other agencies—national and international—for rural development. In this, he had to make a special effort to organize the poor to take advantage from the bounties provided by the government and other agencies, national and international.

The next phase is that of expansion. The orientation of the worker becomes careerist when professional expertise is required for specialized services. The original worker now moves to a higher position and he/she is not able to keep in close contact with the people. The three steps necessary in this phase are: (i) Evaluating effectiveness; (ii) Development of infrastructure to provide specialized services and (iii) Increase of workload. The most critical issue is that the expansion of work should not be just for the asking but should be based on proper evaluation. But most of the workers do not follow this principle. They just expand work without preparing or training the workers for the various tasks. The infrastructures are built to ensure the flow of services and provide opportunities to professionals who take to work as a career. The facilitation of this task depends upon the availability of funds.

The expansion phase poses certain risks. It increases the workload which can create problems as regards maintenance of values and standards of the services. By the fourth phase, the worker begins to consolidate the work by giving an institutional shape such as creating buildings and other physical structures. At this phase, the risk is that the activities may become programme-orientated and no longer people-oriented. When that happens, the people are fitted into programmes. People's participation becomes minimal. They mostly become users of services.

This is done to provide stability and operational continuity and for conserving the organization. The institutional order is one of the most important functions in any work to crystallise forces. But without proper checks and balances, some of the people who manage institutions become powerful. They may misuse funds as well as workers to their advantage, especially if they aspire to get into the political arena.

The fourth phase has survival orientation, that is, the maintenance of institutions. The hazard of this phase is that of goal-displacement. Emphasis is likely to be placed on protecting the institutional ethos rather than mobilising, the confidence and faith reposed by the people in the institution. The goal thus gets displaced from people to the programme.

In order that the undesirable aspects, associated with the different phases of development work, may be deliberately warded off, work with the people has to be planned along four steps : (a) Involve the villagers in systematic discussion of their felt needs; (b) Systematic planning to carry out the first self-help project selected by the community; (c) Harnessing the resources of the community for carrying out a concrete project; and (d) Creation of community appreciation and determination to take up additional projects to maintain enthusiasm and spirit of the people.

VIII
THE ROLE OF WORKERS

The role of the worker is, first of all, to help initiate this process in the community and guide the community through the above four steps. Second, he must supply the technical information and know-how for executing certain projects. Third he must be prepared to give material aid where these materials and resources are beyond the reach of villagers.

Some workers, inspired by Gandhian ideals, took to village work 40 to 50 years ago. The dedication and devotion gave them enormous confidence in themselves and evoked the response and acceptance of villagers. Consequently, their work has become institutionalized, e.g. educational and other institutions. In fact, a good number of the villagers have developed a feeling that the institutions have grown at their expense or cost. The workers of these institutions are dominating the socio-political lives of the villagers. The villagers had reposed full faith in the workers; but instead of passing the power to the people, the workers themselves have occupied the power positions. Some of them have risen to occupy as high a position as MLAs or MPs or Ministers either in the State or at the Centre. The missionary zeal, with which the work had started has almost evaporated. The money for the programmes and activities was brought by these workers or leaders, either from the government or foreign sources. The villagers had hardly contributed anything except that they were made conscious and aware of using modern techniques to raise agricultural production. In the management of the institutions, they had hardly any voice. The programmes were no longer tailored to suit their requirements. Most of the programmes, or projects or schemes, were to suit the purpose of the aid giving agencies. The preservation of the institution had become the main goal. This displacement of the goal of building a society, from the bottom up, has alienated people from these institutions.

The workers cannot afford to sit back on their past laurels and continue to work in the name of the people. The workers must develop appropriate methodologies and communication techniques so as not to allow either, their, or the people's enthusiasm to dampen. The interest of the people must be sustained despite the missionary worker moving away to other positions. This continuous interest is necessary for renewal and for invigorating the institutions and workers. A worker can be effective only if he works with a sense of devotion, dedication, and competency acquired through training and practice.

IX
PROFESSIONAL SOCIAL WORK AND PEOPLE'S PARTICIPATION

In the foregoing paragraph, it has been made clear that development is essentially a programme of human development. In such a programme, social work has a vital role to play. Social work has a body of knowledge and skills that are basic to people's participation. Social work education includes knowledge about and understanding of the dynamic forces that motivate human behaviour towards acceptance or resistance to change. In addition, as part of their training, the social workers learn by practical application of this knowledge the special skills required for helping individuals, groups and communities to discover their own needs and to engage in constructive action to meet them.

The other important point about social work training is that it lays great emphasis on self-knowledge the special skills required for helping individuals, groups and communities to discover their own needs and to engage in constructive action to meet them.

The social worker's techniques are described as case work, group work and community organization. Through these techniques he may play an important role in promoting a desire for constructive change on the part of the people, receptivity to other technical services and fuller participation in activities designed for the common good.

The other important point about social work training is that it lays great emphasis on self-knowledge and self-understanding as essential in the process of helping others. The social worker learns, not only to perceive what motivates other human beings, but what his own motives are in his relationships to and dealing with them. If his motives are appropriate and in keeping with the good of community development, he will be able to elicit from the people the expression of their felt needs and help them to take action to meet these needs.

The basic philosophy and thinking of social work is particularly relevant to enlist people's participation in their own development, and especially, rural development. Appreciation of the dignity and value of the individual, his right to determine his own affairs, must surely be the basis of such endeavours because villagers are after all individual human beings.

However, whether the skills of social work can be applied in the practical situation depends on how we look at social work. If a narrow definition is adopted, i.e. social work is considered as dealing only with the socially disabled, physically and mentally handicapped people, then the skill of social work will only have a limited application in the context of development. On the other hand, if social work is taken to include such work as leading to desirable social change, then professional social work discipline and training are invaluable and are essential requirements for enlisting people's participation.

A good number of institutions imparting training in social work education have now gradually moved to the new position, that the profession's main concern would have to be social change and the removal of poverty rather than adjustment to the social process. It has now been recognized that social work has to transcend its limited concern with social welfare in the context of urban-based problems and industry to shift its attention to a wider spectrum of welfare and development.

X
A NOBLE IDEAL

The country cannot have a better ideal than that provided by Gandhiji to work with the people. This ideal has to be emulated both by constructive workers as well as professional social workers. People who came to Gandhiji, whether they came in personal contact with him or not, were inspired either by his total philosophy or some particular action in which he was engaged at that time. Their coming to him had no relation to their being looked after by one organization or another. Not that they did not need maintenance; they did. But it was not for the sake of maintenance that they joined him. They joined him because of an ideal and a commitment. Such a commitment is absent in most of the present social work-professionals or voluntary workers. They are mostly committed to their own self-professional or political advancement.

The various associations of the workers have also not provided necessary impetus to become a guild of workers dedicated to build the new society. There are a very few workers who have accepted the challenge. They are working in difficult places, especially in remote villages and tribal belts. Some of these places can be reached only by arduous journey, and during the rains these areas are quite unapproachable and they remain isolated.

It is to the credit of some of the young activists, whether enthused by Gandhian ideals or otherwise, that they are able to do as much as they are doing. The physical resources at their command are very small. In accomplishing anything, they have to rely on their own wits and powers of persuasion. Even when the cooperation or the support they receive from the local people is small, they persist in their efforts. They are loyal to the various goals and philosophy of their various programmes on which they are engaged. In some places they have been able to show astonishing results in terms of people's participation and work.

There is an erosion of social, moral and political values. Perhaps nobody could be held directly responsible for it. Yet, it is imperative that this is realized by all those concerned with the Gandhian ideals, professional ethics, and standards of social work. Both the constructive workers and the professional workers today need to be given a feeling of hope that the Gandhian ideal can influence the people of the country, that they are not working for a lost cause, that they stand for a noble ideal.

In a democratic society, the people should be made a part of the decision that effect their lives. Their active participation will reduce power differences and will contribute to equalization and social justice. It is a potent force of reducing disparities and inequalities in society. The collective wisdom and commitment generated through effective people's participation have the greatest capacity of controlling unintended effects of planning and development. Let us not treat people as "voters" and every community as "vote-banks". We have all become ruthless in the pursuit of power. This speaks volumes for the participatory democracy and our 'concern' and let us not create "Community divide" by spreading fear among the people for the disadvantaged sections of the society (Gangrade, 1991).

Gandhi taught us that Indian Culture is that of compassion, service to others and love. It is sinful to inflict pain on others.

XI
GANDHI'S POLITICAL PARADIGM

Once Mahatma Gandhi was asked by a journalist to explain his "politics". Gandhi replied: "Life of all human beings living on the globe is my politics" . Through this political thought Gandhi wanted to introduce a new and more human dimension to modern polity. After the French Political Revolution, Gandhi was the first socio-spiritual leader who had conceptualized a new political theory and had very successfully experimented into action, first, in a foreign land, South Africa (1894-1915) and thereafter in India (1916-1947). This new and innovative political thought was for higher and noble concept of self-government in comparison to then prevailing political systems as were being controlled and governed by the Feudal and Colonial rulers. The rule of majority *versus* minority within the framework of a Nation-State was born in Britain with the emergence of Industrial Revolution of the 18th century. This new system is popularly known as Westminster Parliamentary System of Democracy (WPSD). This system at present is considered the best. It could not be replaced by what Gandhi had thought and experimented in his life time (1869-1948). The 11th September, 2001 terrorist's self-immolating attacks in New York and Washington, USA, and on 13th December, 2001 on Indian Parliament is an alarm signal for thinking minds. It is a global warning for us all to seriously think about the limitations of the WPSD, which has been promoting the cult of negative thinking in the minds of ordinary people and rendering them helpless, frustrated, insecure and fear stricken. Gandhi had given this warning in the beginning of the last century. (*Indian Home Rule* 1909, Navjeevan Publications, Ahmedabad, originally published in Gujarati as *Hind Swaraj*; also see 'MMDS' (Money, Market, Development and Material Success) *versus* 'AFSJ' (Awakening-Enlightenment, Freedom and Socio-economic Justice, Gandhi's Political Paradigm by A.B. Bharadwaj, Gandhi-in-Action, Constructive Workers Home, New Delhi, 2002). The MMDS paradigm is being mooted as the 'summum bonum' of the modern "Technological-civilization", World Trade Organization is the latest tool that has been devised by the powerful lobby to establish their economic and political hegemony.

While Gandhi had struggled for Awakening, Enlightment, Freedom and Socio-economic Justice for one and all, his utmost priority had been to serve the weakest of the weak. He tirelessly worked to strengthen the "Weakest Link" the poorest of the poor. This basic principle of human and social policy should be the aim of Professional Social Workers (PSW).

In the absence of such a policy the disparity ratio has gone from 1:27 to 1:74 from the year 1960 to 2000. Wars and Terrorism have become order of the day under so called democratic system. Such inhuman political phenomenon are on the increase in almost all the countries, developed as well as developing countries.

The four foundation pillars of MMDS paradigm are: First, the War Industry, 37 per cent of all the human resources available on this globe are being spent on arms, armaments and to promote the cult of militarism in the name of maintaining geo-political boundaries of the nation-state.

Second, is the Chemical-Drug Industry (legal as well as illegal).

Third, is the Real Estate Industry (by perpetuating the institution of private property).

Fourth, is the Global Share Stock Markets Industry, which is considered to be the nerve-centre of modern economic growth.

The MMDS paradigm is not only misleading ordinary innocent masses, but also making them slaves as well of their own physical and mental weakness like blindly following the senseless cult of consumerism. Perverted sex and violence is being injected into the minds of the youth through electronic and print media. The Information Technology (IT) further pushes us into the vicious 'web net' of mad race of cut throat competition. Competition breeds exploitation and finally, results in mental and physical violence. We are being compelled to consider our own fellow human beings as our enemies.

The challenge before all of us is as to how could human beings be helped to discover, recognize and feel concern for the suffering of his or her fellow human beings. How to hold firmly the rays of love and compassion for others by withdrawing the mind from all visible and vain imaginings.

Satish Kumar, editor of UK's *Resurgence* magazine, says people's activities have contributed to more environmental destruction in the last 50 years than in the 5,000 years before. Plus we hear of global warmings' dark predictions that within 60 years coastal inundation will force a billion people to relocate their hearths and home. Well, Gandhian philosophy is the medium and meaningful way to come out of this situation.

XII
COOPERATION *VS.* COMPETETION

Flashback to an ancient parable, sometimes referred to as *andha-pangu-maya* or the logic of the lame and the blind. The story is about a lame man who has keen eyesight, but can't walk, and strong a man who is blind cannot see or has no vision.

Individually they are very limited. But when the lame person climbs on the shoulders of the sightless one, they function as a unit, and by cooperating achieve many wonderful things. That's a fable.

With a minor stretch of imagination we might think of India—metaphorically of course—as the visionary but economically weaker country. And the US as a culturally blind but financially strong nation, temporary as these designations are.

Cooperation is the key. "If there is to be such a thing as a world-wide human family", working together for the common good has to be more than mere formality. Carrying each other's burden is part of love. The ability to trust comes from practical experience, and from being trusted.

Leaders of nations can make a conscious effort to work together, or atleast encourage their respective entrepreneurs to do so.

Integrating the wealth of India's culture with the strength of American technological progress can benefit millions?

XIII
TWO TYPES OF GROWTH

There are two types of growth—Horizontal and Vertical. Horizontal growth means more money, name, fame. People's yardstick of growth is more in the horizontal domain. People come and tell me (Swami Sukhabodhavanda). "I have grown"—which means five year back I earned five million dollars a year and now I earn 10 million dollars a year. This type of growth is not fulfilling.

The second type of growth is vertical growth. The yardstick for this is: Five years back how calm was I, and how calm am I now. The growth is measured in the depth and not in the width. The more one grows in love, kindness and compassion, the more one is truly growing. Such a growth is fulfilling.

In order to grow vertically, one has to cultivate the art of relaxation, be balanced, and stay aware in the present. Life is fulfilling only with such a type of growth. Happiness and joy flower forth in this state of consciousness. This approach has to be adopted by the social workers to bring the Kingdom of God on the earth to achieve peace in the world.

XIV
QUALITIES OF SOCIAL WORKERS

Empowering leadership is a conscious process of building capacity in an organization. As the German poet Goethe once said: "If you treat an individual as he is, he will remain as he is. But if you treat him as if he were what he ought to be, could be he will become what he ought to be and could be." This is what Gandhi did in his life-span in South Africa and India.

Social workers must develop ability to foster and discover potential within an individual and allow the potential to become a fire of inspiration for pursuing the demonstrative and organizational goal. Leadership facilitates the conscious, evolution of the followers' (individual, group and community) capacity for action. On the other hand it is also an evolution of consciousness. Consciousness is the edge that separates the mediocre from the heroic. Gandhi, talking about the enlightened leader said, "There comes a time when an individual becomes irresistible and his action becomes all-pervasive in its effect" (Fischer, 1962).

When Buddha was asked whether he was a human being, an angel or a God, he replied, "I am conscious" (Smith, 1991). The Vedantic psychology tells us that the ultimate source of human consciousness is a centre of bliss. The Sanskrit word for this state is *ananda.* A leader should be seen to be honest, He ought to be unbiased He must be ethically above-board. There are two different orientations—management and leader.

Values Needed

Management Orientation	*Leadership Orientation*
1. Strong work-ethic 2. Predominatly skill based 3. Motivated by love for power 4. Disciplined by organizational control 5. Effective communicator	1. Strong ethics in work 2. Primarily value based 3. Inspired by power of love 4. Relies on self-discipline and self-control 5. Authentic communicator Principle centred Focused on character

Gandhiji in his work subscribed to leadership orientation rather than management orientation. This should be the orientation and motto of workers to make policies, plans, activities pro-people-centred and not self-centred. Let us become unself-consciously and simply then things become special when touched with love. Grumbling and brooding over failures and weaknesses will not help. Do not think you are helpless. Strength has to come from within. Gandhi was neither a system builder nor a theoretician. He responded to situations of injustice and developed strategies and methods to deal with them based on truth and nonviolence. An effort to talk and write on Gandhian work will go in vain until it becomes a science of experience. We as social workers know that theory followed by a practical (field work) truly affirms and solidifies the abstract truth or theory that is sought to be instructed. It is the vision in practical sense which would arouse unflinching faith.

An in-depth study of Gandhian movements will provide a perennial source of inspiration. It should be made an integral part of a programme of social work education.

The Gandhian and Professional Social workers should join together so that the issues relating to injustice are not swept under the carpet.

XV
GANDHIJI'S GOSPEL OF SERVICE

Gandhi drew strength and inspiration from the *Bhagwad Gita*. He says, "The Gita contains the *gospel of work*, the *gospel of Bhakti* or devotion, and the *gospel of Gyan* or knowledge. Life should be a harmonious whole of these three.

He is not saying anything new. This is stated by other Acharyas and Scholars. But, Gandhiji's originality lies in the great stress that he places on *Karma-Yoga*.

He says : "The human body is meant for service, never for indulgence. Renunciation is life. Indulgence spells death."

Service to humanity has been the ideal of all saints and prophets of peace and so for is Gandhiji. He, therefore, specifically states: "the gospel of service is the basis of all, and what can be more necessary for those who want to serve the country than that they begin with the chapter enunciating the Gospel of work".

Gandhiji states that renunciation of the fruits of one's actions is the basic teachings of the *Gita*. Action is not to be avoided and cannot be avoided. For a man who follows the teachings of the *Gita*, *Sanayas* is not actual renunciation of all actions. It is renunciation of the fruits of action as Gandhiji states, and it is also renunciation of the mental attachment to fruits. The *Sanyas* is a state of mind and the true *Sanyasi* makes no difference between human beings. He spends his time for the betterment of all. Gandhiji is clear in saying that,

> The life of Gandhiji is the history of a man who became a greater and nobler day by day, ultimately to become an ideal man.

XVI
NEGLECTED DIMENSION

Schools of social work mostly attract students from middle-class. These students are career-oriented and a very few of them join services that demand change of system. The location of schools of social work is also a deterrent in preparing students to go to rural and tribal areas to render services. This requires an immediate attention on the part of social work educationists.

I am, in general agreement with Sam Pitroda who said: "Unfortunately, Indian talent (Professional Social Worker no exception) so far has been busy creating solutions for the West. India needs solutions specific to this country. These solutions do not have to be directed to the two per cent of the auto economy (cream), or the 18 per cent of the bicycle economy. They have to look at the 80 per cent of the bullock-cart economy".

XVII
MORAL DECLINE

The point is that the moral sensibility in the real world is contrary to what the glib proponents of *Vasudhaiv Kutumbakam* might say is neither universal nor absolute. It is both selective and conditional. For well over a decade, ordinary Germans, brought up on generations of Enlightenment discourse, were shown to be perfectly capable of condoning the systematic extermination of millions of their fellow Jews. The same Americans who view 9-11-2001 as ultimate expression of evil in the world wouldn't probably loose too much sleep over the "mistaken" hundreds of "innocent : Afghans".

The fact is that as humans we experience the pain of the others only when he or she is part of our moral community. In simple terms, this means that biological identity alone is not a sufficient condition for us to recognize someone else as human and deserving the same dignity as us. In our increasingly divided polity, that sense of shared moral community across religious and ethnic boundaries—is today under severe strain.

When there is a breakdown of moral order in society the PSWs cannot remain just a "conscienceless scientism". It is the duty of the PSWs as the upholder of universal norms to step in as shown by Gandhi.

Thought and Action

Gandhi always emphasized that "India lives in her villages." He practiced whatever he preached. His thoughts and actions always went together. He used to say that one ounce of action is better than tonnes of thought without any action. For example, Gandhi was once talking to some villagers on the need for keeping their villages and environment clean for better health and aesthetic values. The people listening to Gandhi understood what he said: But he realized that what he said had little impact on his audience. So suddenly he got up, took a broom and started the cleaning operation himself to the utter surprise of everyone present. It had tremendous impact.

I am not sure how many Professional Social Workers (PSWs) would be ready to emulate such an example. He carried out constructive programmes and did not call them social work programmes. He carried them alongside the freedom movement. His constructive programmes included, Abolition of untouchability, promoting community amity through the removal of all distinctions among the communities, Introduction of prohibition, Popularizing Khadi and hand-woven cloth, Development of rural industries, like hand-grinding, hand-pounding, match-making, tanning, oil processing; Introduction of Basic Education; Emancipation of women, Organization of the peasantry, Improvement of village sanitation, Upliftment of the Adivasis; and Improvement of the cattle.

CONCLUSIONS

The social workers would find these programmes enriching Indian Society in general and rural society in particular. We know that human consciousness contains a sense of both the ideal and real. Both are vital to the shaping of relationships between peoples. A mere descriptive and explanatory exercise does not make for a critical examination of real issues involved in working with people. It does not provide a theoretical framework which could make for a better understanding and appropriate strategies for fighting a deleterious and bewildering complex situation in terms of theoretical and structural changes required to reduce the tensions, conflicts, and violence (both direct and structural) perpetrated by the prevailing system. As long as relationships are a symmetrical for whatever reason, positive peace cannot prevail. At best the resolution of conflict can restore the *status quo*, it cannot create an enduring peaceful society. It is necessary to transform society through the individual and by social values of love, non-violence and justice. Social workers must create the conditions which would help the people to be self-reliant and realize the ideals of the purity, honesty and righteousness, fair play, justice and *universal to tolerance* without the loss of individual freedom.

Gandhi challenged the arrogant imperialist West-centric model of development. His vision of society does not recognize man-made barriers. But at the same time, he often insisted that while we should welcome all that is best in other traditions, while allowing the winds of other cultures to sweep in we should refuse to be swept off our feet. In other words, one cannot be an internationalist without being a nationalist.

Globally the gap between the rich and poor is increasing. In 1970 the ratio was 30:1, today it is 74:1. Drawing upon the Gandhian ideals, the Narmada Bachao Andolan (NBA) is a clear articulation of an environmental movement in terms of "the values of the people" as opposed to "the values of goods *per se*" who are the recipients of such goods. The NBA experience led by Medha Patkar, a professional social worker has shown the limitations of the state-led development package at the cost of the values of the people, in this case the displaced tribals. Service to the people is to be considered as duty. I am reminded of the inspiring words of wisdom of late Abdul Gaffar Khan, that the Pathans (substitute by Indians) are not sheep but tigers. You have been reared in slavery. Don't bleat, roar like a Tiger. This type of confidence is needed by the social workers to make their contribution.

Professional social work has to be a way of life not just a mere profession to earn money, name and fame.

REFERENCES

Betai, Ramesh S., *Gita and Gandhiji*, National Gandhi Museum, Rajghat, New Delhi, in association with Gyan Publishing House, New Delhi, 2002, p. 115.

Gandhi, M.K., *Young India*, 3-11-1937.

Gandhi, M.K., *Harijan*, 24-2-1946.

Gandhi, M.K., *Young India*, 3-1-1927.

Gandhi, M.K., *Young India*, 6-8-1931.

Gandhi, M.K., *Essays on the Gita*, pp. 42-43.

Mahesh, Daya, 'Psyche of the Aggressor'—No Kalinga Effect in Gujarat, *The Times of India*, July 13, 2002, p. 4.

Pasricha, Ashu, Gandhi the communicator, *Gandhi Marg*, Vol. XXIV, No. 3, Oct., December, 2003, pp. 315-26.

Pitroda, Sam, 'Indian Telecom Industry needs a few more price warriors', The *Hindustan Times*, Monday, January 13, 2003, New Delhi, p. 7.

2

Gandhian Perspective on Development

I
INTRODUCTION

Gandhi's vision was to consider whole world as a single family. Therefore, his perspective, ideal and concept were to develop all: *Sarvodaya* (Rise of all). His principles were based on purity of means, truth and non-violence. His method to fight injustice was *Satyagraha*. His approach to development was not pyramidal but of concentric circles. But today's development concentrates more on Economic Development than Social Development. I have developed a formula as stated below:

$$D = (ED - SD) = ND$$

Development = Economic Development – Social Development = No Development. On the contrary it should be:

$$D = (ED + SD) = GD$$

Development = Economic Development + Social Development = Gandhian Development.

The result of pattern of development has been critically examined in this study.

II
GROWING DISPARITY

Globally, 20 per cent of the world's richest people account for 86 per cent of total private consumption expenditures; the poorest 20 per cent only 1.3 per cent. The richest fifth consume 45 per cent of all meat and fish, the poorest fifth 5 per cent; the richest consume 58 per cent of total energy, the poorest less than 4 per cent; the richest have 74 per cent of all telephone lines, the poorest 1.5 per cent; the richest consume 84 per cent of all paper, the poorest 1.1 per cent; the richest own 87 per cent of the world's vehicle fleet, the poorest less than 1 per cent. Worse, the gap between the rich and the poor is growing. In 1970 the ratio was 30:1, today it is 74:1.

The fifth of the world's population in the highest-income countries account for 53 per cent of carbon dioxide emissions, the poorest fifth for 3 per cent. The human consequences of the global warming from carbon dioxide can be devastating for poor countries, playing havoc with harvests, rise in sea-levels, permanent flooding of large areas, increased frequency of storms and droughts, extinction of some species, spread of infectious diseases and possibly sudden and savage flips in the world's climates. Thirdly, excessive consumption of the affluent on the one hand and the poverty-environment-population problem triad on the other is causing an unbearable strain on natural resources. The number of water scarce people is expected to soar from 550 million to 3 billion by the year 2025. Global water availability has dropped from 17,000 cubic metres per capita to 7000 today.

A sixth of the world's land area is now degraded as a result of overgrazing and poor farming practices. Forest area per 1000 inhabitants has fallen from 11.4 square kilometres to 7.3. Fish stocks are declining by about a quarter currently depleted or in danger of depletion and another 44 per cent being fished at their biological limit. Wild species are becoming extinct 50-100 times faster than they would naturally. The cost of this environmental damage is the heaviest and the most severe on the poor.

The remarkable scientific advances that have contributed to food production globally have been achieved at some cost. Over the past 50 years there has been a loss of 25 per cent top-soil and 20 per cent less agricultural land. We have spent the capital rather than used the interest. In 1961 the amount of cultivated land supporting food production was 0.44 ha per person; today it is about 0.26 ha; based on population projections, by 2050 it will be somewhere near 0.15 ha per person. Irrigation has become increasingly important with about

16 per cent of arable land being irrigated and producing one-third of the world's crops, but it has produced problems of salination and soil degradation.

The point of elaborating the global trends in some detail is to highlight the urgency of developing a paradigm for sustainable consumption on a global scale. Local and regional efforts to achieve sustainability are vital but have limited chances of success in the absence of a global consensus.

III
DEVELOPMENT : SOME ISSUES

Maldevelopment, peacelessness and violence are stalking the globe today. While by the year 2100, 13 per cent of the people of the world will be consuming 90 per cent of its resources, a craze for 'development' which is another name for the acquisition of wealth by a few at the cost of the rest is expanding the areas of absolute poverty everywhere, both in the rich and the poor nations. Technologies, institutions, professions and practices borrowed from the rich society create such problems and project the phantoms of violence.

The health problem is a "preventable tragedy" because the developed world has the resources and technology to end common diseases world-wide. Twenty per cent of the world's population or one billion people are diseased or malnourished. The greatest health problems are in sub-Saharan Africa where 160 million are ill and undernourished. Forty per cent of the population in South and East Asia—India, Bangladesh, Indonesia, Nepal and Sri Lanka—were characterized as having 'serious health problems'.

Challenges of Development

The third world comprises 141 nations and has a large population of 3 billion living in villages. That is, 60 per cent of the world population is living in villages and out of this 85 per cent or 2.5 billion live in Asia and Africa. The living standard of villages is far behind that of the cities as the national income of these countries is much less than that of the affluent countries. UN data shows that in these countries the urban population consists of 35 to 65 per cent of rural migrants.

The affluent nations are basically urban and the poor nations rural. Rural development is a critical factor to be tackled which would bring about a less exploitative and more satisfying system of all-round development. Gandhi in the context of India aptly said, "If India is not to perish, we have to begin with the lower rung of ladder. If that was rotten, all work done at the top or at the intermediate rungs are bound to ultimately fall" (*Harijan,* 13 April 1935, p. 68). Gandhi in his writings further dramatized the problems of city-village antagonism. He said: "The blood of the villages is the cement with which the edifice of the city is built. I want this blood that is today inflating the arteries of the cities to run once again in the blood vessels of the villages" (*Harijan,* 23 April 1946, p. 198). Gandhi did not talk simply in terms of city-village dichotomy. In addition to referring to the village exploitation and role of the city, he spoke of alienation of city dweller. He referred to village as a 'community', rather than a socially and culturally structured unit.

The purpose of the chapter is to rescue Social Sciences from this plight and to help to investigate the causes that create these problems. Naturally our main task will be to evolve a theory of social change that may lead to a no-poverty, no-affluence and a non-violent society. It will also draw heavily from the experience of both the cultures of poverty and affluence of the North and the South world. The purpose is to find global solutions to the problems of human settlements that function at the level of the small community and *vice versa.*

We would thus discuss a quest for the logical fruition and some of the ideas and processes that lie germane in history and have found repeated expressions in the contributions of many a leader of thought and action. The latter include, among others, Ruskin, Tolstoy, Gandhi, Martin Luther King, Schumacher, Jawaharlal Nehru and Jayaprakash Narayan. Some of their thoughts had once helped, and could help again, in rediscovering the community that lies at the root of our culture and seems to be withering away. We shall not search for alternatives to the existing distortions of cultures that the world of the megalomaniac, megalopolises, dreaded multi-nationals and super-technologies have now introduced in a bid to react to them. It would indeed look beyond the movement of alternatives to the logical conclusion of a heritage that might yet survive, despite all efforts at its mutilation. The purpose is to analyse the macro and the micro social environs of both the cultures of affluence and poverty, the objective being to provide an integrated overview of the struggles, aspirations and experiments that are being conducted the world over in the field of community building and constructive work that arise logically out of the culture in which the humankind has grown.

In my opinion our ultimate aim should be to have a no-poverty society. Man exploiting man should cease to have place in the world. The process of planning and development should be to raise the standard of living and quality of life of masses. It should not lead to inequitable distribution of resources, creating of inequalities, and uprooting them from their present environment without providing for their adequate rehabilitation.

The main philosophy of modem development, specially economic development, has been one of maximization of current or future consumption. Given the limited production capacities and iniquitous distribution of purchasing power, development activities have tended to create avenues for excessive consumerism of some as against the continued deprivation of many others. Gandhiji had clearly advocated the restrictions of wants voluntarily. In fact he had said that there is enough in this world to meet the needs of everybody, but not enough to meet even a single man's greed.

The market economy is based on the principle of maximizing profit and it relegates the issue of inter-human relations and human welfare to the background. Taking the case of 'need', as defined by economists, it should override the principle of maximizing profits. Profits are not to be used to build a hierarchical business in which there are masters and servants.

The distinction between growth and development has to be specifically remembered. Growth is no longer a guarantor of trickle down effect. It is now being increasingly recognized in the developing world that there is need for special attention to that group of population which has been left behind in the process of growth. The basic needs approach enunciated by the planning process in India needs to be adopted as a major plank of development strategies. Improvement in facilities for education, health and infrastructure welfare should receive priority attention in the development process.

Unfortunately, since the beginning of the process of industrialization in Europe towards the end of the 18th and early 19th century, development is defined in terms of *shifting* from *agriculture* towards *industry* and later towards *service* activities. Developing countries have followed blindly this model of development. This has created two types of problems. Often the labour share in agriculture may not fall to the same extent as share of agriculture in GDP. This means labour dependent on agriculture continues to be substantial while the share of agriculture in GDP accruing to the labour force dependent on it falls more sharply. This leads to uneven distribution of benefits of development in two segments of population. The second problem arises out of the nature of linkages between agriculture and industry, both due to production linkages of backward and forward kinds or income induced linkages of demand for each other's goods.

Many developing countries have permitted weakening of these linkages in their over-enthusiasm for rapid industrialization in a highly diversified structure. With the majority of the population still dependent on agriculture and still also with a highly rural bias in the culture of population, weakening of these linkages is a serious matter of concern.

The present-day social scene either at the level of individual nations or in the global context is beyond doubt one of crisis and disarray. The situation has become complex partly because of the simultaneous operation of a multitude of factors and partly because received theories and analytical tools have lost their relevance. Development can no longer be identified as a process of shifting surplus labour from agriculture to the industrial sector.

In the present stage of world economy, no country can remain delinked from the rest of the world. There are different approaches for getting a nation integrated with the rest of the world. Integration with the international environment should not necessarily mean total opening of the economies. It is a twin process of learning from external development and at the same time strengthening the internal capabilities for endogenising the process of development. This requires strengthening of the human resource element and institutional basis of the developing countries.

IV
CONCEPT OF DEVELOPMENT

The word 'Development' like the phrase 'Third World', is an Anglo-Saxon concept. Few ideas in our time have been invested with as much respectability or historic significance as the concept of development. How to make poor people rich and undeveloped countries advanced?

By and large, the philosophy of development has restricted its concerns to the poor of the Third World. Development schemes are formulated by experts, planners and voluntary agencies to deprive 'these people' of their poverty and to wrench them above the poverty line. Gunnar Myrdal defines development as follows:

> "By development I mean the movement upward of the entire social system, and I believe this is the only logically tenable definition. The social system endorses besides the so-called economic factors, all non-economic factors, including all sorts of consumption by various groups of people, consumptions provided collectively; educational and health facilities at all levels; the distribution of power in society; and more generally economic, social and political stratification; broadly speaking institutions and attitudes to which we must add an exogenous set of factors, induced policy measures applied in order to change one or several of these endogenous factors."

Fundamentally, development implies the replacement of general competence and abundant subsistence activities by the use and consumption of commodities. Development implies the monopoly of wage labourer over all other work. It implies the redefinition of needs in terms of goals and services, produced on a mass basis according to expert design. Ivan Illich says:

> "the development paradigm is more easily repudiated by those of us who were adults on 10th January, 1949. That day most of us came to know the term development in its present meaning for the first time when President Truman announced his Point Four programme. Until then we used the term development to refer to species, real estate, and moves in chess and only thereafter to people, countries, and economic strategies. Since then we have been flooded by development theories... We will remember, for example, growth, catching up, modernization, dualism, dependency, basic needs, transfer of technology, world system, industrialization."

Common Factors of Development

Development is neither a static nor a uniform concept. As a historical fact, the classical model remained the only model in the West until

1913. After World War I, especially after the Russian Revolution and the Great Depression, the classical model declined and alternative forms emerged. After World War II, the world entered another new stage of development. Development must be defined in each of these stages. Furthermore, development always varies widely in different countries. Yet there are important features of development common to all phases and to all types of modernization. The most important common feature is that of growth. To develop means to advance, to further, to evolve, or to expand by a process of growth. A modern society is one which is growing, expanding or advancing.

Development is a process of societal transformation from a traditional society to a modern society, and such a transformation is also known as modernization. A modern society is also a rational society. While all societies have rational and irrational elements, modern society is rational in the sense that it is not dominated by super-natural factors or by tradition and that it assigns high value to making decisions on the basis of reason and performing tasks in accordance with rational methods and procedures. Another common feature is the building of nation state as the unit of development. This is why modern development is often known as national development. Development involves institutional changes. Institution is a significant element in the life of a culture which is persistent and enduring, which regulates pattern of behaviour; and which is widely tolerated, sanctioned or legitimized by the society.

Development is considered to be a process of improving the capability of a nation's institutions and value system to meet increasing and different demands—social, political and economic. Development has also been defined as economic growth *plus* social change as bread *plus* dignity, as a technical solution to under-development; as institutional building; human development, a more equitable spread of distribution and development resources.

Value Base

The basic values of development are human dignity, equality, and social justice. These three concepts are not separate and distinct but inter-related and dependent on each other. Another principle implied in social development is the emphasis on cooperation as against competition. It lays emphasis on collectivity as against rugged individualism. It does not deny the right of full development expression of the individual and his/her role in decision-making that affects their lives. It lays greater emphasis on the well-being of the total society and all its individuals.

Development based on the principles of human dignity, equality and social justice, can be defined as a goal and process that aims to achieve an integrated, balanced and unified (social and economic) development of society. It is international in scope and has a holistic, interdisciplinary, inter-sectoral and inter-regional approach to societal issues and problems. It focuses on "qualitative" development as measured by: (a) the participation of people in matters affecting their lives, (b) the nature of social and inter-personal relations, and (c) the relationship of people to their environment. Quantitatively, social development aims at structural and institutional reforms to bring about changes in the distribution of income, wealth and services.

In fact, social development means something more than merely economic, political, social and environmental development. It is not merely an effort to provide *ad hoc* growth targets in each of the sectors of planning. Social development planning requires the perception and delineation of the nature of inter-relationships between the different sectors. Social development is an integrative concept and this integration depends upon clear enunciation of the values and the type of society towards which planning is to be undertaken.

Briefly stated, the word 'development' has its origin in an Italian word "Velupara" of the 12th or 13th century. It means to unwrap, to disentangle, to rid of something. The opposite of "develop" is "envelop", which means to hide, to cover-up, to put-up constraints—that we do when we envelop something. When we develop something, we do the reverse—we remove these constraints, whatever they may be. The word 'develop' is a positive term meaning progress, and when applied to man, indicates a comprehensive growth which enables an individual to feel that he is as much a part of mankind as anybody else.

V

DEVELOPMENT—PHILOSOPHY AND OBJECTIVES

Our view of development is a process by which one's overall personality is enhanced. This is so for society as well as for an individual. For society, the identity is collective. Thus development for society means development of the collective personality of society.

Development of collective personality requires physical, material and economic development, but it is above all the development and application of consciousness and faculties. A child may grow physically while his personality does not develop. So is it with society. Thus, economic development, while it is vitally necessary, cannot be treated as an independent variable divorced from its social bearings. Development of a society is social development, a process in which 'economic' and 'non-economic' elements interact organically with each other. Attempts to isolate the economic elements and fit them into hypothetical model of 'economic development' are therefore unscientific. Development thus defined is a multi-variate quantitative and qualitative change. It would be futile to attempt to measure any country's social development quantitatively and expect consensus on it. The world's richest society may be considered to be its sickest, and hence not developed at all. Such positions can be understood but cannot be refuted, and yet scientific judgements may be given on such a basis. While scientific judgements about social development need to be reasoned, cardinal quantification has often served as a fetish that has detracted from rather than helped evaluate the more essential qualitative attributes.

Individual and the Collective

The individual and the collective might be thought to have conflicting interests. Our concept of the collective rules this out. The collective exists to the extent that individuals acquiesce in its sovereignty, and develops as individual's acquire more of this collective spirit. Thus a nation of 'self-seekers' may be a collective one in the sense that its members have agreed to hold a common passport. However, if there is no 'collective spirit', it would be a very weak collective, indeed.

The 'collective spirit' is not necessarily an abnegation of individual interest in favour of a mystified concept of 'society'. We view the collective as a method of serving individual interests while at the same time raising individual consciousness, so that one progressively aspires to fulfil higher orders including fulfilment in developing together.

Aspirations Frontier

Within the framework of the above philosophy, development has to have its operational objectives. One of these is growth of the collective spirit. Stimulating the spirit of cooperation is another, by means of which the collective consciousness may be promoted and the quantity of social good to be produced may be raised. Creativity and innovativeness, and a problem-solving approach to life, are essential attributes of a dynamic personality and have to be cultivated. Improvement of knowledge is a basic requirement. A will to develop and faith in the collective creative potential of man are fundamental prerequisites with which society must be equipped.

Somewhat more complex is the question of attaining an 'aspirations frontier'. At any point of time, individuals in a society have certain natural aspirations, such as minimum of nourishment, clothing and shelter, some leisure and opportunity for cultural-scientific pursuits. For India, this may have to be set as a long-term objective, beyond the material possibilities in the short run. This leaves the problem of sustaining morale in the short run.

The solution lies in the direction of creating values that give a sense of fulfilment in the very austerity that is necessary in the short run. Such fulfilment is possible only if the austerity is shared in a framework of collective effort for progress.

Self-Reliance

Of all the new values to be created, self-reliance is the most important one. India has depended too long on external masters. This is much more true of Rural India which has depended too long on external masters. Rural India has depended too long on the city. The rural poor have been subservient, too long, to the rural rich and to the 'officer' sent from the city, a subservience that has been forced upon them; in the process their own initiative and vitality have been sapped. The result is a history of exploitation of the 'dependent' by the 'master'. The dependent, appearing to have no self-respect, commands no respect from others. He is laughed at by the world and despised at the same time as he is squeezed.

India cannot develop unless it rejects the soft option and resolves to be self-reliant. This means building up a combination of material and mental reserves that enable one to choose one's own course of evolution, uninhibited by what others desire. It requires maximum mobilization of domestic resources for poor societies, but above all it requires psychological and institutional staying power to meet crisis situations when the supply of essential materials is too short. This staying power is best attained collectively. Individually a hungry man feels isolated and his mental reserve wanes; collectively this reserve is reinforced for each and collective resolve gives individuals strength to fight a calamity with their heads high.

Self-reliance does not necessarily mean self-sufficiency. With psychological staying power, a self-reliant society can open up and negotiate from a position of strength. But some measure of self-sufficiency in strategic areas that are easily prone to manipulation by exploitative interests is desirable. Such vulnerable areas are staple food production, technology and spare parts, and military resistance power.

All these make the development of appropriate technology indispensable. While development of a modern sector is imperative, the technological revolution has to be primarily internally achieved.

Participatory Democracy

The 'collective' as we conceive it functions through the active participation of the people. Without this the individual would not belong organically to the collective and the collective itself would not be to that extent a reality. Hence collective and participatory democracy are inseparable concepts. Participatory democracy is not the formal voting of leaders into power once every five years and passive obedience in between; it is not merely government of the people but also, and more fundamentally, 'by the people'. Participatory democracy rules out the dominance of any minority group over the broad masses of people. In the Indian context it precludes, therefore dictatorship of the 'elite' over the masses, of the city over the countryside, and of the modern sector over the traditional, and new forms of external control which would dilute the processes of democracy. Moreover, there is no room in this participatory system for power-wielding, which is alien to the broad masses of the people and tends to strengthen its own position at the expense of the latter; nor is there a place for the unaccountable and unresponsive bureaucrat who considers it beneath his dignity to have any interaction with the masses.

Consciousness Gap

The problem of a 'consciousness gap' between the leaders of a society and the masses of the people remains. In concrete historical conditions in any society some persons may be ahead of others in perceptions of the need for social change, in their ability to systematize ideas whose origins are in the masses themselves, in seeing through complex relationships and in relevant technical expertise. Such men are natural leaders of society, whom the masses of the people tend to follow without coercion. Participatory democracy in such situations would not yet be complete, nor would the leaders be fully accountable to the people in a real sense. Such a relationship may be formally 'democratic', but in the depth of the situation lies the seed of leadership ego which may grow and gradually alienate the leader from his people, so that finally he leads them to a vision that is more his than theirs. This would, in turn, alienate the people and inhibit the growth of their collective personality. The leadership and masses must, therefore, move in a mutually interacting process that systematically reduces the consciousness gap. Democracy in this sense is not a system to be implanted, but an objective to be realized through a process.

De-alienation

Many of the above objectives imply a regeneration and development of values that man has lost or nearly lost through ages of subordination to exploitation, maladministration and misdirection. Regressive social relations and cultural taboos have paved the way for such alienation from man's original and inherent potentials.

In essence, the development philosophy and objectives which we have enunciated centre around five core concepts which stand inseparably together :

1. Man as the end of development which is, therefore, to be judged by what it does to him.
2. De-alienation of man, in the sense that he feels at home with the process of development in which he becomes the subject as well as the object.
3. Development of collective personality of man in which he finds his fullest expression.
4. Participation as the true form of democracy.
5. Self-reliance as the expression of man's faith in his own abilities.

In India, whose situation we are reviewing, rural development is the key to its overall social development.

The personality of India cannot be enhanced without raising the personality of rural India. This leads us to a strategy of development which points that the countryside should be centre of activity for contemporary India. The inner-directed strategy that we are seeking encompasses the city, but the focus and driving spirit is the village where the new Indian drama will inevitably have to be played.

VI
GANDHI'S PHILOSOPHY OF DEVELOPMENT

Gandhi's development philosophy revolves round man, his society and nature and their respective and simultaneous development. He had a philosophy of work, wealth and happiness of man in line with the religious and ethical philosophies of the East as well as the West. His philosophy was governed by two fundamental and inter-related principles—truth and non-violence (*ahimsa*). In recent years, his vision of life, society and civilization has been increasingly shared and practiced in various parts of the country and the world with reference to several basic and contingent problems, like poverty, violence, discrimination based on caste and religion, ecology, centralization of wealth and power. This has created a tremendous interest in the people to know and understand his philosophy of development.

As already stated in general terms the word 'development' in brief can be explained in the following ways:

1. Development is a term which is applicable to man only. Both society and nature are merely regarded as factors facilitating the development of man. The term, when used with a prefix or a suffix, refers to a superstructure or to an infrastructure, necessary for development of man.
2. Human development has three complementary aspects—physical, mental and spiritual development (not co-terminous with religious development).
3. A comprehensive development programme is a combination of all the three aspects of development.

Physical development depends basically on proper nutrition, treatment of ailments, healthy living surroundings and enough clothings to protect the body from the ravages of nature. As long as a minimum quantity of these are not made available to the individual, he remains much too preoccupied with the problems of survival. A person dependent on others for primary necessities of life can hardly declare that all men are equal and he is a part of a society of equals. The word 'development' because of this emphasis on economic condition in the developing region particularly, has thus been regarded mainly as an economic concept concerned with the increased production and distribution of goods and services in a more or less integrated system controlled by various agencies as partners in the exercise of state power. It still means affluence and is growth-oriented. Its maturation logically aspires after affluence. This development is planned mostly by state which, with the help of bureaucracy and technology, carries out development tasks and projects.

Gandhi's Concept of Development

Affluence as a goal of development was not in Gandhi's mind. He believed that there is sufficient to meet the needs of people, but not their greed. He, therefore, refused to accept any move towards affluence as the goal of Indian society. He believed that the type of development that had been achieved in Europe was the result of a systematic colonization and exploitation of both the people and nature. He, therefore, rejected not only supportive mechanism of development such as bureaucracy, technology and elitist education but also the whole idea of development as conceived by the builders of the industrial society.

His opposition to this approach should be understood in relation to his philosophy of development, which is closely linked with his life philosophy. As a great unifier not only of persons but also of ideas, his social, economic and political ideas are all interrelated and interdependent.

Gandhi had a holistic view of life. Accordingly, his development philosophy revolved round man, his society and environment (nature) and their respective and simultaneous development. He believed that, instead of man exploiting the society and both exploiting nature, there is a symbiotic way of life which is in harmony with each other. In his frame of reference for development, man is the centre of attention. The objective is the moral and spiritual development of man. Man is primarily his consciousness, his capacity to be self-conscious and his inbuilt-potentiality to judge between good and evil, between what will help him in his evolution to higher levels of being and what will obstruct his path. This gives him a leverage, not only to aspire after higher levels but to endeavour to attain the same. Gandhi believed in this self-effort and the path he outlined lay through ethical, moral and spiritual disciplines. The key-note of his ethics is love, which means near identity or interest with every sentiment. This love has to be expressed in the form of service and sacrifice. His ethics in relation to material things and property consisted in his concept of trusteeship. Every human being is a trustee not only of his faculties and attainments but of everything he comes by, and trusteeship consists not only in using his powers and goods properly, but in using them selflessly and for the well-being of all others.

The concepts popularised by Gandhi during his socio-political *yojana* in India's freedom and prosperity are as follows:

- Truth
- *Ahimsa* (non-violence)
- Prohibition
- Self-control
- Worship
- Eradication of Untouchability
- Women's emancipation
- National integration
- Village uplift
- *Khaddar* (*Khadi*)
- *Swadeshi*
- Manual labour

Gandhi's Programmes of Development

Purity of ends and of means formed an important aspect of his thinking. He believed that means must justify the ends and refused to accept the maxim, that ends should justify the means. He stressed on means because he felt that it is within the individual's control and not the ends. It should, however, be remembered that there is no rigid dichotomy between the two; sometimes end is changed into means to another end. Ends and means are interrelated and interdependent—means is the end in making the "end in embryo". It is determined and conditioned by the end. As a man of action, Gandhi tried to work out the means to achieve his desired ends—*Sarvodaya* and *Swaraj*— the new society of his thinking. Gandhi was non only a man of ideas. He could not rest by merely enunciating his idea on development. He tried to practice it.

Based on his own experiments, he worked out the details regarding a wide variety of things which he named as "Constructive Programme" and which he considered as vital for building a new society.

VII
GOVERNMENT POLICIES

The poverty of India was linked to the British exploitation of Indian resources through trade and transfer, described as Drain Theory. The British refused to permit the growth of industries, the British policy of land settlement in India and even the British educational system which was alleged to be meant to produce clerks for the Raj rather than to train people to solve the country's problems. In independent India Systematic Approach to poverty seems to be that growth is for the rich and distributive justice for the poor. Some believe in having authority to govern through ownership.

In terms of the distribution of resources, the vast majority of people in our economic system can at best expect to survive while a small minority almost automatically have a surplus and can get this surplus to grow. The natural propensity of the system, therefore, is to respond to the requirements of those who own and control resources, and in that process make those who have little resources even more dispossessed. This is the paradox. It is, therefore, necessary that a substantial reduction in the existing concentration of the ownership of resources, especially land takes place to effectively solve the problem of poverty. In this sense the eradication of poverty is a political task, and the prospects for the future will depend on the extent to which the political processes are geared to the purposive mobilization of social power to achieve a major transformation in the socio-economic order. Is it possible to expect such a human act from our politicians? They are spending over one trillion US dollars in armaments. Winston Churchill had said, "... if the human race wishes to have a prolonged and indefinite period of material prosperity, they have only got to behave in a peaceful and helpful way towards one another and science will do for them all they wish and more than they can dream."

Role of Leadership

The type of leadership required at the grassroots to organize people to help themselves is of two types—leadership from outside and leadership from within. The outside leaders are bearers of new ideas and specialized skills. In my own work I found that the skill most called for is that of patience in working with communities. This is hard to acquire and harder to practice. In my case study of "School is Built", I have highlighted the need for patience, idealism, resourcefulness and above all a skill in relationship on the part of a community organizer. Here, I had to begin with an apathetic, if not hostile, community. I had to find out a project that will appeal to all, induce the need for it, organize the material and human resources of the community and patiently pursue my objective of bringing together the various groups in the community despite many reverses. In a large countrywide programme the factors of time and skill both tend to be sacrificed in the interests of time coverage and the urgency of target achievement. We substitute short term 'trained' workers for adequately qualified personnel and use a 'multi purpose' functionary in place of a team of development professionals. The type of training input needed and the kind of workers or officials required to eradicate poverty has to receive proper attention.

I feel that training, research and extension must become an integral part of any system of work with people. It is wrong to artificially separate them from one another. There is possibility of a degree of variance depending on the interest of an individual or a set of workers.

VIII
EDUCATING THE EDUCATED

The central problem in the world today is not so much the development of the so-called underdeveloped, as it is one of educating the educated.

The task is verily one of educating or developing the so-called 'developed' and the educated. To use a new coinage, one that has, by now, become almost a neo-classical expression in the field of social change, we need to de-school or de-educate the leaders, the vanguard or the elite of the global society first. If the poor and the deprived, the sick and those awaiting self-determination, have to be helped, the task needs to be redefined.

What is called for is not to help those who apparently stand in need on a priority basis, but to offer succour to all those who think that they are qualified enough to meet the needs of the afflicted.

It is the doctor that needs to heal himself. For, it is the projection of the values of the systems, most of whom are still the products of a colonial, imperialist past, which continues to haunt the process of give and take that is involved in any helping process. Unless the helper is healed, the persons or cultures at the receiving end cannot be helped at all. The following extracts from a recent news item will make our contention clear. It will make it evident how much of help the 'giver' so-called needs.

> "A vaccine against primary liver cancer caused by Hepatitis B virus (HBV) has been developed by Australian scientists. The vaccine has been tested on chimpanzees and young children in Taiwan, Burundi, Senegal and South Africa, and it has been found 90 per cent effective in preventing cancer, according to Prof. Gordon L. Ada, Department of Microbiology, the Australian National University. But, the vaccine is difficult to make, expensive to produce, and requires a course of three injections, says an Australian Science Newsletter, quoting Prof. Ada" (*Indian Express,* 2nd July, 1984, New Delhi).

Are the Australian researchers, at Canberra, trying to invent a vaccine or are they elucidating the Darwinian theory interpreting it in their own way? Have they come to believe that the chimpanzees and the children of Taiwan, Burundi, Senegal and South Africa (of course the Blacks of South Africa) belong to an earlier breed of human species to which the wasps of Australia or South Africa do not? Or are they trying to avoid any risks that lie germane in the experiment? They may, in turn endanger the life of their own species. Does not the Australian National University get a grant from the government to try these experiments? Does not the funding come from a source that is unable to provide the required number of jobs in Australia? Then why waste the precious funds of the Australian exchequer, some parts of which are diverted towards scientific experiments, to pay for the travelling spree of the scientists from Taiwan to South Africa? Can they not find their guineapigs nearer home? Are there no scientists who are prepared to try it themselves on their own anatomy?

Here lies the main issue and the matter does not emanate only from the Australian elite. It is the psyche of the elite of the whole world, including that of the do-gooders of the Third World that plans such exercises.

Charity has to begin at home. The helpers and the educators must be de-educated. They must learn certain basic facts about human anatomy, society and culture which constitute the A, B, C, D of human civilization. They must know that what is true of the poor is also true of the rich elite of any society.

Unless the elite learn this basic grammar of civilization they cannot help anyone and not even themselves. All that they can do in the eventuality of failing to learn this grammar is to move away from the poor and block their sun. This is the advice that one of the starving sages had given to Alexander the Great. When the latter had introduced himself as the emperor of the world to the former, he generously asked the sage, "What can I do to help your situation? You have only to ask for it".

"Don't block my sun," came the quick reply, "Please stand aside. That is the only help that you can offer." Multinationals have become the greatest obstacle to all-round development.

IX
MULTI-NATIONAL CORPORATIONS (MNCS)

Majid Tehranian says: "Although capitalism has always been an international system, with the demise of Soviet Union in 1991 and the opening of Eastern Europe and China to trade and foreign investment in the 1980s and 1990s, a new form of global capitalism has emerged. Some 1,000 biggest Trade National Corporations (TNCs) and Transnational Media Corporations (MNCs) manage the global market. Their loyalty is primarily to their stock holders who are spread around the world. Regardless of their national origin, the TNCs are multinational in their sources of capital, investment, and employment. To survive, they need to have a global strategy beyond national boundaries and loyalties. They frequently come into conflict with national governments but need to cooperate with them. TNCs use their power to locate wherever taxes, wages, rents and government regulations are lowest and profits are highest. Whereas national sovereignty is territorially defined, corporate sovereignty is global."

David Chappell has beautifully summed up thus: "The rapid growth of the global economy in recent decades is perhaps most clearly shown by the fact that in 1970 the total number of transnational corporations (TNCs) was about 700 but grew by 1998 to atleast 53,607

TNCs that were contracted with atleast 448,917 foreign subsidiaries. The six largest corporations in the world (Exyon, General Motors, Ford, Mitsu, Daimiler Chrysler and Mitsubishi) have combined revenues larger than the combined budgets of 64 nations that include 58 per cent of the world's population (including India, Indonesia, Brazil, Russia, Pakistan, Bangladesh, Nigeria and Mexico). Only seven nations have budgets larger than Ford, Exyon or General Motors, namely France, the United Kingdom, Italy, China, Japan, Germany and the United States. Size of individual corporations in comparison to nations is impressive. However, there growing influence based on their growing number makes them even more powerful." In listing the 200 largest financial budgets in the world, Charles Gray found that only 39 were nations whereas 161 were corporations. The Fortune 500 companies in 1999 consisted of companies that have budget over US$ 9 billion, but only 57 national governments have budgets as large as these 500 corporations. In other words, corporatives are increasingly "ruling the World".

We are at the edge of new civilization that demands, nay necessitates a new vision of our common destiny to save the spaceship Earth by the Gandhian way of development which believes in "sharing".

X
TERRORISM

Terrorism is the greatest obstacle to development and world peace. K.C. Pant, Deputy Chairman, Planning Commission, Government of India, says: "The act of terrorism is one which is designed to strike terror into innocent non-combatants and cannot be condoned by any yardstick." He further gives the factual position regarding various attempts made to define the act of terrorism.

The European Union agreed in December 2001 that "terrorist offences" constitute those "intentional acts that may" seriously damage a country or an international organization when committed with the aim of "seriously intimidating a government or an international organisation to perform or abstain from performing any act, or seriously destabilizing or destroying, economic or social structure of a country or an international organisation".

Section 2331 of Title 18 of United Sates Code defines "international terrorism as occurring primarily outside the United States and involving violent acts or acts dangerous to human life that are a violation of the criminal laws of the United States or any State, or riot would be a criminal violation if committed within the jurisdiction of the United States or of any State and that appear to be intended to intimate or coerce a civilian population; to influence the policy of a government by intimidation or coercion; or to affect the conduct of a government by assassination or kidnapping."

The U.K. Terrorism Act of 2000 defines terrorism as "the use or threat of action *inter alia* involving serious violence against a person, serious damage to property, serious risk to health or safety of the public etc. for the purpose of advancing a political, religious or ideological cause or to influence the government or intimidate the public or a section of the public."

Under the Indian Prevention of Terrorism Act, a terrorist act is defined as an act committed by a person or persons with the intention of threatening the unity, integrity, security or sovereignty of India or striking terror that results in death or injuries (or likelihood thereof), destruction or damage to property, destructive of essential supplies or services, damage or destruction of equipment to be used for the defence of India or for other purposes of government, or destruction of any person with the intention of compelling the Government of India to abstain from or do any act. A terrorist act also includes the raising of funds intended for the purpose of terrorism.

Based on the above definitions, Pant arrives at the following agreed principles as constituting an act of terrorism:

1. Terrorism involves the act of threat of use of violence to intimidate,
2. Such violence may be directed against innocent civilians, the Government or Government facilities or both, and
3. Terrorism always has an agenda designed to advance a particular cause.

However, differences on what constitutes terror among nations has prevented the development of an internationally accepted definition of terrorism. Pant stresses that it will be impossible for the international community to successfully combat terrorism without first arriving at an international and universally acceptable definition of terrorism. Without such a consensus, one man's terrorist will remain another man's freedom fighter. There should be no "good" and "bad" terrorist and no double standards.

If terrorism is to be tackled, it is imperative that the sources of their finance and money laundering operations are traced, identified and neutralized.

Terrorists do not fight fair. They hit below the belt. Pant suggests following measures to combat terrorism:

- Root out the financial resources and support to terrorist outfits. Greater transparency and monitoring of banking transactions would be necessary to achieve this.
- Ensure international cooperation to track down sources of terrorist finance including hawala transactions and laundering of drug money.
- Compile and regularly update data on terrorism and terrorist organisations and share this in real time with concerned countries.
- Plan and carry out joint intelligence based operations to neutralize terrorist outfits and undertake as necessary operations to retaliate against terrorist acts committed in any part of the world.
- Institutionalise cooperation against the threat of Weapons of Mass Destruction terrorism and encourage international co-operation in tactics and methodologies to deal with the threat.
- Conduct a media campaign that creates awareness among people in general and the young in particular about how damaging to themselves and self-defeating it could be to provide any kind of support to terrorists or terrorist organizations.
- Develop multi-purpose international cooperation to facilitate action—administrative, police, economic and judicial—against terrorism and terrorists.
- Enact analogous legislation against terrorism in all member countries of the international coalition to facilitate and arrest, extradition, trial, and punishment of terrorists cutting across international boundaries and barriers.
- Finally, the international coalition against terrorism should ensure that any State not cooperating or that is continuing to aid and abet terrorists anywhere should be appropriately penalized.

Satish Kumar has aptly said: "The deepest cause behind any conflict or terrorism is rooted in the idea of dualism, in the notion of 'us' *versus* 'them'—'good' *versus* 'evil'. The line dividing the good and evil cuts through the heart of every human being. Once the world is divided into 'self and the other', we are forced to act in self-interest and self-defence. We create artificial concepts such as "national interests".

If we are serious about dealing with the deep causes of terrorism and war, we need to make a fundamental shift from seeing the world in fragmentation, in pieces, in divisions and see the world as a seamless continuum. This holistic view of reality is the essential ground on which a new world order must be built if we are to free ourselves from perpetual spectra of conflict, war and terrorism.

XI
POSSIBLE STRATEGIES

In many societies, the majority of the people were still confined within the remnants of a feudal past. Feudalism could often mean that the control of society was vested in a few powerful individuals who regulated it, maintained the *status quo*, with the majority of the people remaining below the poverty line and being denied basic human rights.

The purpose here is to identify the barriers and to develop a strategy for their removal. Mentioned in this connection are certain possible strategies that would help the situation. Some of these could be stated as follows:

1. Identification of a target group: a whole village or some specific community in the village?
2. Target in terms of women: a special desire to reach women as a target group?
3. Priorities and objectives: what is more important? To work with a village to acquire greater share of the resources of the country or the internal process of redistributing the internal resources and power within the village?
4. What is the point of entry?
5. What is the attitude towards confrontation? Is confrontation central and desirable or harmful?

6. Is there an attempt in one's work to integrate the villages/communities into the government system, e.g. in the areas of health, education, agriculture or, to develop a parallel system, more effective than the governmental one?
7. What is the value of foreign aid as an alternative to helping communities to take a greater share of the existing government schemes? Which is favoured?

Regarding strategy number 7, relating to foreign aid, one feels that a judicious investment of foreign aid by a conscientious and powerful non-governmental organisation can save a nation form the de-liberating and destabilizing forces of colonial rule more effectively than what indigenous governments that are mostly flooded with foreign funds can do.

In a recently published analysis of the Sarvodaya Shramdana Movement in Sri Lanka entitled "Sarvodaya at Sri Lanka—A Rapid Appraisal" the truth of the above statement has been borne out. When we consider the totality of the political situation of the contemporary world, it becomes evident that no nation is really sovereign and that most of them belong to the client system of either of the Super Powers.

Moreover, the armaments that limit their sovereignty are not guns but the lure of free flowing 'butter and consumerism', available in 'duty free' economic zones, as in Hongkong, Singapore and Sri Lanka. If the concept of sovereignty is to be revived and the small nations have to become really sovereign, it can only be done through the achievement of the Swaraj society at the grassroots of the national pyramid. By liberating the local communities, such a process can travel upwards and finally free the nation from the shackles of consumerism.

The clientele that the Sarvodaya Shramdana Movement of Sri Lanka serves and belongs to the weaker sections. They live below the poverty line. It becomes difficult for the normal channel of supplies and the workers to reach the have-nots. A similar question can be asked again—how do the workers of Sarvodaya Shramdana Movement, quite a few of whom hail from the Nalanda culture, get de-classed and reach the poor? Gandhian values, and the infusion of values among the classes and the masses, seem to be the only answer to that question.

XII
CONCLUSIONS

The planning and development process may not yield any result unless it goes whole hog to build a 'no poverty society'; otherwise poverty will remain a shibboleth. This would mean nothing short of the leopard changing his spots. But can we? This can be done, if we have political will backed by a plan of action. Failing that, development plans will remain like the famous sun-stone kept surrounded by a bundle of cotton wool. The stone by itself cannot reduce the cotton but when the sun's rays are so focused through it, as to fall on the wool, by virtue of the heat that generates on the focal point the latter is turned to ash. So too "Plan of Action" properly drawn and put into action may help us to reach our cherished goal of 'no poverty society' by having active participation of people.

Wolfgang Sacks writing on development says, "The time is ripe to write its development/obituary—delusion, disappointment, failures and crimes have been the steady companions of development and they tell a common story—it did not work." Further, he adds, "the advanced societies are no model rather they are most likely to be seen in the end as aberration in the course of history.

The adoption of the western economic and development model globally has meant a certain death of the ecosystem and of the Earth itself. It is imperative that we transfer our ways of life so that the Earth is saved from man's greed and his murderous ways. Almost a century ago Gandhi had questioned the very foundation of western civilization, namely the modern industrial growth centred materialistic and self-centred view of life. He emphasized the spiritual aspects at the individual as well as the global level. If we wish to protect the Earth and its eco-systems, we will have to change our worldview, its prodigies of domination and perpetual growth and focus more on sustainability and spirituality of life.

Among the tributes received in New Delhi within hours of Mahatma Gandhi's assassination on 30th January, 1948 was one by Sarojini Naidu who said: "May the soul of my master, my leader, my father rest not in peace. Not in peace my father. Do not rest, keep us to our pledge. Give us strength to fulfil our promise to your heirs, your descendants, guardians of your dreams, fulfillers of India's destiny."

The force of her words reminds us that we should not rest till we are able to internalize in ourselves twin principles of Truth and Non-violence in our thought, work and deed. We should be optimistic and hope that we would be able to overcome the moral crisis facing the world in general and India in particular.

Although Gandhi had experienced many ups and downs in his life, even in the midst of extremely adverse circumstances, he was never a pessimist. He said, "Assassinating the body does not matter, for out of my ashes thousand Gandhis will arise." It is the duty of those who aspire to follow Gandhi's footsteps to create these thousand Gandhis by trying to apply in present day life some of his principles he taught. This will be one of the best tributes we could pay to Gandhiji while entering in the twenty-first century.

The phases of development followed in India are: First, consists of formulation of values and traditions; the Second, deals with the stabilization of those values and traditions; and the last leads to superannuation of these values. That is, either realizing the highest goal or decay and disintegration. We are at present in a decaying and disintegrating stage. In other words, India's development after Independence can be compared to an analogy: the grandfather "creates wealth", son/daughter "consolidates" it, and the grandson/daughter either "furthers" or "maintains" or "evaporates" it.

We have to reverse the process. We have to make India based on Gandhian Ideals, economically and spiritually strong, and to get its past glory to be called a "Golden Bird". Let us hope, as the saying goes, that night is the darkest when the light is the nearest.

No Change in Living Conditions

Bisheshwar Mishra has critically examined the census data of 2001. His findings are between 1991 and 2001 in India. No change has taken place in living conditions of people.

The availability of basic amenities like dwelling units, potable water, electricity and latrine facility has not shown any significant improvement as is evident from comparative figures of Census 1991 and 2001.

While in 1991, only 63 million households—i.e. 41.7 per cent of households—lived in 'pucca' or permanent houses (based on material of roof and wall), this figure stood at 51.8 per cent in 2001.

In other words, the remaining household lived in 'kacha' or semi-permanent structures.

About 74 million families were living in single-room houses in 2001 as compared to 61 million in 1991—an increase of 20.8 per cent.

Though the overall proportion of families living in a single room declined from 40.5 per cent in 1991 to 38.5 per cent in 2001, roughly one in three families was living in single-room accommodations.

In terms of drinking water availability, there has been a significant increase in households using tap water—from 49 million in 1991 to 70 million in 2001 (an increase of 44.5 per cent).

Yet, tap served only 36.7 per cent or roughly one in three households as source of drinking water in 2001 at the national level.

It is worth noting that about 39 per cent households in the country in 2001 had drinking water facility of any kind available within premises. Of the remaining, 44.3 per cent had drinking water facilities near the premises while for 16.7 per cent households, it was far away from the premises.

The Census figures also disclose that "more than three out of five households in 2001 are bereft of availability of latrine within the house".

The figure shows that at the national level, there was an increase in the number of households having latrine within their house from 36 million in 1991 to 70 million in 2001—an increase of 95 per cent.

However, the number of households where the latrine facility is not available also increased from 115 million in 1991 to 122 million in 2001

The proportion of households having electricity as source of lighting improved from 42.4 per cent in 1991 to 55.9 per cent in 2001.

Leaders who have a false sense of ego and pride, and want to take revenge by waging war should learn a lesson from poem of Ayodhya Singh "Harioudh". Let me quote from his poem:

> "Bloated with ego, one day I was standing over the roof of my house;
> Where suddenly a floating piece of straw fell into my eye;
> I was terribly upset, and my eye also became red;
> When my friends offered me a swab of cotton;
> My ego vanished into the air;
> I heard my intellect mercilessly retort;
> Of what use is your taking on false air;
> When a piece of straw is all that is needed to puncher your ego!"

May I trust and hope that all of us like Gandhi would consider the whole world as our family and live lovingly as its members.

The soul of India is not wholly out of its prolonged suppression. And that will remain so, until freedom is translated into empowerment and optimum equality of life for every Indian citizen.

REFERENCES

Banerjee, Kalyan, World Development Report, in *The Economic Times* Vol. XVI, No. 174, September 21, 1989, New Delhi, p.5, and Vol. XVI, No. 175, September 22, 1989, New Delhi, p. 7.

Chekki, Dan A., *Participatory Democracy in Action—International Profiles of Community Development*, Vikas Publishing House Pvt. Ltd., Sahibabad, U.P., 1979.

Gangrade, K.D., *Dimensions of Social Work in India—Case Study,* Marwah, New Delhi, 1976.

Gangrade, K.D. *Gandhian Ideal of Development and Social Changes,* Northern Book Centre, New Delhi, 1991.

Kumar, Mahendra and Low, Peter (Eds.) *Legacy and Future of Non-Violence*, Gandhi Peace Foundation, New Delhi, 1996.

Mishra, Lakhwinder, "Education for Secularism and National Integration", *Indian Journal of Adult Education*, Vol. 3, No. 4, October-December 1993, pp. 5-18.

Mishra, R.K., "Dirty War on Democracy", *Patriot,* Vol. XXVII, No. 176, September, 21, 1989, New Delhi, p. 4.

Mishra, R.P., *Gandhian Model of Development and World Peace,* Concept Publishing Company, New Delhi, 1989.

Nakajima, Hiroshi, "One Billion People in Poor Health". *The Times of India,* Section 2, Vol. CL 11, No. 268, September *26,* 1989, New Delhi.

Dassgupta, Sugata, *Writings in Continuum*, A Journal of Jayaprakash Narayan Institute of Social Change, Calcutta.

Social Work and Social Change, A Case Study in Grediu Village Development, Expanding Horizons Books, Boston, U.S.A., 1968.

Radhakrishnan, N., *Gandhi : The Quest for Tolerance and Survival* Gandhi, Smriti and Darshan Samiti & Gandhi Media Centre, New Delhi, 1995.

Singh, Ramjee, *Gandhi and the Future of Humanity*, Institute of Gandhian Studies, Rajghat. Varanasi, 1997.

Tehranian, Majid, *Third Civilization : Promises, Perils and Prospects*, Gandhi Marg, Vol. XXII, No. 2, July-September, 2000, pp. 173-86, sp. 181-182.

Chappell, David, *Lotus in a Corporate World: Buddhism in a Global Economy*, paper presented at a Rissho University, Tokyo, 11 November, 1999.

Joshi, Murli Manohar, *Sustainable Consumption: Issues of a Paradigm Shift*, ICSSR Occasional Monographs Series, No. 1, 2002, pp. 10-14.

Pant, K.C., *Combating Terrorism*, Key Note Address, International Parliamentary Conference to Mark the Golden Jubilee of the Parliament of India, New Delhi (India), 22-24 January, 2003, pp. 1-20.

Kumar, Satish, *Tough on Terrorism, Resurgence* reproduced in Relevances, Vol 3, No. 7, February 2003, p. 4.

Wolfgang Sacks (ed.), *The Development Dictionary*, Zed Books Ltd., London, 1992, quoted by Kamla Chowdhry in her paper on *Ecological Security—A View from Gandhi's Window*, Lecture at the Sasakawa Peace Foundation, Tokyo, 5th Mark, 2003, p.2.

Kamla Chowdhry, *Ibid.*, p. 6.

Mishra, Bisheshwar, In Ten Years, No Change in Living Conditions, *The Times of India*, April 19, 2003, New Delhi, p. 9.

3

Social Work Education in India

A New Look

ABSTRACT

Unless we worked for rejuvenating for the 'common man' we should write obituary of Social Work Education in India. Root has to grow from Indian soil to make it an effective profession of social change and justice. Blind imitation of Western paradigm would not help us much. Unfortunately, our education system and talent so far has been creating solutions for the West. India needs solutions specific to this country. These solutions do not have to be directed at the 2 per cent of the Auto Economy (Cream), or the 18 per cent of the Bicycle Economy. They have to look at the 80 per cent of the Bullock-Economy wherein "common man" is found to struggle even for survival. Social worker has to become the Parasmani, which turns metal into gold. Similarly, social workers' intervention or touch must make a 'common man' a capable and an effective citizen fully participating and decision-making in governance of his own affairs. The world is today dominated by a particular vision of globalization. We must reject both an ungoverned free-market and an old-style socialism with the mind-set of "One-Shoe" fits all. We want and should have a world in which different countries can pursue social and economic policies of their own choice.

I
INTRODUCTION

Training for professional social work in India began some time in 1936. In its more than six and a half decades of existence the number of schools is growing in geometrical progression. Under the self-financing scheme, with only one professional social work teacher the training in social work is imparted with almost no fieldwork. Some schools or departments just manage with a teacher of sociology as a coordinator who invites social work teachers on a per lecture basis. I call them "casual teachers". We would be soon facing the Gresham's Law in which "bad coin drives out good." While jobs are not growing even in arithmetic progression, with the exception of reputed schools of social work, job market for other students is shrinking day by day. Despite this situation competition for admission is very severe. It is calculated that out of every ten students applying for admission only one gets in.

It is also true that professional social workers have risen to the highest positions in academic, social development, and welfare fields in national and international organisations.

A lamentable factor is that despite significant contribution by professional social workers the profession even today faces 'identity crisis'. The problem gets further accentuated and complicated as most of the politicians and some of the leaders who are not able to identify either their occupation or vocation or profession call themselves social workers.

The highest or lowest position occupied by professionals do not generally revert to professionals when vacancies arise as anybody having a degree in sociology, psychology or in any field of social sciences is considered competent and suitable for these posts. Thus, many positions requiring professionally qualified manpower have neither been clearly identified nor professionalized nor, to use the modern language, 'marketed'.

Indian schools have been largely using American material unabashedly to teach their students. They make only a peripheral grafting of the thoughts of the great social reformers and activists of the country. Most of the Indian teachers dismiss Gandhi as totally irrelevant to the practice of social work. Gandhi was a great social activist but our social work educators and practitioners do not find any material relevance in Gandhian literature that would enrich the methods of the profession. On the contrary, American Professor Alinsky, has elaborately quoted Gandhi to draw sanction for his theory of social action and methods (Gangrade, 2002).

II
GANDHI'S GOSPEL OF SERVICE

Gandhi says: "The *Gita* contains the gospel of work, the gospel of *Bhakti* or Devotion, and gospel of *Janana* or Knowledge. Life should be a harmonious whole of the three." (*Young India*, 3-11-1937). In fact, he is not saying anything new which has not been stated by other scholars and Acharyas. But, Gandhiji's originality lies in the great stress that he places on *Karma-Yoga* that he knows as Gospel of Service. It was the guiding principle of his life. He says: "The human body is meant for service, never for indulgence, Renunciation is life, "Indulgence is death" (*Harijan*, 24-2-1946). Service to humanity has been the ideal of all saints and prophets of peace and so it is with Gandhiji. He therefore specifically states: "But the gospel of service is the basis of all, and what can be more necessary for those who want to serve the country then they begin with the chapter enunciating the Gospel of Work"? (*Young India*, 3-1-1927). Thus Gandhi's ideals and experiments provide much needed strength and inspiration to professional social workers.

III
WESTERN SOCIAL WORK AND THE INDIAN WORLD

Jan F. de Jongh in his article "Western Social Work and the Afro-Asian World" (1969), has raised many pertinent and important questions. Social work has been imported to almost all the Afro-Asian countries from the West, especially from America. This is to some extent responsible for its stunted growth in the countries of its adoption.

The profession of social work has not yet taken roots in the Afro-Asian countries. It continues to draw inspiration and guidance from the country of its origin. This makes many wonders as to whether what they have learned in the schools could be practised in the field in their own countries, where they begin to feel alien. However, thanks to the employment opportunities available in the Western world, most of the social workers trained in the countries of their origin, find their training more relevant and useful in Western countries, which they may soon adopt. This calls for a serious and critical look at the profession of social work, especially in Afro-Asian countries.

Social work, in India, and in the whole of Asia, stands at a different level than in the West. Its professionalisation must make its way in opposition to certain deep-rooted and ancient conceptions. The act of helping a person in trouble is considered in Asiatic culture to be a personal equation. The thought of being paid a salary for helping others is, to many, repugnant. The empirical knowledge that those who strive to assist often do much more harm than good is itself an accompaniment of technical scientific experience, hence we should not expect to find it in places where such experience has been scarce. When these facts are taken into consideration it becomes clear that American case-work, group-work and community organization skills cannot be taught or applied in India without adaptation. The end must belong to the Indian people. American social work may furnish some of the means, but the purposes and goals for which those instruments are to be used must be determined by Indian citizens.

The principles developed in the United States are much less relevant than the ways of attaining this knowledge; the attempt to develop a scientific approach for dealing with the inter-play of objective and subjective factors in the everyday life of people; that is, "bringing science to the aid of art". Some of the principles of social work have been criticised as not concerning social work exclusively, but referring to ethical and aesthetic value-systems which hold good for any profession and, in fact, for every responsible citizen. In so far as these principles are concerned with methods of work, some of them are so much related to the American social, economic and cultural patterns of life that they have little significance or possibility of application for social workers elsewhere. But main and most important principle to accept is the commitment to a scientific approach to the problems which our profession is called to deal with. Let us think for a moment of the applicability of the principle of "self-determination"; although this may be applicable in India, it may necessitate a new definition of the "self." Who is to decide? We have been wondering all along whether this would still be the same principle, or whether it would not be good to attempt a new formulation which would also apply to the Indian ego in the accepted sense of the term, rather than to redefine a concept from another culture.

In the Hindu way of life, self-reliance is the ultimate goal of life. We will like to quote from Radhakrishnan, our former President:

"That the Hindu solution of the problem of conflict of religions is likely to be accepted in the future seems to be fairly certain. The spirit of democracy with its immense faith in the freedom to choose one's ends and direct one's course in the effect to realize them makes for it. Nothing is good which is not self-choosen; no determination is valuable which is not self-determination."

IV
SOCIAL WORK—A CULTURE COMPOSITE

Social Work is a culture composite, and the wholesale transplanting of social work evolved out of American culture cannot be expected to work so effectively in other countries. While material resources are undoubtedly important in the development of social work programmes, the more intangible cultural aspects should not and cannot be neglected.

From experience in teaching case work in the Netherlands, it has been realized to a greater extent that the difference in the "cultural and scientific atmosphere" in Europe and in the United States is a major factor in preventing the importation of many American casework methods to Europe (de Jongh, 1953). Doubt has been expressed by an Indian of the value of the "individual casework approach" for all social problems in the East (Bulsara, 1952). In Czechoslovakia a psychological approach to casework has been developed. The underlying philosophy and principles have been drawn from American case-work, *but* the theoretical formulation and actual method are indigenous. This approach stresses "treatment through authority and educational but forceful action." (Karkesova-Doskora, 1948).

American social workers are also of the opinion that many practices generally accepted in the United States are not appropriate for transfer to other countries. The dependence of the individual from birth to adulthood upon authority in Germany is at variance with the non-authoritarian emphasis of social work. The individual in such a culture is seeking for substitute authority even in his contact with social workers. The opportunities for personal gratification are limited by concepts of duty. Severe moral standards tend to block the social worker's ability to handle such "psychological principles as emotional gratification, sexual satisfaction, dependency needs or aggression"

(Kesius,1951). The democratic participation of children may run against the accepted standards of obedience to authority. The reliance upon authority in Japan becomes a problem in arousing the interest of local leaders in local planning and action, for they look up to the highest figure of authority for—the improvement of their lot. Respect for the aged in Eastern countries make it culturally improper for a young individual to ask personal questions from a much older person.

Difficulties in social work practice are to be expected because social work itself is a manifestation of principles and practice drawn from an integral part of culture. The social worker is an agent of society, and should work within and through the limits and conditions imposed by that society.

V
SOME DOMINANT FEATURES OF THE INDIAN AND AMERICAN SOCIETIES

In Indian society, the family is considered a more significant entity than the individual. It is difficult for the individual to conceive of himself—as a person separate from or even with in the family. For these reasons it is rare for a social worker to meet a client alone. The neighbours or members of the family will not only be present, but will be actively involved in such situation. The worker who wishes to be helpful, therefore must be skilled in "capitalizing" on the interaction within this group. This is the characteristic skill much needed of a social case worker working in India.

Social organization in America is dominated by attributes of the husband-wife relationship which feed "individual-centred orientation" of the American culture characterized by self-reliance. Whereas Indian social organization is dominated by the father-son relationship and attributes of this relationship feed the 'situation-centred orientation' of the culture, expressed in the form of mutual dependence. These varying patterns of psycho-cultural orientation affect the inter-personal relationship in the two societies, so that the relationship between the individual and his family vary with them.

For an Indian, specially for a Hindu of North India, his family and its direct and wider extension, the caste and the sub-caste are the beginning and end of his human universe. He can find in that kinship group all that is meaningful in his relationship, his sociability, his security and his status. He will attribute his success to what his parents did for him, and repay his debts to them by honoring them and sharing with them all that success brings. He and his wife will, in due course, be the recipients of similar benefits from their sons. The cardinal measure of his worth as a human being is to be found in that group with which he is affiliated by birth.

The outstanding characteristics of Indian society, primarily held together by the kinship principle, is the centripetal outlook fostered among its members. Men belong to their deceased ancestors and their unborn descendents. So strong is this centripetal orientation that women loose their own kinship affiliation upon marriage and merge into their husbands, and patrilineal family groups.

For the American, his family is strictly a *sort* of nursery to prepare him for future on his own. By express definition, the family consists of man, his wife, whom he finds for himself, and his unmarried children whom he and his wife plan to *beget, often* with an eye on their desired standard of living. His parents have no permanent hold on him. Even more tenuous are relationships with his remoter relatives. His life aspirations are his individual advancement and achievements, preferably as a completely free agent. He resents being dependent on anyone.

The American outlook, linked to his individual-centred orientation, and reinformed each generation by a kinship organization dominated by the husband-wife relationship, thus compels him to satisfy his social needs, outside the family. Although trained to be independent, he has to depend upon other fellow human beings, not only for nourishment and support but also for their faith in him, and even for trivial conversation. This poses some basic problems which he tries to solve by developing elaborate usages, rules and regulations governing inter-personal relations of all kinds. These usages, rules and regulations are designed for two purposes. On the one hand they must guarantee his individual privacy, his right to associate with fellow human beings and to terminate such associations. On the other hand, they must assure him that such association is in his best interests, and advance them or at least maintain them. Neither of these ends is always attainable to the complete satisfaction of all concerned, for the best interests of one individual do not as a rule accord with those of others. Furthermore, as often as not, the individual objects to the bondage of prevailing customs, practice or morality and attempts to break out of them. It is this process of eternal American conflicts which make American society so dynamic and exuberant.

The ideological foundation, the theological sinew, the thousand and one organizational details of society and the consciously repeated educational economic and political slogans in America, all point to the horizontal emphasis on, equality and freedom. Such inequality and lack of freedom as exist at present are nothing but temporary imperfections to be swept away in time. And there is no question but that the political, religious, economic and even social forces shaping the society as a whole are moving in spite of many signs to the contrary, in the direction of more freedom and greater equality for the underdog. However, the result of this dominant equalitarian approach is often inevitably and unsuspectedly hierarchic. When the individual is propelled by his centrifugality out of his primary group, he has to seek some other group in its place. When his affiliation with a non-kinship group is loose because of equality and freedom, he must resort to more groups, bigger groups or better groups in order to ensure his desired share of sociability, security and status. The inevitable consequence is a perpetual competition among individuals and groups for higher status and a realignment of individuals into new groups for the same purposes.

The basic difference between the two orientations is that the Hindu centripetal tendency is channeled within the same ideological framework, so that no matter into how many castes the Hindus are divided, the desired end-results are similar and accommodative; whereas the centrifugal American tendency makes for a diversity of free associations of clubs with a variety of totally different objectives, which may have no reference to each other or may be mutually destructive.

There is a tendency in America to assume that change is always for the better. A manifestation of change is the nobility of population, both geographically and socially. Constant change heightens the need for acceptance and emotional security. There is also great emphasis on the value of the security. There is also great emphasis on the value of the individual in this society. The family, as it is, seems to be less valuable, except as a means roduction of happy and healthy individuals. The privacy of the individual gives a claim to the right of self-determination, his right to participate in the solution of his problems to express his needs to feel as comfortable as is realistically possible. Viewed against the concept of equal opportunity, it becomes essential to stress the necessity for the highly valuable individual to be economically responsible for himself. Social programmes are set up to give individuals equal opportunities.

American society is also characterized by the quantification of values, or the emphasis on delimitation. It has been suggested that the concept of sibling rivalry is a manifestation of this tendency to regard acts, situation, and relationships as finite and measurable (Lee, 1950). Parental love in this context is seen as exhaustible, so that the arrival of a new love-object diminishes what can be given to the other children.

From these cultural bases it can be easily understood why American social work has developed as it has, with value placed on client participation, the client's right to self-determination, and the constant expectation of change. From emphasis on the individual, the right to utilize existing resources increasingly, comes the belief that a client seeking help is close to treatment. It has been said that the concept of the desirability of an element of choice for the individual, and an emphasis on non-authoritarianism in the development of new ways of acting are peculiarly American.

VI
NEED FOR TRAINING

All over the world there is growing awareness of the need for trained professional social workers. The United Nation's survey shows a wide variety of content in the education of social workers, but there seems to be a general unanimity that some kind of training is important (U.N., 1950). This movement is being stimulated and facilitated by international fellowships such as those offered by the United Nations, by the United States, by various governments and organizations and by regional conventions. Because of the relatively advanced development of social work in the United States and the greater availability of financial assistance, many foreign students, teachers, social workers and other people interested in social *work* come every year to this country.

The Orientation of Foreign Students

As long as facilities for the training of social workers are not available in their own countries, foreign governments will continue to send students to the United States (Friedlander, 1949). These students from other lands have to keep in mind the fact that schools in the United States are designed for the preparation of American social workers according to the demands of American social welfare. This necessitates that the foreign students should be analytical and selective. Ashton, writing about United Nations' fellowships in the United States, made a very wise comment :

> If he is focused on learning how to be a United States social worker, has been poorly selected by his government and accepted by the United Nations in error (Ashton, 1949).

An Attempt to identify International Aspects of Social Work

The growing insight into the cultural determination of social work and the growing body of social work knowledge constitute a challenge to identify the international aspects of social *work*. This attempt may have had its first impetus from the establishment of the International Migration Service, an agency giving casework services to immigrant families whose relatives were in their native countries.

Active participation of American social workers in the development of social welfare programmes in foreign countries has made a major contribution to the development of professional social work and stimulates reflection on what can be done. Schools of social work and agencies in this country have also assumed responsibility for training programmes for foreign students, and for making their facilities available to observers.

The exchange of students, workers, and teachers helps to identify the international aspects of social work. More than thirty years ago the belief was expressed that the philosophy of social welfare programmes developed in the United States could be applicable to other countries with some adaptations. A simple hypothesis has been presented to explain why part of the knowledge can be transferred from one country to another.

> "In every country social work may be seen as a product of two separate sets of factors. One set should be generally valid because it represents concepts of those needs, hopes and demands that are characteristic of human being as such of the common man everywhere. The other set represents elements of political, economic and sociological development of the specific objectives and values of a given society." (Friedlander, 1949)

Friedlander has tried to underscore the international aspects of social work, especially as they refer to social work education.

> "Varied as the social, economic and cultural conditions in the different nations are, there remain certain factors that even in international social welfare may be considered the generic features of the social work profession. From social workers everywhere we shall require the ability to understand the basic personal and social needs, the emotions and the behaviour of people, and the willingness to aid them with sincere sympathy and respect for their human dignity. Those groups of population in greatest want of aid—widows; orphans; the homeless; the aged; sick; infirm; and disabled; the refugees and handicapped will everywhere require priority in social services...social workers always deal with human beings. They have to maintain their basic professional aim to comprehend the needs of the human beings. They serve and desire for self-support. They will attempt to secure for these people the wellbeing and social and economic security that the present status of the surrounding society permits." (Friedlander, 1949)

Thus he takes the view that considerable agreement exists among social workers everywhere as to the purpose and goal of social work. The difficulty seems to lie in identifying the ingredients the social work process through which the purposes and goals are to be met. The current phase of this struggle is reflected by the scarcity of materials identifying what American social work has found applicable and useful in other countries.

For the foreign student there is a certain amount of anxiety around the roots of social work process itself. What are the cultural ingredients of American Social Work? Which of these are found in my homeland. This is fascinating but will it work at home? Why and why not? The foreign student has to work in quite a different setting from that he has been used to in his homeland. The material presented, its analysis, the frame of reference of this analysis, are all oriented to helping students to become functioning professional social workers in the United States. The foreign student is concerned with developing social work knowledge and skills for practice in his country of origin, it is largely left to him to work towards that end.

The foreign student's analysis will have to be done with the native culture as frame of reference. This implies that he should know both his culture and that of the United States. Unfortunately for foreign students, especially those coming from the Orient, very little sociological literature is available. Living in a different culture gives them a new experience, and sensing this they start to compare.

The student's reactions to the foreign culture will determine how much he can usė the knowledge of the two cultures in making his social work learning more meaningful. Two extreme reactions sometimes occur, both self-defeating. Some foreign students cannot see anything good in America; others, after being exposed to American ideas, beliefs and conditions, cannot see any thing good in their own countries.

VII
SIMILARITIES AND DIFFERENCES IN INDIA AND AMERICA

The recent development of social work education in India has helped her to find a body of knowledge not only in the US and Canada, but in other countries as well, on which it was possible to draw in educational planning, and a body of formulated theory which could be used in teaching.

If we look at the setting in which social work education is carried on, we find one factor in common—the governments in both countries are founded on democratic principles, and in both, the ideology of democracy is predominant. In material resources and their development, America has many advantages, while India's available resources are not sufficient to meet more than a fraction of the reasonable legitimate demands on them.

If we look at the groups for whom services are provided we find that in both areas, services are provided for delinquents, both children and adults; for orphans and other dependent children; for widows; for the mentally ill; for the physically handicapped; for the sick in hospitals. Two striking differences are that in India there is no provision for the unemployed or, with a few exceptions for the family in acute financial distress, while there is widespread provision for a labour welfare officer in industrial establishments. In India the service provided consists almost exclusively of institutional care, with very little attempt to rehabilitate people in their own homes.

VIII
THE CONCEPT OF EDUCATION FOR SOCIAL WORK

The first similarity to .be noted is that of concepts. For example, the concept of the responsibilities of a social worker, concept of the qualities required to meet these responsibilities; the concept of professional education and the concept of its place in the educational system. More specifically the schools of social work in both regions see the social worker as a person who renders service to disadvantaged people and who participates in social reform movements to remove the disadvantages. We see essentially the same qualities of mind and heart; we believe in an educational programme of academic courses with practical experience of fieldwork.

Problems are encountered in both regions in putting these ideals into practice and devising an educational programme that gives it expression, but those in India differ to some extent in kind and intensity from those in America. We will discuss below three problems which seem to us to be of particular importance: (i) Certain problems of curriculum construction; (ii) Problems of teaching social work methods—casework, group work, and community organization; and (iii) Problems of fieldwork.

Problems Related to Curriculum Construction

We will limit our discussion to a few selected problems : (i) the place of social science; (ii) the place of content relating to the nature and organization of social services; and (iii) the place of basic social work methods, especially casework, group work and community organization.

It appears that in both countries, there is a common agreement that a professional social worker should have at least a minimum understanding of the social, economical, and political institutions of the society in which he practices. In America, however, the schools have decided that this should be obtained before entering a school of social work, and have built their curricula on the assumption that students come with this background. In India we proceed on the assumption that student enter with no previous study of any social science. Hence, our curricula contain much content from those sciences which think a social worker should have.

The striking differences in acquainting students with the nature and variety of social services is that in India it is scattered over different courses.

The other salient agreement in both regions is that student should have experience in more than one method, preferably in all three. In America, however, the student is generally expected to do fairly intensive work in one of the three, with more than an introduction to the other two. In India, the tendency is to give all students more or less the same amount of work in all three, or at least in casework and group with slightly less in community organization.

Problems Relating to Teaching the Method Courses

The Indian teacher of casework, group work or community organization has a much harder task than his American counterpart, owing to the lack of teaching material that is well adapted to his needs. The books which expound the principles of casework and community organization have all been written in America for Americans. Articles that develop a particular aspect of theory or show its application to specific problems are likewise, with a few exceptions in casework and community organization, of American origin.

Problems Relating to Fieldwork

The importance of fieldwork in education for social work is recognized in both regions; although time allotted to it is not appreciably different, it is hard to generalize, as there are variations from school to school.

In both countries, it is believed that fieldwork is expected to sensitize the student to human suffering, to give reality to the social problems discussed in the classroom and to help the student develop skill in the helping process and gain a deeper understanding of the theories studied in class.

A concept of what fieldwork should be is only emerging. Problems inevitably arise in arranging for the student the experience that implements the concept. The basic problems are the same in India and America: (i) that of finding suitable agencies where the student can get good experience, and (ii) that of finding supervisors who can help them learn from this experience.

The dearth of social agencies in India creates a special problem. What the Indian schools have had to do over and over again is to create an agency administered by the schools; or to create a service in an agency. Neither of these devices has proved entirely satisfactory.

There are some established agencies in which students are placed for field experience, but the quality of the work is below that which the school expects of students. However, the student may be supervised by a member of the school staff, who will be able to give better supervision than the employed worker. In India, with negligible exceptions, the supervisor is a member of the school faculty, engaged in classroom teaching, thesis supervision, and the many duties that fall on a member of any faculty, in addition to his field supervision. The number of students whom he supervises varies from school to school; it may be as high as twenty or as low as eight. In America, probably the most usual pattern is for the supervision of eight students in a single agency to constitute a full-time job, and very few schools rely so much on their own faculty for fieldwork supervision. As regards the qualifications of Indian supervisors, most of them have had a professional education in India or abroad. But relatively few had an opportunity to supplement their education by a work experience in the type of service in which they are supervising students; and even fewer have had a chance to do this work under the supervision of a more experienced worker.

IX
CONCLUSION

The need for social work to clarify its values is so great because its core is relationship between human beings; social workers cannot be purely scientific observers, but must also be active conditioners and helpers.

What is social work? To what extent should cultural factors be taken into account in understanding the individual and his problems? Should they be tackled? How far should the social worker go in handling cultural contents? These and many similar questions are continuously raised by practitioners of social work and social welfare, specially in India and other countries who attempt to adopt this new profession, developed and refined in the United States. This is not to imply that the American Welfare Programme is superior either in philosophy or methods, to similar programmes in other countries. It merely means that the technical aspects of social work have received more attention here. These skills should not, however, be directly transplanted to other cultures. The way in which technical knowledge and skill operates in differing cultures has its own underlaying concepts of value. Techniques should not violate these cultural patterns. Technical skills, like visitors, need to be acclimatized.

Three Types of Economy

Sam Pitroda says : unfortunately, Indian talent so far has been busy creating solutions for the West. India needs solutions specific to this country. These solutions do not have to be directed at 2 per cent of the Auto-Economy (Cream) or the 18 per cent of the Bicycle Economy. They have to look at the 80 per cent of the Bullock-cart Economy which needs technological and holding to get their day-to-day process right. (Pitroda, 2003).

Andha-Pangu-Nyaya (Cooperation)

This has compelled me to think unless we worked for the rejuvenating of the "common man" we should write the obituary of professional social work education. There is a story of *Andha-Pangu-Nyaya* or the logic of the lame and the blind. The story is about a lame man who has keen-eyesight, but can't walk, and a strong man who is blind. Individually they are very limited. But when the lame person climb on the shoulders of the sightless one, they function as a unit, and by cooperating achieve many wonderful things.

With minor stretch of imagination we might think of India, metaphorically, of course as the visionary but economically weaker country, and the US—as a culturally blind but financially strong nation, temporary as these designations are cooperation is the key. If there is to be such a thing as a world-wide, human family, working together for the common good has to be more than formality. Carrying each other's burden is part of love. The ability to trust comes from practical experience and from being trusted (Mukunda Goswami, 2003). The quality of humanity should be an integral part of social worker's personality.

Globalization

Let me give an example to illustrate the point. There are two brothers; Ramu and Shyamu, Ramu is elder, cunning, very clever and manipulative, while Shyamu is simple, obedient and respectful to elders. Symbolically Ramu represents developed world and Shyamu developing and least developed world. Their father had died. His wealth was a coconut tree, a cow and a blanket. In his "will" he had written that these three assets may be equally distributed between the two brothers.

The elder brother, as far as the coconut tree was concerned, gave the lower part to the younger and kept the upper part with him. Thus he would eat the fruits and the younger one would water and tender the tree. When the turn of the cow came he reverse the process. The younger was required to feed the cow and elder to get the milk. In regard to the blanket he kept it for himself to use it in the night and asked the younger to use it in the day. Thus he (elder one) would have comfortable sleep during the winter season.

The younger brother accepted the decision of the elder and went on working as required. But with the intervention of a Social Worker he became conscious that he was being exploited by the elder brother. He challenged the elder brother. However, his arguments were that division was as per the "will". All pressure on the elder brother proved futile to resolve conflict. He did not yield to social worker's advice as well as of village leader.

The head of the village devised a method to bring elder brother to his senses. He asked younger brother to cut the root of the tree, and beat the cow as lower portions belonged to him. He was advised to keep the blanket in the tub so that in the night wet blanket would be available to the elder.

Shyamu armed with an axe started cutting the root of the tree. Ramu immediately rushed and requested him not to fell the tree. He promised him to give the equal share of the fruits as well as giving his helping hand to take care of the tree.

Shyamu now turned to cow as he saw Ramu was milking the cow. He gave two Lathi blows to the lower portion of the cow which belonged to him. The blows were so severe that cow hit Ramu. He was thrown and got severely injured. He felt pained all over the body. In the night he wanted to cover his body. He was aghast to find that the blanket was in the water tub. He was unable to use it.

He realized that he had not been fair to his younger brother. He was willing to cooperate fully. Thus, peace, solidarity and happiness was brought by working together. Similarly, Developed, and

Developing world should work to remove inequalities and imbalances. The developed world must learn to share and sacrifice to achieve world peace.

Disparity

Nobel laureate Joseph Stiglitz states in Globalisation and its Discontents that in the last decade of the 20th century, the number of people living in poverty has increased by 100 million. At the same time the total world income has increased by an average of 2.5 per cent annually. Further, the assets of the world's three richest persons exceed the combined GDP of the poorest 48 countries and the richest 225 persons are richer than the poorest 2.5 billion people across the developing world.

Dr. Clifford Manshard, the first Director of the Tata Institute of Social Sciences, in his inaugural address said: "With the rapid increase of knowledge in all fields we have lost the ability to see life as a whole. There are many specialists, but few can correlate the specialization to our large life." He concluded by exhorting the students of the Institute with these words : "Over and above serving society let us be Social Engineers." These words of wisdom are as valid today as they were years ago.

We must have complete knowledge of the whole. In order to work as a social engineer or social worker, we must have general understanding of the 'total life'.

Just as Parasmani, which turns metal into gold, can covert an idol of God into Gold as well as the knife of a butcher. Similarly, a true Social Worker does not distinguish between the people based on caste, creed and religion. He works for the betterment of all.

Walder F. Bello, a world renowned professor of sociology writes that the world today is dominated by a particular vision of globalization that has no place for real politics. This is an unnatural World which is destructive of nature and of communities. Corporate capitalism is a destructive monopoly. We must have the courage and conviction to oppose this vision of the world. Our emphasis should be on community equity, democracy, diversity and equilibrium between community and environment, and local production... Our emphasis on the local is not meant to be parochial. We must recognize universality of universal human rights.

The first step is to delegitimise the existing power structures such as multinational corporations, the WTO, the IMF and the World Bank. These institutions are deeply embedded in the existing order and cannot be reformed. They must be deconstructed. We reject the models both of an ungoverned free-market and old style socialism with its mind-set of "one shoe fits all" (Bello, 2003).

We do not have blue-print for how to get from here to goal of a more equitable and ecologically sustainable world. But we do possess the necessary values in which different countries can put together institutions that realize these goals. Throughout history there have been struggles between ideals and interests. The interests tend to prevail in the short run but ideals prevail in the long run. So we must see social work profession in a more strategic and long term sense.

Social Work Educators must realize that a lip-service to incompatible or ill-understood ideas of another culture specially of Western will only take the form of imitation.

Swami Chaitananda Keerti rightly says: "That man has no future if India gets drowned in darkness. India is the heart and soul of the east that is where the sun rises. In the West the sun always sets."

This is an "awakening call" to social workers to draw theory, methods and practice from the rich literature and experience already available in India. Social Worker cannot tie himself with any 'ism' and his school of thought has to be humanity. That is, what education has to project. Our work should make people to stand on their own feet and stop looking at others for help.

The words of wisdom of the Indian President A.P.J. Abdul Kalam would be highly useful to social workers to determine their goal. He while addressing the three-day International Conference on the occasion of Golden Jubilee of Indian Parliament on 23-1-2003 said: "that poverty, illiteracy and unemployment were sowing seeds of terrorism world-wide. He exhorted the delegates that *Global sharing of resources* to address these issues for world peace and development is essential. In other words, when there is "a will" in the leaders, there is a way and the way as shown by Gandhiji.

Gandhiji said : "I am endeavouring to see God who is neither in heaven, nor down below, but in everyone" (*Young India*, 4-8-1927).

In everything that he did therefore the "common man" was before his eyes. The common man has lost his self-respect and his soul. Can

Social Worker help him to struggle to regain both? It is most unfortunate that Gandhiji's ideals and words not commanded attention from PSWs that is justly due.

REFERENCES

Apton, Elma H., "As UN Fellows See Us", *Social Work Journal*, October 1949, p. 155.

Bulsaia, Jal F., "Toward Human Welfare...The Eastern Way", *The Survey*, February 1952, p. 59.

de Jongh, Jan F., "A European Experiment in Case Work Teaching", *Social Casework*, January 1953, p. 17.

Friedlander, Walter A., "Some International Aspects of Social Work Education", *The Social Service Review*, June 1949, p. 205.

Gangrade, K.D., "Continuum Social Work; Social Work Today," (Ed) P.K. Visvesvaran, *The Madras School of Social Work*, Golden Jubilee Commemorative Volume, 2002, pp 173-178.

Karkesova, Doskora Marrice. "Psychopedagogical to Social Case Work in Prague," *Journal of Social Case Work*, June 1948, pp. 233-34.

Kasius, Cora, "Case Work Development in Europe," *Social Case Work*, July 1951, pp. 282-83.

Lee, Dorothy. "Some Implications of Culture of Interpersonal Relations", *Journal of Social Case Work*, November 1950, p. 358.

Mukunanda Goswami, True, Strength Needs Humality, *The Hindustan Times*, December 2, 2002, p.2.

Pitroda, Sam, "Indian Telecom Industry Needs a Few more Price Warriers," *The Hindustan Times*, January 13, 2003, New Delhi; p.17.

Radhakrishnan, *The Hindu View of Life*, George Allen & Unwin Ltd., London, 1959, p. 59.

Swami Chaitananda Keerti, "Meditations", *The Hindustan Times*, December 20, 2002, New Delhi, p. 2.

Stiglitz, Joseph, *The Hindustan Times*, January 24, 2003, p. 16 (given to you Noble laureate Joseph Stiglitz and quoted by Jayshree Sengupta).

U.N. Department of Social Affairs, *Training for Social Work : An International Survey* (Lake Success, N.Y.), 1950.

4

Gandhi and Human Relationships

Concerned alone with the upholding of the world, you should act. Whatever the best man does, others do that also. The world follows the standard he sets for himself (*Bhagvad Gita* 3-20-21) .

In the Name of People

It is people who make war against another people. It is always vested political, military and economic interests which wage war in the name of the people who must then suffer the consequences of their leaders' action. The life and death business of war is far too serious to be left to the political and military class. This simple but fundamental realization could be the first step towards that consummation devoutly to the wished; What if they gave a War and no one came? What do the Pope, the Archbishop of Canterbury, Susa Sarandon, Noam Chowsky, US columnist Maureen Down and many millions of marchers from Sydney to San Francisco have in common? They have all said no to a war on Iraq (War on War, *The Times of India*, p. 16, March 6, 2003, New Delhi).

In my view, US is engaged in to thrust war in a race for technical supremacy. What is the principal purpose of the race? To prevent one nation—one part of humanity—from dominating or destroying another. Much intelligence and much energy is going into this effort. Yet it seems more important than ever that an ever greater effort be made to achieve positive and mutually helpful relations of loving each other rather than hating or revenging. This cannot be accomplished by harnessing technical forces for war, but only through man himself, working with other men. Let me give two examples, one praiseworthy revenge and another loaves of gold for Alexander the great.

Praiseworthy Revenge

King Maug Fu of China was informed that his opponents had risen in revolt. He immediately set out to annihilate them. He took a pledge that he would return to the capital only after achieving his goal. As soon as he reached near the insurgents, they surrendered. Everybody thought that the king could kill everyone of them. They were however surprised at the courteous behaviour of the king with the insurgents who were all spared. Mustering up courage, the chief minister said to the king, "Sir! how can you violate your pledge in this manner." The king replied, "I am firm on my pledge. I have annihilated my opponents by abolishing animosity from their hearts. See, they are now my friends." Feeling sorry for his conduct, the minister said, "Without doubt, my lord, you have taken the revenge which is praiseworthy and worth emulation."

Loaves of Gold

When pride hath a fall, one never knows the depths to which one may sink. Pride destroys the faculty of reasoning and a person full of pride is not able to discriminate right from wrong, truth from untruth and *dharma* (righteous course of conduct) from *adharma*. He becomes selfish, considers everyone before him lowly and his own powers matchless. Misuse of his powers becomes his nature.

Alexander the Great had left his country to conquer the whole world. He had extraordinary talent and ability, but successive successes made him haughty. He trampled many a city. He killed masses mercilessly and plundered unbounded wealth. He would also reward his soldiers with the booty so acquired.

Once Alexander mounted attack on a town inhabited only by hapless women and children. The menfolk had already been killed in the battle. The women accompanied by a few soldiers had no means to protect themselves. Alexander could not decide whether he should or should not attack the unarmed women.

At noon Alexander felt hungry. He stopped before a house. After many knocks at the door of the house, an old woman supported by a stick came out. Alexander commanded, "Get me the food that you have, I am extremely hungry." The old woman went inside and brought a covered plate which she presented to Alexander. On removing the cover from the plate, Alexander found that it contained some old jewellery. He was greatly irritated and was red with rage? In a fit of anger, he said, "You old wretch, what have you brought? Shall I eat this jewellery? I had asked you for food."

The old woman coolly retorted, "Aren't you Alexander the Great? I have heard a great deal about you. I am glad I could have a look at you today. I learn that your food consists of gold, and it is in search of this food that you have been wandering, plundering gold and wealth and killing innocent people mercilessly. If ordinary loaves could satiate your hunger, didn't you have enough, in your own country? Otherwise why should you have felt the need to snatch other people's loaves?"

Alexander was stunned on hearing the old woman. His pride was shattered to pieces. The old woman then served food to him with great affection.

Alexander was now a changed man. He did not harm anybody in the town. While leaving the town, he got a stone plaque installed on the main highway. The plaque had the following words inscribed on it: "The ignorant Alexander learnt a good lesson from an old woman of this town."

II
WAR AND PEACE

It is most unfortunate that leaders of America believe in propagating the idea that war alone can make the world a safe place. The discourse of development, which America has initiated after World War II, is now obsolete. Some saw it as a fraud from the beginning; others tried to use it for what good it could be. Development now means equipping the poor to buy the technology of war from the rich. Ivan Illich pointed out disassociation of technology from human ends had begun in the early 12th century, and this process is now reached completion. Now that the terror is both a threat and policy, weapons of mass destruction have become an obsession for both rich and poor. America appears to have no sense of history, or perhaps it wants us to forget all history including its role in empowering the Taliban and Saddam Hussein. Worse still, America has no vision for the future, or else it would worry about the enhanced hatred it would face worldwide if it attacked Iraq. We as a country are not in a position to dissuade to the US not to attack Iraq. We have lost the moral clout we once possessed. And we cannot be treated as an economic power merely because we are about to plan a big order for deadly weapon system. If India opts to be land of poor hungry and restive people, kept under control by jingoistic politics and hard laws, the world will not care for its opinion. A visible return to welfarism (or Gandhism) alone can put substance into our claim of moral responsibility in world affairs (Krishna Kumar, We All Fall Down, *The Times of India,* March 6, 2003, p. 16, New Delhi). It has already attacked war ignoring world opinion.

All the people of the world who love peace and humanity, and they constitute an overwhelming majority, need to be united to raise their voice from all platforms to resist the Bush-Blair War- mongering. Messers Bush and Blair are a great threat to world peace and stability then all terrorist combined. The war against Iraq needs to be opposed tooth and nail since apart from being a threat to world economy causing suffering to the Iraqi people, it might assume catastrophic proportions with its chemical, biological and nuclear dimensions (Arun Bhagat, Faridabad, Conversations with readers, *The Times of India*, March 6, 2003, New Delhi; p. 16).

Gandhi and Events of September 11, 2001

A question is generally asked what would have been the response of Gandhi to the September 11th, 2001, attack in America on Empire building and World Trade Centre and December 13th, 2001 attack on Indian Parliament. Let me cite an interview which the Mahatma gave in the early afternoon on 30th January, 1948, to *Margaret* Bourke White. She had come to interview him for *LIFE* magazine. She asked the question: Would he persist in his theory of non-violence in the event of a nuclear attack on a city ? The Mahatma's reply was that if the defenceless citizens died in a spirit of non-violence, their sacrifice would not be in vain; they might all pray for the soul of the pilot who had thoughtlessly sprayed death on the city. This was his last message of compassion to mankind. He said "Non-violence is the greatest force at the disposal of mankind. It is mightier than the mightiest weapon of destruction devised by the ingenuity of man."

He further said : "I do not believe in shortcuts which involve violence. However, much I sympathize with admire worthy motives, I am an uncompromising opponent of violent methods even to serve the noblest causes. There is, therefore, really no meeting ground between the school of violence and myself."

The heart that bled at the sight of the misery of other was bled to death on 30th January, 1948 with three-death dealing slugs buried deep in it. The Mahatma has gone the way of all saints. India has lost her soul, but his spirit lives and that spirit will continue to live among us, as long as India survives. Swami Vivekananda, speaking in New York, had said "Since death is invincible, let it go in a noble conquest, and what conquest is nobler than the conquest of the lower instinct of man? Unless we are prepared to pay the price to achieve mastery over our lower self, the highest self to achieve mastery over our lower self, the highest cannot be unfolded and revealed to us. The goal of human life is to manifest the divinity which is within us. Arise, awake and stop not till the goal is reached. For centuries we have seen change. From the Unreal lead me to Real; From Darkness lead me to the Light. From Death lead me to Immortality.

With the modern day inventions we are able to fly like birds faster than the speed of sound, swim faster than fishes and remain alive under water. Man has walked even on the surface of the Moon. But as human beings we are not at peace with ourselves nor with the world around us. In fact we are under tremendous stress in the present time. On the one hand the world talks about globalisation and aims at a borderless world. On the other, we worry about petty personal gains. The only solution to this problem is that we need to work towards changing our mind-sets. We must wage a war against anger, hunger and illiteracy.

Remove Seeds of Hatred

It is no doubt, December 13, 2001, saw a reprehensible terrorist attack on Indian Parliament. Our legislators were shocked because they were the target. And we were shocked because militancy had reached the heart of Power in our country (India) and many more lives could have been lost.

In India, many of us are familiar with the theory of *Karma* or belief that every cause created has an equal and opposite effect. If we have a problem in Kashmir today, we need to just go back to our role in the creation of Bangladesh. If Bhindranwale was nurtured, Indira Gandhi had to die for it; the LTTE was armed and Rajiv Gandhi paid for it with his life. The analogies do not end there: If there were riots in Bombay (Mumbai), Ayodhya has to answer for it and if Z.A. Bhutto was murdered, what happened to his assassins? The latest addition to violent causes was the destruction of Bamiyan Buddhas and the havoc of Afghanistan before our eyes.

There is a common notion that violence is essential for demonstrating the strength of our response. An idea we have absorbed for too long from angry people around us. But are they the ones who inspire our deepest respect? Or the happiness? Violence is a response of frustration and weakness, when we are at our creative worst. Ruchira Mukherjee (The writer of novel : *Toad in My Garden*) asks us to call upon our people to come up with their ingenuity and compassion with solutions that will match a Gandhi, a Buddha, and later Ashoka, Akbar and other great people of our land. Were they weak people? The results they have achieved are still here for us to see. The nation's leaders are merely our reflection and reflection of present society.

The only answer is every Indian (or people of the world) to introspect and remove the seeds of hatred we have within us for other communities, nations, people of a different caste or colour. By focusing not on the differences but what makes us alike, a common humanity. *Let us first kill the hatred and anger within us and prepare for a future of genuine good, future for the whole continent and the world.* (emphasis added)

IV
GLOBALISATION

Daisaku Ikeda in his article "Spirit of Dialogue must for Peace" while elaborating on Globalisation, says that: "I (Ikeda) think we must recognise that the present movement towards globalisation contains within it the danger of becoming yet another ideological battle. Specifically, I am concerned that the inflexible application of so called "global standards" can cause the logic of conflict, exclusion and pressure brought to bear on those societies and parts of the world, that do not follow a particular model of development. More than enough warning signs have already emerged to temper the enthusiasm of the most dedicated proponents of globalisation. By this I mean the shocking disparity of wealth between and within societies as well as purely speculative non-productive global movements of money that are sometimes referred to as "Casino Capitalism". We must replace unrestrained competition with ethos of co-existence, the application of external pressure and force with the autonomous decisions of people and societies. The Buddhist teaching of dependent origin which places ultimate emphasis on inter-relatedness and interdependence."

Relevance of Gandhi

Indian systems and ideologies may be relevant at one time and irrelevant at others. But teachings of Gandhi—the great and benign lamp of wisdom and humanity are for eternity. He gave us the priceless gift of self-respect and sense of dignity as a nation... Gandhi was the leader of the people, unsupported by any authority, a politician whose success rested, not upon craft or guile, but simply upon the moral grandeur of his soul; a fighter who pushed back the mightiest empire on earth without the use of force, a spirit of profound. wisdom and captivating humility, armed with only an iron will and inflexible resolve, and a frail man who confronted the brutality of military strength with the dignity of a simple human being. ...We must go back to the spirit and ideals of those halcyon days when we practised the philosophy of nation first and foremost; when we spoke the language of the heart, when we breathed the air of idealism, when we walked hand-in-hand on the path of self-less service and sacrifice, when all sons and daughters of the motherland prided themselves in being "Indian first, Indian last and Indian always". The need of the hour is that leaders and people should get inspired by Gandhi's teachings.

Among the tributes received in New Delhi within hours of Mahatma Gandhi's assassination on 30 January, 1948 was one from Sarojini Naidu who said: "May the soul of my master, my leader, my father, rest not in peace. Not in peace—my father—do not rest. Keep us to our pledge. Give us strength to fulfil our promises to your heirs, your descendants, guardians of your dreams, fulfillers of India's destiny."

The force of her words reminds us that we should not rest till we are able to internalize in ourselves the twin principles of Truth and Non-violence in our thought and action. We should be optimistic and hope that we would be able to overcome the present crisis facing the world.

Gandhi is believed to have greater relevance in the present world of Modern Science and Technology. Modern Science and Technology has produced geographical neighbourhood but the distance between man and man has increased. We have become highly individualistic. We feel no longer concerned with each other's welfare, except in commercial and business terms. Cooperation has been replaced by competition and consumerism. Much intelligence and much energy are going in this effort.

Yet it seems more important than ever that an even greater effort be made to achieve positive and mutually helpful human relationship. This cannot be accomplished by harnessing technical forces but only through man himself, working with other men based on Gandhian ideals. Nobel Laureate Rabindranath Tagore had put it beautifully: "Every child brings proof that God has not lost faith in man." The message of Surdas, the blind Vaishnava Saint and poet was: *"O Lord, look not upon my evil qualities. Thy name, O Lord, is Same-sighted. One piece of iron is in the image in the temple, and another in the butcher's hand, but when they touch the philosopher's stone, both alike turn into gold. So Lord, Look not upon my evil qualities."*

The whole song expresses the truth that God dwells in everyone and in everything. This had touched Mahatma Gandhi deeply. The way to happiness and prosperity has never been through despair. Only the one who never despairs can have hope and enthusiasm in work. Gandhiji used to often illustrate his enthusiasm and hope with the help of table of 'nine'. Nine represents determination and not to lose heart even if one has no good quality. Let us take the table of '9'; 0 + 9 = 9, 1 + 8 = 9, 2 + 7 = 9, 3 + 6 = 9, 4 + 5 = 9, 6 + 3 = 9, 7 + 2 = 9, 8 + 1 = 9, 9 + 0 = 9. Thus, we began with a zero value and came to 90 at the end by our determination. This demonstrates that there is no duality in our thoughts and deeds. Just as we cannot live without the 'sun' we cannot live in 'peace' in the world without Gandhi's twin ideals of Truth and Non-violence.

Contemporary Social Data

The contemporary social data of the international community indicates increasingly a decline in its ability to hold and maintain its order and stability. The charismatic non-violent integrative clan of the founding fathers of model society, which had remarkably succeeded in welding varieties of heterogeneous groups, communities and ethnic groups together into a single humanity in different countries is under a serious process of erosion. The unifying moral imperatives of social and cultural values are being replaced by division and disintegrative forces in almost all countries of the world. Something vital is missing today.

There seems to have emerged a great divide within social settings such as family, village, town, ethnic groups and communities, creating splits in them, despite liberalisation and globalisation of economy. Collectivities are being individualized and jointness and communal values are getting broken and privatised. Such a social divide tends to place individual against individual, group against group. Such horizontal and vertical cleavages are further increased and accentuated by the monopoly of all the resources enjoyed by the so-called "elite" who show a tendency to amass wealth and power at the cost of ethics and morality. A thinker once said, that truth is a scarce commodity but its supply has always outstripped its demand. While truth does not seem to be triumphing all around us somehow, somewhere, someway, something is working which is bringing the human race to say about truth and nonviolence.

'Truth alone will endure, all the rest will be swept away before the tide of time'. Nonviolence is the law of our species, as violence is the law of the brute. Nonviolence is the greatest force at the disposal of mankind. It is mightier than the mightiest weapon of destruction devised by man.

The disturbing social data of violence all over the world do not make it worthwhile to live on this earth despite man's ability to conquer space.

The series of violence and unrest show decadence of higher moral and ethical values. The lack of spirit, trust, faith and inter-personal and inter-group involvement and concerns for each other, is suggestive of the fact that the tested path of tolerance, justice, morality and trusteeship shown by the former leaders and specially by Gandhi has been forsaken by the present leaders all over the world.

According to Gandhi, real democracy should have meaning not for a few but for all including the poorest and even for the maimed, the blind and the deaf. He did not believe in mere lip sympathy for the ideal which comes so easily. The entire social order should be such that this ideal should be achieved in practice. A genuine democracy calls for a higher degree of seriousness of purpose and a sense of urgency. Gandhi realized that once people are awakened, they would become a revolutionary force. Their minimum expectations would have to be satisfied, otherwise they would explode. This explosion could take many unpleasant and ugly forms. Despite many laws the whole electoral process and system in India is becoming less and less an honest mirror of public opinion. This is true of all other parts of the world as well. Even criminals are acquiring political respectability. This power is assuming more and more credible forms. The situation in other countries is not bright either. The voters are bribed and often elections are rigged. The candidates are merchandised rather than elected. One of the saddest aspects of election times is that politics overrides all human considerations.

Of course, in order to come out of the present malaise and dilemma, the only remedy lies in adopting the Gandhian path to resolve conflicts. Arnold Toynbee has rightly observed: "At this supremely dangerous moment in human history, the only way of salvation for mankind is the Indian way—Emperor Ashoka's and Mahatma Gandhi's principles of nonviolence and Sri Ramakrishna's testimony to the harmony of religions. Here we have an attitude and spirit that can make it possible for the human race to grow together into a single family and in the Atomic Age this is the only alternative to destroying ourselves."

Nonviolent Behaviour

The nonviolent behaviour on the part of humanity requires the highest form of civilization. Civilization is an act of the spirit. Ancient India was far more civilized than modern India with its satellites in space. The recurrent looting of banks in broad daylight arouses as little public attention as the sun setting in the west every evening. Our legal system has made life too easy for criminals and too difficult for law-abiding citizens. The country has forgotten that crime is not a problem to be handled by the police only but by the whole society. The two basic lessons which we have to learn from Indian history are: (i) Indian people have always taken their moral standards from their rulers and people have risen to great heights whenever they have followed in the glow of noble kings or leaders; and (ii) regions and kingdoms have been destroyed not by adversity but by abasement and corruption is the greatest solvent of public institutions, and that poverty poses a far smaller threat.

Politicians should give moral leadership for which people are yearning and waiting, instead of maintaining a system which is poisoned by collective bad faith and polluted by individual self-interest. People are served by deception and craftiness instead of by vision and imagination. The duty of a citizen is not merely to vote but to vote wisely. He must be guided by reason and by reason alone. He must vote for the best man, irrespective of any other consideration and irrespective of the party label.

There is a saying that reason is more important than emotion and action is more important than thought. That is why, I consider Shivaji greater than Ramdas, Jyotiba Phule greater than Justice Ranade, and Mother Teresa greater than J. Krishnamurti. An ideal situation is to integrate thought and action. A frequent saying is that nothing is more practical than a good theory of action.

Indians, by and large, are "low arousal" people. They tolerate injustice and unfairness with feudalistic servility and fatalistic resignation. On 15 August, 1947 India achieved Independence. But Gandhiji was not present in New Delhi. At that time, he was working among the poor people of Bengal. The reason for his absence was simple. He had two dreams in his life. The first dream was liberation of India from the British rule, while the second was liberation of India from oppression and injustice, from inequity and inequality, from discord and disharmony. While we have achieved the former in his life time, the latter is still a dream after more than 56 years of independence of the country.

To quote his own words: *I shall work for an India in which the poorest feel that it is their country in whose making they have effective voice, an India in which there should be no rich class and no poor class of people and an India in which all communities shall live in perfect harmony. This is the India of my dreams.* His first dream was fulfilled but the second was not. According to the Mahatma the true time for celebration would be when the second dream is fulfilled.

Gandhi was a leader of his people, unsupported by any authority; a politician whose success rested, not upon craft or guile, but simply upon the moral grandeur of his soul; a fighter who pushed back the mightiest empire on earth without the use of force; a spirit of profound wisdom and captivating humility, armed with only an iron will and inflexible resolve and a frail man who confronted the brutality of military strength with the dignity of a simple human being.

To Mahatma, Truth was God and Non-violence was religion. At his memorable trial for sedition in 1922, he said: Non-violence is the first article of my faith. It is also, the last article of my creed. In non-violence bravery consists of dying, not in killing. His compassion and humanity were as boundless as the universe. "Gather together", he said, "under *one banner all men from all religions, and races of India and infuse into them the spirit of solidarity and oneness to the utter exclusion of all communal and parochial sentiments.*" And again, *"My Hinduism is not secularism. It includes all that I know to the best of Islam, Christianity, Buddhism and Zoroastrianism. Truth is my religion and ahimsa (the principle of nonviolence) is the only way of its realization.*

Gandhi held the view that the life of a good citizen was the life *of Karma*—action in the service of the country *"My writings should be cremated with my body", he said. "What I have done will endure, not what I have said or written."*

Indian systems and ideologies may be relevant at one time and irrelevant at others. But teachings of this great and benign lamp of wisdom and humanity are for eternity. He gave us the priceless gift of self-respect and the sense of dignity as a nation.

Gandhiji completely identified himself with the Indian masses. He observed: *We must first come in living touch—with them by working—with them and in their midst, we must share their sorrows, understand their difficulties and anticipate their wants. With the pariahs we must be pariahs and see how we feel to clean the closets of the upper classes and have the remains of theirs to be thrown at us. We must see haw we like being in the boxes, miscalled houses, of the labourers of Mumbai. We must identify with the villagers who toil under the hot sun beating on their bent back and see how we would like to drink water from the pool in which the villagers bathe, wash their clothes and pots, and in which their cattle drink and roll. Then and not till then shall we truly represent the masses and they will, as surely as I am writing this, respond to every call.*

The Indian masses responded to the Mahatma's call in a spirit of total surrender. He said to them that *real Swaraj will come not by the acquisition of authority by a few but by the acquisition of the capacity by all to resist authority when it is abused.*

He repeatedly used to mention that through realization of freedom for India, we would try to carry on and fulfil the mission of universal brotherhood. He was really involved in achieving the broadest good of humanity at large.

Indeed in India, the manner in which intolerance has begun to manifest itself is obvious. Disagreement is no longer reflected in a mere angry letter to the editor or a cross-table debate, violence has become the fashionable way to settle "disputes" and "conflicts". The ruthless destruction of the liberal temper and its replacement by authoritarianism has not occurred overnight.

The rising tide of intolerance has forced even those committed to free speech to look over their shoulders every time they say or write anything. The Indian nation is gripped by the worst cynicism when the nexus between criminals and those in authority is dismissed as global phenomenon. The Union and the State governments are not called upon to account for communal carnage nor do voters exercise their right to recall defecting politicians. Hypocrisy, the hatred sign of a morally drained society, is still the trademark of India's political parties. Insincerity and sycophancy are the hallmark of Indian politics. Is there any political party which can claim steadfastness to its politics?

The problem of identifying forces which will work for community integration at the global level is one of considerable complexity. The global community is divided into developed and underdeveloped communities. It must learn to live together on the principle of interdependence. There are many Third World countries which are in no position to pursue an independent path of development as they do not have the necessary capital and skills nor, for that matter, the appropriate political environment. Many are already involved in debt trap. Quite a few have been ruined by civil wars. The poor can never hope to catch up. The technological lag grows bigger every year. The poor are expected to provide sites for polluting industries, markets for surplus goods and arms.

There are three factors responsible which have distorted a rational development of citizenship in India. One is poverty, creating the need for economic security at any price and its corollary, the widening gap between the rich and the poor, the second is the galloping population growth and the third is the conflict between ethnicity and the doctrine of unity. Reconciling the implications of the pressures upon the public psyche, a self-centred society has emerged. This society seems unable to look farther than narrow self-interest, self-promotion and self-ambition. This is the rule rather than the exception which leaves a particularly heavy burden on all disinterested citizens who are acutely aware that we shall have no nation worth the name in the near future unless we can do something to restore the confidence of the people in a lifestyle that shows concern for others.

A moral person or a citizen is one who is concerned with the welfare and happiness of his or her fellow beings. He subordinates his individual goals in the larger interest of society. He is expected to move from the ego-centric self to a decentring activity, leading to the formation of a harmonious and reciprocal relationship. These ideals and values are inculcated and transmitted into an individual by the society in which he lives.

VII
FAILED SOCIAL ORDER

We must understand that we have now reached the end of our resources in speech making and it is not enough that our ears and eyes are filed with speeches and declarations but it is necessary that our hands and acts have got to move towards a society which will really feed, clothe and provide shelter to everybody and treat everybody in the world as equal and pave the way to live in peace. We should move towards a society where everyone will live in harmony with his neighbour, where everyone will be treated with equal respect, will feel secure, self-respect and self-confidence and feels he/she is wanted. Everyone realizes that it is only global peace that will make the human race feel safe and happy.

In the new social order human race will not be determined and divided by caste, class, religion, race, colour, and the rich and the poor. Towards that social order, we have to march through in a peaceful way without hating and without killing anybody. The society, will then have sustainable economy. People will participate in planning and executing. It is from the bottom to the top and people to government not top to bottom. This is the non-violent approach to achieve a new social order.

Scientists should realize their social responsibility. They should focus on the global issues threatening mankind like population explosion, the environment and control of biological, chemical and conventional weapons and should stop the race against mankind. Peace to millions people means satisfaction of basic needs food, shelter, health, education and a place to live. It means that there is justice, freedom of opportunity for education, employment, recreation. We need to have a dynamic, democratic leaders who could guide the people towards this new social order. We need a living and vibrant leader who is fearless.

There is a story of a drowning boy and a philosopher or a leader. When the philosopher was lecturing him, the boy cried "take me out of the water first". Similarly lectures enough, meetings enough, papers and books enough; where is the man who will lend us a hand to drag us out? Where is the man who really loves us? Where is the man who has sympathy for us? 'Ah! that man is wanted. That is, Gandhi, who was voted as the greatest human being of the 20th century.' His message was "My Life is My Message".

If conflict arises from divergence and opposition accommodation and cooperation arise from complements balance of power and consensus. Complementarity means the possibility of mutual advantage and cooperative interdependence is likely to be highly advantageous. The more integrated into the society are parties to conflict, the less likely will be the chances of conflict being violent. This is the Gandhian way to create a peaceful society.

Power can be political or economic in its nature, it may emerge from the sword or the pen, or from the common voice of a collective people. Power can also come out of faith, one's conviction that one's way is the right or righteous way. It is this belief in oneself that we see at work in the mission of Mahatma Gandhi, in his practice of *Satyagraha Satya-agrahi,* insistence on truth.

Ethical values, however, sound they are, must have a bucking *of* *Samarthya* (strong) power, otherwise they are like a bow and arrow without an anchor to use them. The weapon has neither strength, nor accuracy, nor purpose by itself. *A* leader of the nation has the responsibility of uniting the people. He must constantly remind himself of his responsibilities as a ruler. He should not be engrossed in his own life and in the pursuit of self-gratification. He must not become an uncaring and callous leader towards citizens. He must turn power from a gratification into responsibility. This is expected of all leaders from top to bottom, or bottom to top, to serve people and build a peaceful society.

At a Washington meeting, some years ago, Peter Drucker, the Management Guru was asked who would make an ideal chief. Several possibilities had been suggested by earlier speakers. Why not an accountant, said one; and what about a marketing expert, asked another. What Corporation needs is an efficient manager, said a third. Drucker disagreed with them all. His vote went for a Doctor of Divinity. A man such as that, argued Drucker, would stand for values. We need a man of values at the head of a government or an organisation. We need a philosopher king, whose head is clear and whose heart is in the right place.

The twenty-first century has come with this challenge before voter(s) and people of India. If the right type of leaders or representatives come to power they will be able to accept the challenge and lead the nation. If India accepts the challenge as a nation to give a lead it will emerge as a world leader of peace.

Gandhi believed that there is divinity in all life, and there is, thus fundamental unity in diversity. The Gandhian model envisaged that development and governance should be bottom-up and not be topdown; goal should be self-defined and not stranger-defined, production should be aimed at basic goods to fulfil basic needs with useful value and not at non-basic and greed-oriented luxury goods; the process of production should be by the masses and not through mass production and the whole approach should be holistic and not sectoral. The Model of industrial development is relevant primarily to the industrial economic sector. This model needs refinement and has to be made sustainable. The Gandhian Model in the words of J.C. Kumarappa, leads to decentralized economic planning and actually 'Economic of Permanence', while in the Model of industrial economy there is the danger that the rich becomes richer.

India's success will be measured not by homogenizing a heterogeneous situation but by the success with which diverse groups can be harmonized and co-exist and become mutually reinforcing and supportive. Where traditions and modernity are appropriately blended, and where man-made capital does not become destructive of the natural capital. Both models have their specific constituencies in India. Thus, following a democratic path, there is a need for creative synthesis of the Gandhian and Western models.

Let us break the word Gandhi into six constituents. The first 'G' stands for Generosity, Second 'A' for Affection; Third 'N' for Non-violence; Fourth 'D' for Dedication; Fifth 'H' for Honesty and Sixth 'I' for Integration. These six lessons will bring down man-made fences that segregate us. The acid test lies in practising these virtues. It will require on our part-steadfastness, self-discipline, patience and faith. Gandhi said:

> If God gave him the chance, he would once again call out the students to take their due share in the task of nation-building as he had done at the begining of the non-cooperation movement, organise and provide them suitable outlets for their idealism and creative energy so that it could find fulfilment in the service of the common man.

We must go back to the spirit and ideals of those halcyon days when we practised the philosophy of nation first and foremost; when we spoke the language of the heart; when we breathed the air of idealism; when we walked hand-in-hand on the path of selfless service and sacrifice; when all sons and daughters of the motherland prided themselves in being "Indians first, Indians last and Indians always." Shri Jayendra Sarswathi, the Kanchi Sankaracharya, said: "First learn to love your country, your people. You can then extend this love to others." The saying, *Janani Janmabhoomischa*

Swargadapi Gariyasi, well illustrates this sentiment. *Janani* (mother) and *Janmabhoomi* (motherland) are more exalted than even *swarg* (heaven).

We must feel proud to be an Indian. India had civilization when others had Jungle Raj. It has incredible heritage of thoughts and deeds. People (freedom fighters) have died to give us this nation. Why can't all this inspire us, give us strength, happiness and pride. The need of the hour is that leaders and people of the country be inspired by the ideals and teachings of Mahatma Gandhi.

REFERENCES

Singhvi, L.M., M.R. Rai and S. Ramakrishnan (Eds) *Nani Palkhiwala—Selected Works*, Viking, Bhavan's Book University, New Delhi, pp. 238-43.

Ibid., 237.

Swami Gokulananda, 'Spiritual Upright is the key to Self-Realisation', *The Hindustan Times*, December 29, 2001, New Delhi, p. 2.

Gupta, J.L., 'Fight off the Devil within yourself', *Times of India*, December 31, 2001, p. 10.

Mukherjee, Ruchira, 'War of Peace-Conflict Interest', *The Hindustan Times*, January 1, 2002, New Delhi, p. 10.

Mukherjee, Ruchira, *Ibid.*

Mukherjee, Ruchira, *Ibid.*

Mukherjee, Ruchira, *Ibid.*

Daisaku, Ikeda, 'Spirit of Dialogue Must for Peace', *The Times of India*, December 29, 2001, p. 10.

5

An Overview and Role of NGOs in Development

I
INTRODUCTION

Today, social scene of international society is suffering from moral atrophy, spiritual decay, materialistic invasion, and dethroning of primordial values of universal brotherhood. The moral-cum-spiritual approach has already been put on the back burner. The cult of violence is growing very fast everywhere.

Both for the affluent as well as developing countries, the 21st century is going to be one of turbulence and far reaching transformation in the world. That refers to example of science and technology, to the changing values in economy and culture and also to global integration coupled with pluralism and tensions and to population size and world ecology. There is a massive effort to involve Non-Government Organizations (NGOs) to meet these challenges. NGOs have moved into front and centre of the world stage. They have become the warp and weft of democracy.

The proliferation of Non-Governmental Organisations (NGOs) itself is an apparent indication to the prominence they gained in a democratic pluralistic country like India. The crucial role of NGOs, albeit at the micro level, has been widely recognised by many.

The recognition is largely due to the advantage they have as against the statutory bodies and governmental agencies in delivering goods. Currently more than one hundred thousand NGOs are involved in diverse activities including development programmes, welfare work and a host of others in the country. The evergrowing relevance of these organisations in matters concerning people's participation and development has constrained the government to acquiesce in the services rendered by them to the society. It even coaxed government to ensure their involvement in a number of government programmes. The NGOs assuming the role as a catalyst of social change have enhanced their own standing in the changing Indian scenario.

II
MEANING

The terms Voluntary Organisations or Associations, Action Groups (AG), Voluntary Agencies (Volags) and Non-Governmental Organisations are used interchangeably. The United Nations (UN) regards all these under the generic name NGOs. The UN nomenclature of NGOs refers to "any international organisation which is not established by inter-governmental agreement shall be considered as a non-governmental organisation including organisations which accept members designated by government authorities, provided that such membership does not interfere with the free expression of views of the organisations".[1]

The concept of voluntary organisation or NGO is one which is easy to comprehend but difficult to expose in precise terms. It has been understood, defined and used in a variety of ways.

The term 'voluntarism,' derived from Latin word 'voluntas' means 'will' or 'freedom'. Harold Laski defined "Freedom of Association" as a recognised legal right on the part of all persons to combine for the promotion of purposes in which they are interested.[2] For Lord Beveridge, a voluntary organisation is an organisation in which whether its workers are paid or unpaid, is initiated and governed by its own members without external control.[3] Modeline Roff adds one more feature to these definitions by saying that voluntary organizations should depend in part at least, upon finding support from voluntary resources.[4] Michael Bonton defines it as a group organised for the pursuit of one interest or several interests in common.[5] Sills explains it as a group of persons organised on the basis of voluntary membership without state control for the furtherance of some common interests of its members.[6] Norman Johnson lists four main characteristics of voluntary organisations. They are: (i) method of formation, which is voluntary on the part of a group of people; (ii) method of government, with self-governing organisation to decide on its constitution, its servicing, its policy and its clients; (iii) method of financing, with at least some of its revenue drawn from voluntary sources, and motives with the pursuit of profit included.[7]

Kulkarni very strongly feels that voluntary action borne out of free will of its initiators and run without any form of external influence is, of course, rarity. For instance, action which is inspired, sponsored or engineered by external agents and its managements dictated or directed or even conditioned by authorities outside the organisation can hardly be called voluntary. The co-existence of myth and reality of voluntary action are pursuit in nature but in actual operation, they are feeble and heavily polluted with bureaucratic effluent.[8] He further warns us that the schism between myth and reality does not confine only to the origin of voluntary action but run throughout its lifetime and sometimes extends to its post-mortem.[9] Chowdhry is of similar opinion when he says voluntary action, as the term applies, is an action initiated on one's own volition. It is directed towards many kinds of actions like welfare of the needy, neglected, destitute, handicapped, aged and infirm, construction and maintenance of religious places, providing jobs to the needy, community service like roads, library services, parks etc.[10] He defines *voluntary* organisation as a group of persons, who have organised themselves as a legal and corporate body based on explicit rules and procedures for giving continuity and permanency to the work of the agency; providing facilities of group thinking ensuring collective action with division of responsibilities and relieving the members from unlimited financial responsibilities. It is initiated usually spontaneously, at least at the level of persons who form it, and governed by its members without any external control.[11]

Voluntary association is essentially a group of individuals that feels itself one, is ready within limits to sacrifice the individual for the group advantage that prospects as a whole. The group is organised on the basis of voluntary membership that is neither mandatory nor gained through birth but purely voluntary.[12] However, that voluntary membership is really psychological willingness, but in general patterned by a complex of social, structural and value considerations. This embodies a statement of explicit purpose of the group and of the way in which the association will be organised to pursue this purpose. Voluntary association is a structurally organised entity and more or less permanent in nature. They may continue to exist till their aims and objectives are met or may identify new areas of operation. The unique characteristic of this kind of association is that the method of control is necessarily one of self-governance precluding the chance of any external control or coercion. The members themselves take part in the decision-making process. The chief feature of voluntary organisations is a set of officials defining the delimited obligations and responsibilities of those who fill the offices. These office-holders or 'officials' are chosen by the members; sometimes only a few members in oligarchy choose the officials, but usually in the voluntary association all the members are given a vote in the election of officials since each and every member is assumed to have an equal interest. The members constituting the association, voluntary workers, would remain as paid or unpaid staff for the services they render willingly and conscientiously. Voluntary organisation is the product of the blood, sweat and toil of few individuals who are known for their persistent efforts and commitment to certain social ideals.[13]

III
BASIS OF NGOS

The quintessence of NGOs is voluntarism. The spirit of voluntarism stems from varied sources. It may arise out of the love of humanity, the belief that the neglected sections need to be helped, and a conviction that social justice is to be distributed in a more equitable manner in the given social circumstances.

Voluntary work has a religious basis too. All religions, needless to say, extol voluntary action and charity. Compassion, charity and duty are the common core elements of religions. Giving alms to the poor, feeding the hungry, caring for the disabled, providing shelter to the homeless, and extending help in exigency all constitute different facets of religious tenets. The followers of Islam, for instance, follow the custom of setting apart one-sixth of their earning, known as *zakat* for charitable purposes. It is a common practice among them in many parts of the country to offer *zakat* during the holy *Ramzan* month.[14]

The craving for voluntary service springs from the social instinct of man. Vilfredo Pareto explained it in terms of social instinct that comprises one of the most important residue inherent in man. The urge to associate with like-minded people for a common purpose and cherished ideals is the beginning of voluntary action at the individual level. The motivation for voluntary action, is the desire to lead a full-life. Many need more than what they can find in their work place or home. This is rather a need to live as members of groups doing things for themselves and their fellow members or for the benefit of others outside the group. The urge to act in groups is fundamental to man.[15] The driving force remains the commitment to some social cause, service mindedness and sacrifice. The motive is seldom profit intention.

Psychologists find reason in impulses that inspire members joining associations and continuing their membership. A broad variety of impulses namely, idealistic, educative, psychological and social is responsible for associations.[16] These impulses may further be influenced by the prevailing social conditions that can result in voluntary action.

Voluntary work includes a wide spectrum of activities. Quite often it is problem-oriented. It is initiated not merely to solve the problem which might show its ugly face constantly but to prevent its recurrence. It is aimed at changing or transforming the socio-economic life of the people particularly the weaker and marginalised sections of the society.[17] Ranging from providing food and shelter to the hapless and to establishing super speciality hospitals, the true spirit of selfless service is reflected. Shelter for the homeless, education for the illiterates, medicare for the sick, assistance to the exploited and poor, protection of the nature and environment from the tide of consumerism, designing plans for the upliftment of those *left* behind in the process of so-called development and in many more areas voluntarism is apparent.

IV
NGOS IN INDIA AND ABROAD

Voluntary association is not a peculiar characteristic of Indian social structure, although there are some distinguishing features. In the US, NGOs are better known as private agencies. People who formed such agencies were in the forefront for assisting the victims of the complex modern social processes like industrialisation, urbanisation and immigration. Playing the role as socially responsible citizens they rendered essential services to the needy through programmes, experimentation and efforts in order to fill the lacuna formed by the work of governmental agencies.

NGOs have been recognised as social welfare organizations in Western countries. Efforts of these organisations are in effect more complementary to that of the State. They act as a link between the government and the needy and the aid they receive from the government are channelised to the people.[18] The approbation of these agencies is largely due to their organisational abilily, managerial efficiency and competence in corrective and curative work they offer to the society.[19]

The extent of voluntarism varies from country to country and time to time. Tocqueville, the French social thinker, observes that the English regard association as only one of several "powerful means of action", the American appears to regard association as the "only means". He viewed Americans as a "nation of joiners" and more addicted to associations than the English.[20] Contrary to this, the French and the Germans, the less enthused in forming associations present a weak tradition of voluntary organization.[21]

Of late, the NGOs originated in Western countries act as anti-state apparatus. *This is* due to the perception that the State is ill-equipped to solve the problems of the neglected sections and so the NGOs are being projected as an alternative to over centralised state system. It is often said that voluntary intervention is needed to keep a check on the modern centralised and militarised systems.[22] Current history of the West gives substantial evidence to this sort of voluntary intervention. The success story of Ralf Nader, who crusaded against the powerful automobile manufacturers in the US is a case in point. He, along with a group of young consumer advocates, fought against the industry which marketed unsafe products. The efforts of these socially committed individuals later grew into a movement and exerted influence on government to make necessary legislation to curb the dangerous and exploitative practices of the industry.

The structural characteristics in one way or other influence the nature of association. In Western society, kinship and occupational roles and their associated interests are, to large extent segregated both from each other and other interests. In the occupational and kinship spheres members of Western society achieve success and happiness by their own individual efforts and achievements. In the Indian society, by contrast, kin, caste and community groups determine many of these interests that are segregated in Western Society. It is for the organised accomplishment of these segregated interests and for such of the interests related to occupation and kinship as cannot be achieved by the individual himself on the job or in his isolated conjugal family, that associations exist in great numbers in Western society.[23]

NGOs in India are identified on the basis of certain criteria. The Seventh Five Year Plan while recognising the role of the NGOs in rural development programme lists out the criteria for organisations to be identified as NGOs. As per the Plan yardstick the NGO should be a legal entity registered under an appropriate Act. The Acts under which the organisations can be registered, depending on the nature and scope of activities, are the Societies Registration Act, 1860; the Indian Trusts Act, 1882; the Cooperative Societies Act, 1904; the Joint Stock Companies Act, 1956, and Charitable and Endowment Trusts Act.

V
VOLUNTARY ACTION IN INDIA : THE BACKGROUND

Voluntary action has its origin in charity, philanthropy and poor relief. India has a glorious history of organised voluntary work for public and social good. Before the nineteenth century charity on a voluntary basis outside the religious channels took place mainly during emergencies like famine and floods. The rich and the ruling extended support to the indigent.[24] Planting trees along the ways for the benefit of travellers and digging tanks and wells for drinking purposes were common and tangible forms of voluntary action.

VI
BEFORE INDEPENDENCE

In the ancient and medieval India, voluntarism was manifest in diverse forms. In the fields of education, medical service, cultural promotion and at crisis like drought, floods and epidemics people volunteered their service and expertise. During this period there was a system of *adheenams* prevailing in the southern parts of the country. Under this system, the community organised and established centres of learning and research where free food and accommodation were given. Communities raised funds through their own organisations to distribute grants to hospitals, schools, colleges and orphanages. The system of *Madhukari,* where students supported themselves by taking food from households on a rotation basis, was in vogue. *Dharamshalas* (rest houses) were constructed for the itinerants.[25]

Voluntarism, found its most human expression at the time of natural calamities. Communities pooled their resources to help those affected in contingencies. The later part of the sixteenth and seventeenth centuries witnessed the outbreak of severe famines. The King responded to the pitiable situation with royal charity doles. Philanthropists came forward out of their ardent belief in *Dhana Dharma.*

In the nineteenth century voluntarism gained new stimulus. Voluntary action was evident in three directions, namely religious reforms, social reforms and voluntary work. Social reformers like Raja Ram Mohun Roy (1772-1883), Devendranath Tagore (1817-1905), Sayyed Ahmed Khan (1817-91), Dayananda Saraswathy (1824-1933), Iswarachandra Vidya Sagar (1826-91), Kesava Chandra Sen (1841-84), Ram Krishna Paramahamsa (1836-86) and Swami Vivekananda (1863-1902) had focused their voluntary efforts against the evil customs and practices to usher in radical reforms. The highly rigid social structure built on the foundation of caste system offered them with extensive opportunities for protest and reform movements. Many influenced by modern western thought began mobilising people against all odds. Large number of people volunteered to work with them. Their voluntary and selfless services were instrumental in organising public opinion against anti-social, caste-directed practices such as *sati* and several other disabilities. The reformers initiated a number of movements with a view to eliminate these age-old practices.

Atmiya Society, founded by Ram Mohun Roy in 1815 in Calcutta, was the first amongst the voluntary associations in India.[26] The Unitarian Committee (1822), Brahmo Samaj (1828), Dharam Samaj (1830), Prarthana Samaj (1864), The National Council for Women in India (1875), Indian Social Conference (1887), Theosophical Movement (1893), Ramakrishna Mission (1897) and Anjuman-Himayat-I-Islam (1898) are other prominent associations.

Ram Mohun Roy, the founder of Brahmo Samaj too, propagated the ideal of *ek dharma, ek jati* and *ek bhagavan* (one religion, one caste, and one God) . He organised and steered vigilance committees of volunteers to fight *sati*. Arya Samaj denounced child marriage and endorsed widow remarriage. Ramakrishna Mission took up humanitarian work. Dadabhai Naoroji in the western parts of India played a pioneering role in the furtherance of education of girls and women. Jyotiba Phule striving for both the emancipation of untouchables and educating girl children started Satya Shodhan Samaj (1873) in Pune. Ranade who founded Prarthana Samaj supported the movements for widow remarriage and women education. All India Mohammdan Educational Conference was formed in 1886 by Sayyed Ahmad Khan. Pandit Ramabai toiled for the education of women. In 1905, Servants of India Society was instituted by Gopala Krishna Gokhale. Aiming the goal of providing education and emancipating women from their hardships, D.K. Karve founded the All India Seva Samiti in 1914.

Programmes of these organisations, which inculcated voluntary spirit included education, relief work and welfare service to the poor and neglected. As a result of the efforts of the reformers a number of associations originated in different parts of the country attracting many people to voluntary work. The Widows Remarriage Association (1850), Widows Home in Mysore (1907), Mahila Silpasrama (1907), Depressed Classes Mission (1906), Gokhale Education Society are noted among them.

Christian missionaries were not far behind the reformers in augmenting voluntary action. Missionaries belonging to several congregations like Baptist, Anglican, Wesleyan and Roman participated in charity work and reform activities. Christian missionaries were in fact the pioneers in setting up orphanages and institutes for the old and infirm. For instance, upto 1895 only Christian missionaries had set up orphanages. Voluntarism of missionaries took concrete shape in the field of education. A network of educational institutions across the country was established. Even in remote and unaccessible areas they set up schools for tribals.[27] Their area of operation was not merely confined to this. Apart from health care services, they protected the tribals who remained as the most disadvantaged section. Missionaries organised tribals in their attempt to protect them from exploitation and land alienation.

Chotanagpur Catholic Mission Cooperative Society, started in 1909, is a solid example in this regard.[28] They extended their work to other tribal belts which yielded good results. Uplifting the poor from their miseries, conscientising them, establishing hospitals, dispensaries and other welfare centres, including rehabilitation centres, constructing roads, helping women to come up, were all part of missionary work.[29] Their contribution in eradicating untouchability and eliminating various disabilities were vital and timely. In the succeeding years they ventured into new areas.

Voluntary action is often directly responsible for state intervention in many realms where the governmental efforts could not be of much help. Voluntary action during this period had policy implications too. The organised effort of voluntary associations paved the way for many a social legislation. There are several instances to substantiate this. The coming of Children Aid Societies in Madras in 1925 and in Bombay in 1927, had led to the enactment of Children Acts. Voluntary action in the field of rehabilitation of fallen women persuaded the government to enact the Madras Suppression of Immoral Traffic Act in 1930. This was mainly the outcome of the work of Madras Vigilance Association.[30]

The enactment of the Literary, Scientific and Charitable Society Registration Act of XIII in 1850 was another significant event in the history of voluntary action. This law came into effect as a result of the situation in which voluntary organisations received growing importance. Later in 1860 it became the Societies Registration Act. In the beginning years of the twentieth century, religious fervour gave way to more rationalist principles. The birth of the Servants of India Society laid the foundation of secular voluntary action in India.[31] The coming of Mahatma Gandhi to the political scene gave a fillip to principle-based voluntary work in India.

VII
GANDHI'S ROLE

Gandhi's strong adherence to high social ideals and practical approach inspired sincere and conscientious workers to follow him with a genuine sense of dedication. His belief in the potential of rural India, and the wisdom that India lives in her villages guided him to concentrate his efforts on villages. Rural reconstruction was his mission. He initiated a large number of constructive social welfare programmes designed to remove the evils that had crept into society.

His constructive programme, which entailed among others *charkha*, *khadi*, *gramodyog*, basic education, removal of untouchability and prohibition found ready acceptance among people.[32] The success of his powerful weapon *satyagraha* too enticed many volunteers. Gandhi used this weapon in Champaran in 1917 against European planters who demanded the peasants to cultivate indigo and sell it at prices arbitrarily fixed by the planters.[33] Educated volunteers also took part in this *satyagraha* with other national leaders.

Gandhi founded Harijan Sevak Sangh, Gramodyog Sangh, Hindustan Talim Sangh, Adivasi Seva Mandals and Kasturba Gandhi National Memorial Trust.[34] Inspired by his ideology, a number of voluntary associations like the All India Spinners Association, the All India Village Industries Association and many others later emerged on the scene. Many leaders were to follow him.

Vinoba Bhave who came forward with the novel idea of *Bhoodan* and *Gramdan* movement (land and village gift) and Jayaprakash Narayan along with others inculcated the Gandhian spirit of voluntarism. A.V. Thakkar, popularly known as Thakkar Bapa, who made a mark in the history of voluntary service, too based his work on Gandhian principles. His attention was drawn to the field of education, health and tribal development.

Prior to Independence, the growth and working of voluntary organisations were greatly influenced by the freedom movement. Three major national forces, namely the secular nationalism as preached by the Indian National Congress, Hindu nationalism and Hindu Maha Sabba, and Muslim nationalism of the Muslim League were at work. These forces too exerted their own influence to the development of voluntary organisations.

VIII
AFTER INDEPENDENCE

A sudden spurt in the growth of organised voluntary action was witnessed soon after Independence. One estimate shows that the increase was five-fold during 1953-80.[35] The impact of Gandhian ideology in the field of voluntary work was evident in the genesis of many voluntary organisations. Following the demise of Gandhi, his constructive work followers met at Sevagram in March 1948. Two things happened in this meeting: One, a fellowship of brotherhood under the Sarvodaya Samaj, and two, a coordinated organisation named 'Sarva Seva Sangh' for all the constructive work institutions were established. A number of freedom fighters motivated by Gandhian social ideal too joined NGOs to participate in the development process.

Acharya Vinoba Bhave's attempt to transform rural India got crystallized into his *Bhoodan* and *Gramdan* movements. This was a major movement for voluntary action. Till 1969, 140,020 villages were declared for *Gramadan*. He further widened the concept of *dan* (gift) for the benefit of the society as a whole. Other forms of *dan* included *Shramdan* (gift of labour), *Sampatidan* (gift of money), *Buddhidan* (gift of mental abilities for the realization of Sarvodaya ideals) and *Jeevandan* (dedication of life). A *Shanti Sena* (Peace Army) was launched in 1957 for all those who pledged themselves to work for truth and nonviolence.

On its part, government embarked on a number of projects to elicit voluntary action. Realising its inability and due to other constraints, government wooed NGOs to participate in the development process. In the First Five Year Plan, an amount of rupees four crore (forty million) was set apart for youth organisations indicating the limited scope of the State in dealing with social problems for which the State cannot provide in sufficient measures.[36] The Plan allocation to voluntary organization continued in an ascending manner Plan after Plan. The Third Plan regarded voluntary action as an aspect of public cooperation. In the Fifth Plan, grant-in-aid has soared to Rs. 83 crores (Rs. 830 million).[37] The Seventh Plan proposed between Rs.100-150 crores (Rs.1000-1500 millions) for voluntary organizations.[38] The separate section in the Seventh Plan document on Rural Development and Poverty Alleviation Programmes involvement of voluntary agencies is remarkable.

The establishment of Indian Council of Social Welfare (ICSW) and Central Social Welfare Board (CSWB) was a major step in this regard. The ICSW started in 1947 and subsequently registered under the Societies Registration Act, 1860 and the Public Trust Act of 1950, functions as a national forum for social welfare activities. The CSWB, set up in 1953 and later got registered under Charitable Companies Act, 1956 promotes voluntary action. Assuming a wide-range of functions in the area of social action the Board encourages the setting up of welfare organisations on voluntary basis. The Board also supplies technical and financial aid to voluntary organisations. Branches of the Board called State Social Welfare Advisory Boards, were opened in all States and Union Territories in the year 1954.[39] The special focus of the Board falls on women and children, the most vulnerable segments of the population. The Board takes up projects like setting up of *Balwadis* and provides maternity and health services in rural areas under its Welfare Extension Projects.

Began in 1969, the National Social Service Scheme provided a volunteer force of young students to work for the amelioration and development of weaker sections of society. The Nehru Yuva Kendras established at district headquarters other than metropolitan area, offered opportunity to rural youth to participate in creative activities and community services such as eradication of illiteracy, health education, sanitation programmes and land reforms.

Freedom from Hunger Campaign Office which came into being under the Ministry of Food and Agriculture during Bihar famine of 1963-67 became People's Action for Development of India (PADI) in 1973, through which government channelised funds to NGOs. Aimed at improving rural conditions by way of innovation and introduction of appropriate technology along with the support of voluntary organisations a new organisation Council for Advancement of Rural Technology (CART) was formed in 1983. Very soon, i.e. in 1986, both PADI and CART merged and found new incarnation in Council for Advancement of People's Action for Rural Technology (CAPART). CAPART was formed for the purpose of encouraging, promoting and assisting voluntary action in the implementation of projects for enhancement of rural prosperity.[40]

The national federations provide a common platform for voluntary action in India. For instance, Association for Voluntary Agencies for Rural Development (AVARD), began in 1958, is consortium of major voluntary agencies to serve as a 'common platform and clearing house' for voluntarism.[41] BASS, acronym for Bharatiya Adimjati Sevak Sangh (1948) coordinates the work of agencies serving the tribal brethern.[42]

During the mid-sixties, voluntary organisations turned again to relief and charity work necessitated by severe drought. This marked the entry of foreign NGOs and foreign funding.[43] Not much later, government amended the Foreign Contribution Regulation Act (FCRA) of 1976, which required the organisation to register in order to be eligible for receiving any foreign grant. It is estimated that there are 15,000 voluntary organisations registered with the Ministry of Home Affairs now. In 1986, nearly Rs.350 crores were pumped into the country as foreign aid.

The approach of the government towards NGOs underwent changes in accordance with the change in political complexion. In this context, the confrontation of NGOs with government in the post-independence era needs some mention. It was in 1973 that number of voluntary organisations rallied behind Jayaprakash Narayan who called for *sampurna kranthy* (total revolution). The call was to build up people's power (*lok-shakti*) parallel to the state power (*raja shakti*) as the latter was becoming suppressive. The government became more repressive and came down heavily on the voluntary organisations.[44] Following this phase, Janata government came to power which assigned special roles to the voluntary organisations. The role of voluntary associations gained new dimensions of development and welfare programmes like adult education, integrated rural development and *Antyodaya* scheme. The changed political situation has given a new boost to their activities. Things again took a reverse course when the Congress government appointed major Inquiry Commission, Kudal Commission, to review the affairs of Gandhian organisations. The report was tabled in 1989 in Parliament.[45] The Inquiry was to malign and harass the Gandhians who turned against the government during Emergency. All this remain black spots in the history of NGO-Government relations.

The relationship between government and NGOs has been continuously evolving and undergoing qualitative changes. While the tensions and conflicts between these agencies are not easily resolved, a growing interdependence of these institutions in their efforts to address the problems of the poor is obvious.

As noted earlier, the area of operation of NGOs covered all aspects of social life and services. As it varies from providing education facilities to construction of latrines, we need not list them all. In other words, the period after Independence witnessed a great momentum in the activities of NGOs resulted out of the situation where the State failed to discharge its functions adequately.

IX
CHANGING SCENARIO

The NGO sector is not a single cohesive entity but a fragmented and sometimes by the nature of its size and resources a peripheral entity. The focus of NGOs so far, as we have seen, has been on relief, charity, education and welfare. Some of them are currently engaged in development and allied activities. Compared to those in the urban and metropolitan centres there are very few that operate in backward rural regions. As per one estimate about 20,000 villages in the country are covered by NGOs and that cover hardly three per cent of the rural India spread over in 6,96,831 villages.

X
NGOs IN DEVELOPMENT

Since Independence some urgency of voluntary action was felt in certain areas where NGOs could work constructively. Attention was thus drawn to reconstruction and development ensuring people's participation. Consequently, many existing as well as newly-born organisations began listing out priorities and strategies towards this end. The policy of the government to encourage voluntary action in this area farther accelerated multiplication of both NGOs and their development-oriented programmes. In fact the shift in the policy of the government explicit in the Seventh Plan document is a landmark in the history of voluntary action in rural development.

The Plan document admits that there has been inadequate recognition of the role of voluntary organisations in accelerating the process of social and economic development. Serious efforts were made to involve them in development programmes, specially in the planning and implementation of rural programmes.[46] The Plan envisaged a number of areas for the voluntary organisations to supplement governmental efforts. Integrated rural development, distribution of surplus land, innovative methods and low-cost alternatives in elementary, primary and middle school education for children, promotion of science and technology are some of the programmes in the Plan that solicited the participation of voluntary organisations.

The integral role of voluntary organisations in development is not restricted to India alone but spreads over to all countries including both developed and developing nations. It is a widely subscribed view that the efficient hand of the NGOs augments governmental efforts. Instances of policy decisions shaped by both innovation and successful implementation of NGOs abound. A number of projects undertaken by government both at the State and the Centre are borrowed very frequently from voluntary organisations pilot projects.[47] The scheme of community health workers, now known as village health guides, is nothing but the adoption of the innovative endeavour of Shah and Aroles who used part-time workers for health programmes. In Korea, government has taken over the experiments of the NGOs engaged in community health programmes and established Korean Health Development Institute.[48]

Indispensibility of NGOs in development is mainly due to their ability for innovation and appropriateness of programmes. No statutory body engulfed in bureaucratic labyrinth could serve the people more effectively than the NGOs. From the beginning of initiating plans and programmes that are remotely related to the immediate needs of people and to the implementation, the governmental agencies are bound to confront with problems. Whereas, the programmes of NGOs are more innovative and adaptive, the creative talent in NGOs is not so obstructed by formalities thus enabling the organization to identify needs and introduce appropriate programmes in the community. The programmes are closely monitored and modifications are made according to the needs of the people. They also have the option to experiment with suitable programmes and evaluate on the basis of their experience in a particular community leading to initiate pioneering approaches to social development.[49] We may explain, in brief, the cases of ASTRA (Application of Science and Technology to Rural Areas), KSSP (Kerala Sasta Sahitya Parishad) and Martandam Centre to highlight this facet of NGOs.

ASTRA originated by the initiative of some socially concerned scientists at the Indian Institute of Science, Bangalore has introduced some innovative programmes in rural areas. In the spheres of rural housing, rural energy and utilizing various locally available resources, ASTRA has been successful. It has developed simple, low cost and hand operated compactor (to make blocks to be used in place of bricks), Astra Ole (fuel efficient mud oven), and many more innovative devices to minimize the hardships of the rural poor.[50]

The KSSP based in Kerala and primarily concerned with popularization of science, has embarked on many innovative projects. Smoke-less Parishad *Chula* which claims to have higher energy-efficient rate has been successfully installed in backward rural regions including remote tribal areas in Kerala.[51] It has gained wide popularity among rural poor and urban middle class as well.

The Rural Development Demonstration Centre at Martandam is another notable NGO. Established in 1921, it started the Martandam Practical Training School of Rural Reconstruction as a pioneering attempt to teach the village leaders the aspects of village reconstruction and development work. It is found to be successful in terms of the number of attendees and its comprehensive approach to social change.[52]

Sulabh International with its main office in Patna is known for its work in the field of health and hygiene. Dedicated to *Bhangi Mukti* (save scavengers) the voluntary organisation centres its activities around the promotion of hand-flush water seal toilets. It introduced the idea of 'pay and use'. Sulabh is generating biogas from human excreta for street lighting.[53]

The NGOs are relatively more sensitive to the needs of the community, which places them in an advantageous position as against the official agencies. Closeness to the immediate needs of the people determines the programmes and policies. Areas are identified, priorities are chosen and programmes are conceived deliberately with the involvement of the beneficiaries concerned in the decision-making process. This, in fact, avoids remote planning which seldom takes into consideration the actual reality. NGOs, in principle aim at long-term benefits so the programmes are conceived not merely for its short-term benefits. This may in turn, help community to become self-reliant.

Governmental agencies cannot be as successful as NGOs in eliciting local participation and mobilising local resources. It is argued that radical community action is unlikely to emerge within the financial arrangements of government bodies as the State has vested interest in maintaining *status quo*. Government agencies are more responsive to pressures exerted on them by the organized groups. As the unorganized and marginalized sections have little chance to influence the government, their interests are never protected nor their demands are met adequately.[54] This lessens the role of the State in transformation. NGOs, the catalysts of social change, trail blazers, and committed to change in *status quo*, initiate the step for transformation. Many are very radical in the true sense of the term. Moreover, the work of NGOs can compel the government to attend to the needs of the deprived.

The specific advantages of NGOs, specially of those in the development activities, do not, however, minimise their weaknesses. As the critics put it voluntary organaisations work in isolation narrowing down their scope of activities. Plans and programmes are usually aimed at the local and communitarian needs. Often NGOs fail to widen the range of programmes extending to make it more beneficial to more people. Strategies and approaches are evolved after giving due consideration to the needs of the populace and the availability and type of resources. The same may hardly have any applicability to other localities or even communities that are in close proximity to the one where it was successfully carried out. NGOs are thus destined to work at the micro level, as far as the experience suggests.

The dependence on funds and assistance from external sources has set in some undesirable practices in the day-to-day functioning of development NGOs. Some of them have virtually become mere outfits of such agencies to help introduce alien ideas to the community. Necessarily programmes are bound to reflect all the inherent handicaps and trivialities. Experience in this regard supports that the organisations have to forgo their own understanding of the community in which they have been working for years. Prospects for future assistance and their very survival itself, at least in certain cases, force them to ignore the beneficiaries and community.

The growing tendency of classification seems to have plagued the spirit of voluntarism in development associations. It has successfully prevented the inflow of creative talents to organisations. The leaders who aggrandise power and authority in the organisation tend to be deaf to innovative ideas; this alone is sufficient to arrest the enterprising mood in the organisation. The situation is further aggravated by the paternalistic attitude of the leader.

Recent studies on the administrative structure of voluntary organisations have revealed the fact that NGOs have increasingly become bureaucratic. Bureaucratisation and institutionalisation may be inevitable, as the argument goes, but how far is it conducive to the effectiveness of NGOs is a moot question. Programmes are implemented for the sake of programmes or for the continuation of activities.

Organisations in the developmental arena start with their own perception about development, upliftment and others. Their programmes are accordingly shaped. Building up of infrastructure and other amenities thus draw the immediate attention of NGOs. As perception varies, programmes and strategies too vary. Conversely, similarity gives rise to similar kind of programmes and policies. Resemblance of purposes is also expected to cause conflict that ultimately lead to duplication of programmes. The corollary of this is ineffectiveness and it may even help polarise the community into groups. Due to diverse strategies, approach and views, NGOs might miss their concern for the beneficiaries. Thus there is a need for proper coordination and networking of organisations that operate in similar areas with similar objectives and targets.

But how far the idea of networking gets translated into action? The answer is quite dissatisfying. Organisations such as Sarva Seva Sangh, Association of Voluntary Agencies for Rural Development (AVARD), Bharat Sewa Sangh, Lokayan, Bharatiya Adimjati Sevak Sangh and a few others are conspicuous in this respect, facilitating coordination among NGOs. The main obstacle in coordination for purposeful operation is reported to be the closed functioning of many associations. Many would prefer to be secretive of the source and quantity of funds, and linkages with international agencies. Interaction between them is thus limited to a considerable extent underlining the opportunity to share and learn from varied experiences. Local, zonal, regional and national levels of interlinking would, to an extent, help reduce the criticism that the NGOs are local-based and follow only micro level working mechanisms. Benefits of constant interaction and interlinking will be evident in successful resource mobilization, adoption of feasible strategy and approach and effective administration. Similarly, networking with international association can have a desirable effect on local organisations. In all the evolutionary stages of NGOs, namely, starting, consolidation, expansion and closing out, the networking effect is manifest.

XI
LINKAGES BETWEEN NGOs AND OTHER ORGANISATIONS

Voluntary organisations in general and those busy with developmental activities seem to face difficulties in raising funds and mobilising resources. This is evident from their increased dependency on government, international organisations and foreign funding agencies for financial assistance. Availability of funds and grants from government has been given as a major reason for the multiplication of NGOs too.

The advent of international voluntary agencies in Indian voluntary scene began in 1965 when the country experienced severe famine requiring relief from varied sources. Since then the flow of funds has been regular. Today the flow of foreign donor agencies to non-governmental agencies in India is more than ever in the past.[55] Foreign contributions now regulated under the Foreign Contribution (Regulation) Act, 1976, continue to soar year after year.[56] In 1986, the amount was estimated to have touched the mark of Rs.350 crore (Rs.3500 million).[57] A great number of NGOs are receiving foreign aid to support their programmes. Of the 11,000 voluntary organisations registered with the Home Ministry, 7,000 are getting foreign contributions.[58] Many foreign agencies list India as the largest single recipient of funds. For instance, more than 50 per cent of the CARE's (Cooperative for American Relief Everywhere) annual contribution is allocated to India. Prominent agencies include Oxford Committee for Famine Relief (OXFAM), Catholic Relief Services (CRS), Community Aid Abroad (CAA), Danish International Development Agency (DANIDA), Christian Children Fund (CCF) and Bread for the World. Countrywise data on funding to voluntary organisations in India records the US as the large source of foreign aid Rs.57 crore (Rs.570 million). The US is followed by Germany, UK, Switzerland, Canada, Holland and Italy.[59]

Obviously, the funds affect the functioning and even the very purpose of organisations. There have been demands in the Parliament to ban one or other agencies on this issue. In 1986, registration of about 27 voluntary organisations was revoked for violation of rules and regulations governing acceptance of donations.

The assistance accompanied by a set of conditions exert undue pressure on NGOs. Projects and programmes get shaped according to the caprice of the funding agencies. The case is similar to government grants. The government grants are tied with the party in power. Grants get stopped as soon as other party comes in power.[60] Most of the grants are form-oriented and not project or people-oriented. If NGOs become agencies responsible for implementing programmes with government funding, then the distinction between NGOs and government may become blurred.

XII
PEOPLES' PARTICIPATION

Close investigations of the empirical data about participation in the voluntary association in India reveals three basic facts:

1. There are countless number of organisations in cities and even those working in rural areas which have their offices in cities and towns;
2. There are a large number of people who have no membership in an association or agency at all; and
3. There exist, in any given association, an active minority and inactive majority among the members.

Each of these facts requires some explanation.

The phenomenon that has been called the proliferation of associations after Independence has been remarked upon countless times. In India principle of association has been more successfully used to get grants from governments and international agencies. Associations are created, extended, and worked in India more quickly and effectively to get into various official positions (President, Vice-President , Treasurer and Secretary) to engrave any of these positions along with their names on their respective letter heads. It is often noticed that this becomes the first and the last work of some of the offices. In fact, some of the office bearers make these associations as their pocket organisations. Such organizations not only bring bad name to their own institution but to whole voluntary effort in the country. This makes bureaucrats to look at all associations with suspicion.

Although in comparative perspective, India may well be proud of having large number of voluntary organisations in urban, suburban, small city, small town or rural areas, a study on membership in voluntary agencies will reveal the little known fact that many have not any affiliation to any agency. The universality of this pattern indicates the all-pervasive effect of Indian kinship and occupational structures in urban and rural areas alike. Even metropolitan areas will yield the same results.

"Who says organisations, says oligarchy", thus has Robert Michels stated in another form in his "Iron law of Oligarch".[61] Gaetano Mosca has also noted "the tendency towards activity and control by a few in all organizations—governmental and non-governmental alike".[62] No matter what interest any particular association represents, one finds the existence of an active minority in control. Although each association has many committees and every member is expected to be active on at least one of them, many members are wholly inactive. Specially many fraternal organisations are subject to democratic control, but the actual formulation of policy is largely the function of a few interested individuals, with the great bulk of the members acquiescing so long as these policies do not interfere with their private lives.

It is estimated that in the most powerful and deeply rooted people's organisations the degree of popular participation is between five and seven per cent. If one was to take figures for attendance at meetings of a wide variety of associations one will find another index of minority participation. This persists despite the frequent attempts to choose a time and place for meetings which least conflicts with the job and family obligations of the members. It persists also despite the enactment of byelaws imposing sanctions for non-attendance. Where they exist, such rules are more observed in breach than in practice.

The relatively peripheral significance of the interests to which associations devote themselves explains in large measure the second and third uniformities: many people have no memberships at all; and among those with membership in any given association, the majority are inactive and participate minimally. Because of individual's cultural pre-occupations in India with obligations to his job and his family, there exists a socially structured pull away from membership in even those voluntary associations relevant to his interests. Further, even when he is a member of an association, the individual's interest is so limited that it lends to minimal participation. The ordinary member sees no particular reason for wasting his time at meetings. "Let the officials run the association, that is what they are elected for or in some case paid for". As long as things go well, the average member of the association does not want self-government, and is annoyed and resentful only when an attempt is made to force its responsibility on him.

There is, in addition, another very important structural factor which contributes to the tendency towards inactive majorities, in voluntary associations. The internal structure of the voluntary associations itself, that is, with its formal organisation and division of functions among members, makes it possible for a minority to achieve the interests of the association with the majority participating very little or not at all. This possibility, however, brings in certain consequences for the executive and the members of voluntary associations alike, consequences which are serious problems for both of them. Since these problems become especially acute in associations which stress democratic values, we need to examine both the sources and the consequences of these problems in such associations.

Beyond a certain point, the size and interests of a voluntary association compel it to have full-time officials. If the voluntary association obliges it to conform with the value that equal participation requires rotation of officers, the formal rules provide for regular election of officials for short terms. It is, however, empirical uniformity that at least a few of the officials serve continuously for a long term. Where the long tenure officials occupy positions below the top most ones, with the top ones being filled with rotating personnel, they are often criticised for usurpation of power.

XIII
CHALLENGES TO NGOS

The role of NGOs is not limited merely to the introduction of innovative ideas. While concentrating their efforts on left-out areas in both rural and urban regions, the objective has to be conceived in a more wider perspective. The NGOs ought to put in their voluntary work in transforming the *minds* of people that are loaded with ill-developed conceptions on equality, justice, development, change, work ethics and others. Any change, if not radical, condition that breeds many current problems is to be initial at the individual level. No one would deny the fact that edradication of undesirable practices and problems in our country should begin at the individual level, more specifically in the mind and conscience. In the given situation of a few enjoying the majority of resources and fruits of development at the cost of the poor, transformation should aim at the minds of the people. Such an attempt, founded firmly on the Indian tradition and ethos, would cherish the feeling of equality and social concern paving the way for an overall change in the society.

Prevalence of socially undesirable practices and evils that appear to erect obstacles on the way to progress needs NGO's intervention. More often than not, the NGOs would have to swim against the stream while they work with the deprived. Combating the powerful cannot necessarily be on a smooth trail. The experience of an NGO called Alternative for India Development (AID) is only the latest illustration. The 18-month old struggle of AID, based at Dharmapuri in Tamil Nadu, has come to the fore recently. The NGO, working among tribal women, runs development projects for promoting micro-level self-employment ventures for SC/ST women. It is fighting to retain its legitimate hold over their 10-acres of land. This is an instance where the local MLA, police and mafia gang work in unison against the NGO to takeover the land and disrupt the programmes.[63] The nexus between the rulers and powerful in the community, however, is bound to lose its binding grip by the voluntary efforts of NGOs targeted at changing the minds of people.

In the changing situation people are not gullible as they can discern the populist policies and its hollowness. Confidence of the people reposed in government organisations and statutory agencies is tapering off paving the way for NGOs. The major advantage of NGOs is that they operate among people and the programmes are people-oriented unlike governmental efforts which very rarely evince any genuine concern for bringing about change in the society.

In the wake of liberalisation the needs of the people are changing in a dramatic way at a great pace. Consumerism has come to be an important phenomenon and it is widespread. In this era of consumerism marketing mechanism works in a very effective and efficient manner to exploit consumers. Ignorant rural consumers inadvertently become the prey of modern market mechanism. A large number of NGOs can enter in this area and many more new avenues are waiting for them.

An important lesson that the NGOs experience has to offer is the social change, especially where it affects gender, class and caste groups is a slow process and must be approached gradually. While grassroots NGO experiments in India have not led to major monolithic movements in people's participation and self-reliance and the voluntary sector cannot hope to play a major *quantitative* role in the national scene the relative advantage of NGOs has been in the *qualitative* role for providing *test bed* for new ideas and methodologies and sounding board for government policies and programmes.

Code of Ethics for Voluntary Organisations as formulated by Mahatma Gandhi is given below :

Success of Organisation

1. Success of any Institution depends on the following conditions:
   (a) Extreme authentic dedication and enthusiasm towards the realisation of the objectives of the institution.
   (b) Not merely observance of the rules and regulations of institutions but also their spirit.
   (c) Feeling of brotherhood and unity among the management, members and subordinate staff.
2. Despite having other favourable conditions the institutions would be lifeless even if a single condition is not followed out of the above mentioned three conditions.

Director of the Organisation

1. The Director of an institution can be termed as the pivot of an institution.
2. The success of the institution depends on the Director's dedication and devotion towards the objective of the institution, his observance of rules and regulations, his behaviour towards other members, his industriousness.
3. If the Director is conceited of his powers or indifferent or disinterested towards other members, it would be harmful for the institution.
4. The Director of the institution should behave in the same way as an efficient Commander-in-chief who is alert and strict about making others follow the rules and at the same time he cares to draw love and respect from his soldiers and feels proud of them.

5. Director should look into the smallest details of the institution. He should take care of the members and other fellow beings of the institute in the same manner as mother takes care of her child.
6. Director should exercise his rights according to the situation. He should consider his subordinates as an equal or his co-worker. He should consider junior most employee as his friend. He should believe that he got his post as a Director not because of his special capabilities but the respect shown to him by his co-workers.
7. He should listen to the suggestions of junior most employee with respect and should be ready to implement them if he agrees with them. If he does not think them proper he should try to make them see his viewpoint.
8. The Director should not be too credulous. He should not form adverse opinion about others in haste. He should take time to understand the person before forming any adverse opinion. In fact he should never form pejorative opinion about others in the absence of clear evidence.
9. He should not shower special favours on a particular person. He should not be partial to people. Also he should not praise one member to down the other.
10. It is not necessary to use the stern behaviour or harsh language to make others follow the rules systematically. The Director who thinks the utility of these harsh measures to maintain the discipline displays his inabilities.

Members of the Institution

(1) The institution cannot continue for a long if there is absence of the feeling of brotherhood and unity among the members. The differences and disputes are bound to occur and the members would indulge in fighting with each other forgetting the real objective of institute.

(2) The institution cannot work for long whose members are not eager to follow their officer. Laziness and careless attitude would spread in the institute and the members would become victim to these vices.

(3) There should not only be outward cooperation among Director and the members but also the mental cooperation. It means

that it is not enough that the members should work according to the will and order of the Director. If they really agree to the will and order of the Director they should behave in a manner so as to show that they themselves want to do that work.

(4) If the members do not believe in a particular rule or are not convinced about certain order they should discuss it with the Director until and unless they are convinced. They should not give wrong impression to their Director.

(5) If the members come across any rule or order which, though, is not against truth and religion but only looks improper in the practical view, the members should follow it. But if it is against truth and religion the members should be ready to leave the organisation.

(6) If a particular rule and order is not against truth and religion but it is difficult to be followed due to personal weakness it is better for the members to leave for the progress of the institute.

(7) If there are mutual differences between the members; if there is doubt about the behaviour of any member; if a particular member is the cause for dissatisfaction or distress or doubt, the matter should be discussed with the concerned person in each and every case in the first place. If the issue is not resolved it should be brought to the notice of the immediate officer and the decision should be left to him.

(8) The disputed matter should not be taken directly to the highest authority without having prior discussion with the concerned member, or intimating the immediate officer.

(9) If you have any doubt about other member, it should be immediately cleared. If you keep it in your heart and do not discuss it with the officer it would lead to the accumulation of vices in the institute.

(10) The institution cannot function properly if the weaknesses and faults of the members are talked about in hushed tones but not disclosed to the officer or the matter is not discussed openly with the concerned member about whom the discussions are taking place. If the situation persists Institute would become lifeless because it would have become an abode of vice, conceit, untruth, vanity.

Economic Condition of the Institute

1. No real work could be delayed due to paucity of funds.
2. It is not appropriate to put the funds in the bank and spend on the interest of the capital. The Director of the institution should firmly believe that the institute is for the welfare of the people and they would get money for its sustenance.
3. The Director would have to work very hard till the people are convinced of the usefulness of the institute. But that hard work would be considered as part of penance and service.
4. After a period of time so much funds are accumulated but this accumulated money could also make the institute lifeless. Therefore, an ideal institution should not fall for the temptation of accumulation of money.
5. It is generally seen that the institute which get public funds to work, becomes careless in spending the money. This is one of the greatest problems before organisations. The voluntary organisations of a poor country like India should spend sparingly.
6. Proper care should be taken to maintain accounts of the institute. Even a single rupee spent should be accounted for and should be regularly audited by certified auditors.

[Translated from Hindi (*Gandhi Marg*, Hindi), Vol.45, No.I, Jan.-Feb., 2000, pp. 1-6]

NOTES

1. ECOSOC Resolution 2S8(X) of 27 February 1950 as amplified by Resolution 1929 (XLIV) of 25 June, 1968. Quoted in Gokhale, S.D. and Sohoni, N.K. (1987), "International Voluntary Organisations in Social Welfare", *Encyclopedia of Social Work in India*, Vol.11, Ministry of Social Welfare, Government of India, New Delhi, p. 123.
2. Laski, Harold (1931), "Freedom of Association", Encyclopaedia of the Social Sciences, Vol. 6. p. 447 quoted in Sachdeva, D.R. (1992-93), *Social Welfare in India*, Kitab Mahal, Allahabad, p. 197.
3. Beveridge, William (1979), *Voluntary Action in a Changing World*, National Council of Social Services, Bedford Square Press, London, p. 100.
4. See Kulkarni, V.M. (1969), *Voluntary Action in a Developing Society*, India Institute of Public Administration, New Delhi, p. 8.

5. Banton, Michal, (1968), "Voluntary Associations Anthropological Aspects", *International Encyclopaedia of Social Sciences*, Vol. 16, p. 358.
6. Sills, David L. (1968), "Voluntary Associations : Sociological Aspects", *International Encyclopaedia of Social Sciences, op.cit.*, pp.362-63.
7. Johnson, Norman (1981), *Voluntary Social Services*, Oxford, Basil Blackwell and Mortin Robertson, p. 14.
8. Kulkarni, P.D. (1984), *Voluntary Action Myth and Reality*, National Institute of Public Cooperation and Child Development, New Delhi, p. 8.
9. *Ibid.*
10. Chowdhry, Paul D., (1971 & 1981), *Voluntary Social Welfare in India.* Sterling Publishers Private Limited, New Delhi, p. 35.
11. *Ibid.*, pp. 51-52.
12. Sills, David L., *op.cit.*, p. 362.
13. Muttalib, M.A. (1987), "Voluntarism and Development Theoretical Perspectives", *The Indian Journal of Public Administration*, Vol. 33, No.3, p. 400.
14. Chatterjee, B. (1977), "Voluntary Agencies for Social Welfare", Ganguli, B.N. (ed). *Social Development*, Sterling Publishers Pvt. Ltd., New Delhi, pp. 248-49.
15. Marry Morris, quoted in Kulkarni, (1969), *op.cit.*, p. 4.
16. Muttalib, *op.cit.*, p. 405.
17. Gangrade, K.D. (1987), "Development of Voluntary Action", *Encyclopaedia of Social Work in India*, Vol. I, Ministry of Social Work, Government of India, New Delhi, p. 219.
18. Pandey, Shashi Ranjan (1991), *Community Action for Social Justice: Grassroots Organisations in India*, Sage Publications. New Delhi, p. 19.
19. Ralston, Lenore, *et al.* (1983), Voluntary Efforts in Decentralised Management. Institute of International Studies, University of California, Berkeley, quoted in: Pandey, *op.cit.*, p. 19.
20. Bourdillon, A.F.C. (1954) (ed.). Voluntary Social Services, quoted in Muttalib, *op.cit.*, p. 410.
21. *Ibid.*
22. Bhambhri, C.P. (1987), "The Modern State and Voluntary Societies", *The Indian Journal of Public Administration*, Vol. 33, No. 3, p. 996.
23. See also, Oommen, T.K. (1984), *Social Structure and Politics: Studies in Independent India.* Hindustan Publishing Corporation (India), Delhi, pp. 27-28.
24. Gangrade, K.D. (1987), "Development of Voluntary Action", *op.cit.*, p. 221.
25. *Ibid.*

26. Pandey, *op.cit.*, p. 17.
27. Prasad, L.M. (1987), "Voluntary Agencies for Development of Scheduled Castes and Scheduled Tribes : Their Role and Function", *The Indian Journal of Public Administration*. Vol. 33, No. 3, p. 591.
28. *Ibid.*
29. Ratnam, D.I.G. (1987), "History of Social Reform among Christians", *Encyclopaedia of Social Work in India*, Vol. II, p. 37.
30. Srivastava, S.P. (1987), "Voluntary Action in Crime Prevention and Control", *Encyclopaedia of Social Work in India*, Vol. III, pp. 274-75.
31. Gangrade, K.D. (1987). *op.cit.*, p. 221.
32. His (Gandhi) compact programme, called Constructive Programme, was evolved during 1915-45. It consisted of evenly areas that visualised for the total transformation of the society. These are: communal unity, removal of untouchability, prohibition, *khadi*, other-village industries, village sanitation, new or basic education, adult education, women, education in health and hygiene, provincial language, national language, economic equality, *kisans*, labour, *adivasis*, leprosy, students,improvement of cattle and nature cure, see Dutt, Dev (1982), *Report to Gandhi*, Gandhi Smarak Nidhi, New Delhi, pp. 2-3.
33. Acharya, N.V.R.K. (1990). *The Gandhian Era*, Cauvery Publications. Hyderabad, p. 82.
34. Sachdeva, D.R. (1992). *Social Welfare Administration in India*, Kitab Mahal, Allahabad, p. 217.
35. Lalitha, N.V. and Madhu Kohli (1992). *Status of Voluntary Effort in Social Welfare*, National Institute of Public Cooperation and Child Development, New Delhi, pp. 15-16.
36. Deo, Mangal Jai (1987). "Voluntary Agencies *vis-a-vis* Government". *Yojana*, 31(4), p. 12.
37. Muttalib, M.A., *op.cit.*, p. 413.
38. Government of India. *Seventh Five Year Plan 1985-90*. Vol. 2, Planning Commission, New Delhi. Chapter 2.
39. *Encyclopaedia of Social Work in India*, Vol. IV, p. 12.
40. Department of Rural Development, Annual Report 1985-86, p. 65, quoted in Maheshwari, Shriram (1987), "Voluntary Action in Rural Development in India". *The Indian Journal of Public Administration*. Vol. 33, No. 3, p. 563.
41. Franda, Marcus (1983), *Voluntary Associations and Local Development in India : The Janata Phase*, Young Asia Publications, New Delhi, p. 19.
42. *Ibid.*
43. Verghese, George B. (1977), "Voluntary Action : A New Mission for the New Missionaries", *Voluntary Action*, Vol. 19, No. I, pp. 3-8.

44. Chaturvedi, H.R. (1987), Role of Voluntary Organisation in Rural Development", *The Indian Journal of Public Administration*, Vol. 33. No. 3, p. 541.
45. Pandey, *op.cit.*, p. 16.
46. *Seventh Five Year Plan*, *op.cit.*, pp. 68-70.
47. Alliband, Terry (1983), *Catalysts of Development: Voluntary Agencies in India*. Kumarian Press, Connecticut, USA, p.x.
48. Hardiman, Margaret (1986), 'People's Involvement in Health and Medical Care, in : Midgley, James *et al.*, (1986), *Community Participation, Social Development and the State*, Methuen and Co. Ltd., London, p. 69.
49. Midgley, James (1986), 'Community Participation, the State and Social Policy', in Midgley, James *et al.*, *Community Participation, Social Development and the State*, Methuen and Co.Ltd.; London, p.154.
50. For more details, see Pandey, *op.cit.*, pp. 81-86.
51. See Zachariah, Mathew and Sooryamoorthy, R. (1994), *Science for Social Revolution? Achievements and Dilemmas of a Development Movement, The Kerala Sasira Sahitya Parishad.* Vistaar (a division of Sage Publications), New Delhi.
52. For a brief account on the Centre, see Alliband, Terry (1983), *Catalysts Development : Voluntlary Agencies in India*, Kumarian Press, Connecticut. USA, pp. 28-30.
53. Pandey, *op.cit.*, pp. 75-80.
54. Marsden, D. and Oakley, P. (1982), Radical Government in the Third World, in G. Craize *et al.* (eds), *Community Work and the State*, Routledge and Kegan Paul, London, quoted in: Midgley, James *et al.*, *op.cit.*, p. 154.
55. Ninan, Sevanti (1986), "Voluntary Agencies : Leave them alone", *Indian Express*, October 31, quoted in: Maheshwari, Shriram (1987), "Voluntary Action in Rural Development in India", *The Indian Journal of Public Administration*. Vol. 33, No 3, p. 565.
56. Maheshwari, *op.cit.*, p. 566.
57. Gangrade, (1987), *op.cit.*, p. 225.
58. *Ibid.*
59. Maheshwari, *op.cit.*, p. 566.
60. Varma, Paripumanad (1992), "Do we need Honest Voluntary Social Workers", *Voluntary Welfare Periodical*. Vol. I, No. 7, p. 3.
61. Michel Robert, (1915), *Political Parties. A Sociological Study of the Oligarchical Tendencies of Modern Democracy*, translated by Eden and Cedar Paul, New York. pp. 377 and 419.
62. Mosca, Gaetano (1939), *The Ruling Class*, translated by Arthur Livingston, New York.
63. Bhagat, Rasheeda (1994), "Goondas Harassing NGO Workers", *Indian Express*, February 12, p. 10.

REFERENCES

Acharya, V.R.K. (1990), *The Gandhian Era*, Cauvery Publications, Hyderabad.

Alliband, Terry (1983), *Catalysts of Development: Voluntary Agencies in India*, Kumarian Press, USA.

AVARD (1991), *Role of NGOs in Development : A Study of the Situation in India*, (Manuscript), New Delhi.

Banton, Michal (1968), "Voluntary Association : Anthropological Aspects", *International Encyclopaedia of Social Sciences*. Vol. 16, Macmillan.

Beveridge, William (1979), "Voluntary Action in a Changing World", National Council of Social Services, Bedford Square Press, London.

Bhagat, Rasheeda (1994). "Goondas Harassing NGO Workers", *Indian Express*, February 12, p.10

Bhambhri, C.P. (1987), "The Modern State and Voluntary Societies", *The Indian Journal of Public Administration*, Vol. 33. No. 3.

Bhattacharya, Mohit (1987). "Voluntary Associations, Development and the State" *The Indian Journal of Public Administration*. Vol. 33, No. 3. pp. 383-94.

Chatterjee, B. (1977). "Voluntary Agencies for Social Welfare" in Ganguli, B.N. (ed). *Social Development*, Sterling Publishers Pvt. Ltd., New Delhi.

Chowdhry, Paul D. (1971), *Voluntary Social Welfare in India*, Sterling Publishers Pvt. Ltd., Jullunder.

Dutt, Dev (1982), *Report to Gandhi*. Gandhi Smarak Nidhi, New Delhi.

Francis, C. (1993), "Rural Development, People's Participation and the Role of NGOs", *Journal of Rural Development*. Vol. 12, No. 2, pp. 205-10.

Franda, Marcus (1983), *Voluntary Associations and Local Development in India : The Janata Phase*, Young Asia Publications, New Delhi.

Gangrade, K. D. (1977) (ed), *Integrated Approach to Rural Development with Social Justice*, National Service Scheme Unit, Delhi School of Social Work, Delhi.

Gangrade, K. D. (1987), "Development of Voluntary Action", *Encyclopaedia of Social Welfare in India*. Vol. I, Ministry of Social Work, Government of India. New Delhi, pp. 219-31.

Gokhale, S.D. and Sohoni, N.K. (1987), "International Voluntary Organisations in Social Welfare", in *Encyclopaedia of Social Work in India*, Vol. II, Ministry of Social Work, Government of India, New Delhi, pp.123-30.

Government of India (1987), *Encyclopaedia of Social Work in India*, Vol. IV, Ministry of Social Welfare, Government of India, New Delhi.

The Hindu (1994), "Plan to Revive Swadeshi Movement", January 25, p. 10.

Hoon, R.S. (1987), "Red Cross", *Encyclopaedia of Social Work in India*, Vol. II, Ministry of Social Welfare, Government of India, New Delhi, pp. 355-60.

Inamdar, N. R. (1987), "Role of Voluntarism in Development", *The Indian Journal of Public Administration*, Vol. 33, No. 3, pp. 420-32.

Kothari, Rajni (1989), *Politics and the People : In Search of a Humane India*. Vol. II, Ajanta Publications, Delhi.

Kulkarni, P. D. (1984), *Voluntary Action Myth and Reality*, National Institute of Public Cooperation and Child Development, New Delhi.

Kulkarni, V.M. (1969), *Voluntary Action in a Developing Society*, Indian Institute of Public Administration, New Delhi.

Lokayan Bulletin (1985), "Dialogues", Vol. 3, No. 2.

Maheshwari, Shriram (1987) , "Voluntary Action in Rural Development in India", *The Indian Journal of Public Administration*, Vol. 33, No. 3, pp. 559-68.

Midgley, James, *et al*. (1986), *Community Participation, Social Development and the State*, Methuen and Co. Ltd., London.

Mohsini, Shamsul Rahman (1987) , "History of Social Reform among Muslims", *Encyclopaedia of Social Work in India*. Vol. II, Ministry of Welfare, Government of India, New Delhi, pp. 58-69.

Muttalib, M.A. (1987) , "Voluntarism and Development Theoretical Perspectives. *The Indian Journal of Public Administration*. Vol. 33, No. 3, pp. 399-419.

Nath, Trilok (1987), *Politics of the Classes*, Deputy Publications, Delhi.

Norman, Johnson (1981), *Voluntary of Social Services*. Oxford, Basil Blackwell and Mortin, Robertson.

Oommen, T.K. (1984), *Social Structure and Politics: Studies in Independent India*, Hindustan Publishing Corporation (India), Delhi.

Prasad, L.M. (1987) , "Voluntary Agencies for Development of Scheduled Castes and Scheduled Tribes: Their Role and Function", *The Indian Journal of Public Administration*. Vol. 33, No. 3. pp. 588-612.

Ratnam, D.L.G. (1987) , "History of Social Refoms among Christians", *Encyclcpaedia of Social Work in India*. Vol. II, Ministry of Welfare, Government of India, New Delhi, pp. 34-42.

Rooff, Madeline (1957), *Voluntary Societies and Social Policy*. Routledge and Kegan Paul Ltd., London.

Roy, Sanjit (Bunker) (1987), "Voluntary Agencies in Development: Their Role, Policies and Programmes", *The Indian Journal of Public Administration*, Vol. 33, No. 3, pp. 454-64.

Sachdeva, D.R. (1992), *Social Welfare Administration in India*, Kitab Mahal, Allahabad.

Sills, David L. (1968), "Voluntary Associations: Sociological Aspects", *International Encyclopaedia of Social Sciences*, Vol. 16, Macmillan.

Singh, Gopal (1987), "Histoiy of Social Reforms among Sikhs", *Encyclopaedia of Social Work in India*, Vol. II, Ministry of Welfare, Government of India, New Delhi, pp. 69-75.

Tope. T.K. (1987), "History of Social Reform among Hindus", *Encyclopaedia of Social Work in India*, Vol. II, Ministry of Welfare in India, Government of India, New Delhi, pp. 43-51.

Thulasi, Swami Sidhanta (1992), "The Need for a Voluntary Organisations in Growing Society", *Vivekananda Kendra Patrika*, Vol. 21, No. I, pp. 1-3.

Varma, Paripurnanand (1992), *Do we need Honest Voluntary Social Voluntary Action*. Vol. 19, No. 7, pp. 2-3.

Verghese, George B. (1977), "Voluntary Action: A New Mission for Missionaries", *Voluntary Action*, Vol. 19, No. I, pp. 3-8.

Vijapurkar, Mahesh (1992), "The Baba Amte Phenomenon", *Vivekananda Kendra Patrika*. Vol. 21, No. I, pp. 178-82.

Zachariah, Mathew and Sooryamoorthy, R. (1994). *Science for Social Achievements and Dilemmas of a Development Movement: The Kerala Sastra Sahitya Prishad*, Vistaar (a division of Sage Publications), New Delhi.

6

'Wake up Call' for India's Environmental Security or Face Collective Suicide

Protest banners hang from a 450-ft. high millennium wheel on Monday, October 25, 1999. A small group of environmental activists scaled the wheel to use banners in protest against dams in India.

[*News Digest, The Times of India*, October 26, 1999, New Delhi; p.1]

Environmentalist activists outside Hong Kong's Legislative Council protest against the slow progress of the government actions to improve air quality. The placards in Chinese reads: "Health equals wealth".

[*News Digest, The Times of India*, November 6, 1999, New Delhi; p.1]

In the nineteenth century the problem was that God is dead; in the twentieth century the problem is that man is dead.

—*Erich Frown*

The problem of the coming century in which pollution has become all pervasive is to rediscover and degenerate man. In the capital city of Delhi itself vehicular pollution accounts for nearly 70 per cent of population while both industrial pollution from thermal plants account for 13 per cent and 4 per cent to households pollution and the remaining to other sources such as burning of shedder leaves.

In the dawn of the new millennium, many of us are not aware that we are heading for "catastrophe" and "collective suicide". The Republic of India gave itself a written Constitution, a document especially treasured for the broadness of its vision and the egalitarian values it promoted. The milestone of the golden jubilee of India's Independence [1997] should have been an occasion for introspection and evaluation as to where we stand with regard to solemn pledges made by our founding fathers. Yet the imagination of those in government will evidently allow none of this. How else can we explain the complete lack of serious debate and "concern" for environmental security? Indeed, environmental security is threatened by three Ps; the first being unbridled population growth, the second, pollution, and the third, an absence of political will to act.

I
POPULATION

Population Bomb and Quality of Life

The latest data indicates that India is sitting on a population time bomb. By 2020 to 2040, India will be the world's most populous nation. It is of very little comfort to know that the birth rate has declined from 34.9 per thousand in 1981 to 32.7 per thousand in 1991.

If the population must stabilize at even a staggering 100 million by 2001-2006, the average birth rate has to be two children per women. So far, Kerala and Tamil Nadu have achieved this goal as will Madhaya Pradesh by 2060, Rajasthan by 2048, Bihar by 2039, and Uttar Pradesh by 2100. The Government of India in its wisdom has removed all family planning targets and left it to the people to decide the norm. However, the truth is that the programme is centrally run and dependent on female sterilization, and ignores the variety of options available.

Enemies of Progress

A human development profile compiled by the National Council of Applied Economics Research [NCAER] confirms that Uttar Pradesh and Bihar are among the worst off states in many areas. Per capita income as well as wage earning households are below the national average. Only 10 per cent of rural households in Bihar and 20 per cent in Uttar Pradesh have electricity, compared to the national average of 43 per cent. The figures for piped water in households nationally is 25 per cent. In Bihar and Uttar Pradesh it is 4 per cent and 15 per cent respectively. The survey also shows that whereas the net purchase of food in rural households through public distribution system [PDS] is Rs.37 per annum nationally, it is as low as Rs.5 in both these states. In Karnataka and Orissa, the comparative figures are Rs.70 and Rs.51 respectively. This speaks volumes about decades of planning and the development process in India.

Details are generally messy; they blur the big picture seen in a wider perspective. Uttar Pradesh and Bihar have begun to resemble the Wild West and Alcapone's Chicago rolled into one. A northern third of contemporary India has capitulated to lawlessness. Not surprisingly the dividing line between politics and crime is a thin one. A policeman remarked wryly : "we are forced to protect those whom we are supposed to prosecute."

Education

As per the 1991 census, the total literacy rate in India was 52.11 per cent which has risen to 62 per cent as per the latest survey. In rural areas, girls' education lags far behind. If 100 girls enroll in first grade, by the time they reach standard five, only 40 girls remain in the education stream; in the eighth grade, there are only 18, in the tenth grade only 9, and in the twelfth grade, only one. The picture changes dramatically in urban areas. There are 82 girls in fifth grade, 62 in eighth grade, 32 in tenth grade and 14 in twelfth grade.

Drinking Water

Only 27 per cent of villages and 21 per cent of cities have safe drinking water. No potable drinking water is available in 162,000 villages while 90 per cent of villages have liquor stores.

Housing

There is a shortage of 13.7 million houses in villages. Living conditions in 36 per cent of cities and 73 per cent of villages are appalling.

Link Roads

Only 112,190 out of the 129,825 villages with a population of 1,000 have link roads.

Availability of food

In 1991, per capita availability of food was 510 grams which has been reduced to 474.2 grams.

Health

There are primary centres in almost all the Development Blocks in the country. An arrangement of 30 hospital beds is available to only 16 per cent of the population in India.

Urban population

In 2016, India's urban population is going to increase from the present 256.8 million to 428.9 million. Constraints on the availability of land for cultivation imposed by the near-doubling of the urban population as well as by other environmental factors such as growing salinity, soil erosion and desertification are also contributing to making food security more challenging in the coming years. Changing cropping patterns are another dimension which needs to be addressed in this context. Other crucial factors include the ability to purchase food. The whole issue comes down to the task of eradicating poverty and creating employment opportunities.

In short, more than a third of India's population still lives below the poverty line. As of 1995, about 665 million people have no access to sanitation, 178 million no access to health services. More than 250 million adults are illiterate, more than half of the children under five years of age are malnourished and under weight. The infant mortality rate in India is still the highest in the world.

Toilet facilities

The 1991 census figures reveal that 3.1 million people in Bombay, 2.8 million in Delhi and 1.2 million in Calcutta and Madras [now Chennai] did not have toilet facilities in their houses. In 1995, when Delhi's population is already estimated to have reached 10 million, as many as 3.3 million persons do not have toilet facilities. In the absence of such amenities, deprived people have nowhere to defecate except in open areas in parks and on railway lines.

In terms of percentages, Delhi is the worst off among India's four mega cities since 33 per cent of Delhi's population do not have toilet facilities, compared to 11 per cent in Calcutta and 23 per cent in Bombay. When every third person in Delhi has to go out to defecate, tensions are bound to arise. In addition, the slums and *jhuggi-jhopri* colonies coexist with communities populated by the middle class and the rich whose moral values and ways of life are in sharp contrast with that of their deprived brethren. Absence of toilet facilities causes urban pollution and spoils the environment.

Flush systems and pollution

Modern technology has brought toilets to bed rooms. But in the absence of proper sewerage systems, rivers are polluted and people drink untreated and contaminated water.

The modern socio-economic context in India reflects a considerable gap between rural and urban communities. The unequal distribution and control of resources has resulted in disparity, but amazingly there are islands of affluence that exist within the country. The basic issue is that population growth is rendering development schemes and projects ineffective as well as damaging the environment.

II
POLLUTION

Gandhi and the Environment

The concept of environmental conservation and survival of human beings was inherent in the ideology of Mahatma Gandhi. Gandhi was ahead of his time and a precursor of environmentalism. As early as 1927, he warned the world that large scale industrialism would create problems of the type we are confronted with today. He said that the world influenced by Western culture was going in the wrong direction and like the proverbial moth would burn itself eventually in the flame around which it was dancing ceaselessly. He saw doom for India and the entire world on the development path it was on. He was not against industrialization, he was against industrialism. And dehumanized machine culture. He emphasized small scale enterprises for "production by masses and not mass-production by an individual". The latter would lead to prosperity for a few and poverty for the rest of the population and that is what happened in India since independence. Small scale enterprises are also free from developmental conflicts between man and nature and economic conflicts between management and labour. They are less energy intensive and therefore less polluting.

His concept of non-violence not only meant absence of injury to the living but also to nature and non-living entities such as air, water and soil. The objective of the ecological movement in the world today is essentially to preserve nature from the onslaught of industrialization but this will be meaningless unless it is simultaneously directed against the stock piling of deadly weapons. Potential threats to the environment and the economy due to arms development are enormous. Besides, polluting the biosphere the world wastes 2,900 river as much scare resources, particularly the fossil fuels on defence preparation as on the internal peace keeping efforts by political department.

Human Greed

Nature is becoming the victim of human greed. Indiscriminate misuse of natural resources in the name of economic development and disregard of the ecological implications, has brought mankind to the present impasse. Gandhi stated that "the earth provides enough to satisfy every man's need but not every man's greed". He was of the view that as long as greed prevailed and the fruits of economic development were not shared equitably among the masses, poverty and hunger would exist. He believed that until the evil of hunger, malnutrition and exploitation of the poor continued anywhere in the world, there could be no economic stability and ecological sustainability of human society. The present ecological crisis demand a different worldview. Giving up the present lifestyle and a reduction in consumerism would directly support the Gandhian ideology of simple living and high thinking.

Gandhi refused to accept affluence as a goal of development and as a goal for Indian society. He believed that the type of development that had been achieved in the West was the result of a systematic colonization and exploitation of the earth and nature. He, therefore, rejected not only supportive modernism of development such as bureaucracy, technology and elites education, but as the whole idea of development as conceived by the builders of the industrial society.

Man must realize that he does not own nature. He is only one of its many offsprings. Nature is not due to man, man is due to nature. He is among its components. More importantly, the wisest animal on earth should play the role of "trustee" of nature's enormous wealth. Exploiting nature ruthlessly amounts to genocide and hence is a crime. Every living component of nature has a right to a dignified existence. Being the most evolved, man should be the "custodian" and "protector" of the dignity of all.

Gandhian Environmentalism

The important elements of Gandhian environmentalism can be summed up as follows: (i) human beings should act as though they are part of nature rather than apart from nature, (ii) materials available on earth should not be used with an element of greed, (iii) human beings should practice non-violence not only towards fellow humans but also towards other living organisms and inanimate materials because over-use of such materials also amounts to violence, (iv) women are to be respected, are to become partners and given their rightful place in all spheres of human behaviour, (v) a bottom-up shared view is preferable to a top-down totalitarian view, (vi) a conservationist and sustainable life-saving approach should prevail over a consumerist self-destructive approach, (vii) human care for and sharing with the poor and destitute in society is a moral obligation towards them, (viii) humans rarely think about how much is enough for a simple, need-based, austere and comfortable life-style, (ix) development should lead, as much as possible, to local self-reliance and equity with social justice and (x) ethics and self-discipline in resource use is an overriding criterion of development.

Urban Pollution Problems

These may be categorized as congestion, transportation, water supply, waste disposal and urban migration.

Congestion

As a rule, third world cities in general and Indian cities in particular are overcrowded. According to the Human Development Report [UNDP, 1993], Calcutta, for example, with a population density of 89,000 persons per kilometre, is the most crowded city in the world...over TEN times more crowded than New York. In the years since then, the population has increased substantially. Other cities are marginally less crowded. Congestion increases pollution, makes shelter beyond the reach of even middle income groups, leads to an increase in crime, reduced perceptivity, human sufferings and converts accidents into disasters. The Bhopal disaster, for example, would have been no more than a minor incident if the Union Carbide factory had been located in an uncongested area, and not surrounded by a heavily populated city. Congestion also breeds slums because it takes land out of the reach of the poor, and even of the middle classes.

Declining Bombay

In his book : *The New landscape of Planning for cities like Bombay*, Charles Correa has compared declining life in Bombay with the state of a frog.

The frog is put in water which is slowly being heated. The frog feels uncomfortable as the temperature gradually rises. The frog "adjusts" to the worsening situation. This process goes on for a long while until a critical stage is reached when the frog goes into a stupor, ceases to struggle, and finally succumbs. Patient Bombayites [Mumbaites] have been undergoing this treatment but can hardly be expected to go on for ever "adjusting" to worsening amenities. Civil disturbances, a rise in organized crime, an increase in the frequency of suburban train disruptions are symptoms of impending collapse. Such events would have been considered inconceivable in the 1950s yet today they are taken for granted.

Transportation

Let us examine the example of Delhi. From a mere 9,803 vehicles in 1947, the number rose to 2.6 million in 1990. Rising at a rate of 11,000 vehicles a month, this figure has reached almost 30 million today. As a result, suspended particulate matter exceeds the prescribed limit while carbon monoxide and nitrogen oxide remain high, causing lung and heart disease. Once a city of gardens, open avenues, and the green ridges of the Aravali hills, Delhi today has become the most pullulated city in India.

Throughout history, since the days of Mahabharta, Delhi has been pillaged, plundered and degraded. It has been polluted. It is being polluted so much that it has the dubious distinction of being the most polluted city in the world perhaps second only to Mexico city. And with a forest cover of only 26 square kilometres in a geographical area of 1483 square kilometres, the capital does not seem to have much hope for clean air in the near future. Indeed, according to available figures, the incidence of respiratory diseases in Delhi is twelve times higher than the national average. Thirty per cent of the capital's population, in particular children, suffer from respiratory disorders. Automobiles account for 70 per cent of Delhi's foul air, while three thermal power stations let out 302 tonnes of ash, smoke and other pollutants into the air everyday.

Water Supply

According to the World Bank Atlas, 1992, India falls under the second best category of nations in regard to water use per capita. Yet, all cities in India suffer from acute water shortages. For instance, the summer water supply in Madras (now renamed Chennai) dwindled to less than 20 litres per capita ; and even worse, water was supplied only once every three days. Yet, rainfall over the city is so substantial that rain water averages over 1,000 litres per family per day. Other Indian cities are in a similar predicament. Nature is bountiful but man's management is evidently incompetent.

Waste Disposal

Indian cities have given up waste disposal as a hopeless task. The difficulty is partly technical and partly cultural. Waste disposal is aggravated both when congestion increases and when a city becomes large. Yet, waste is a source of wealth if technology is employed to convert it into energy and other useful materials.

The Environmental Pollution Control Authority (EPCA) has taken the stand that there should be no new registration of commercial diesel vehicles in the capital city of Delhi. While many environmentalists are against the use of diesel due to the high emission of suspended particulate matter (SPM), a major pollutant, there is a perception in the automobile industry that dieselization need not be considered a negative phenomenon if anti-pollution standards like Euro-II are strictly adhered to. It is the respirable suspended particulate matter (RSPM) below 10 micron size arising mainly from diesel emission that is the cause of great concern. RSPM is considered dangerous as it enters the lungs, instantly aggravating lung disease. The EPCA has recommended that commercial vehicles in Delhi such as buses replace diesel with Compressed Natural Gas [CNG], a much cleaner fuel. The director of the Centre for Science and Environment, late Anil Aggarwal stated: "We will strongly discourage the use of diesel as the SPM generated is 10-100 times the SPM produced by petrol run vehicles." So far, only experiments have been conducted to launch CNG vehicles, and this has had not an iota of impact.

Urban Migration

Migration of the rural population due to poverty in villages is the greatest urban pollutant and has not been checked. Strictly speaking, rural urban migration will be prevented only when villages become as attractive and fruitful with regard to employment as cities are.

Diwali (Festival of Lights)

Every year, the greatest Indian festival, Diwali, becomes a festival of joy accompanied by noise, asthma and air pollution due to the indiscriminate use of crackers and fireworks. A study conducted by the Indian Institute of Medical Sciences reveals that the number of cases of bronchial ailments show a three-fold increase in the week prior to the festival. According to J.S. Kamyotra, a senior environmental engineer at the Central Pollution Control Board (CPCB), most fire crackers are made of Sulphur, a highly poisonous chemical. When crackers are lit, sulphur fumes escape into the atmosphere, increasing sulphur dioxide levels. This is particularly worrying as over exposure to the gas can lead to serious ailments including acute coronary problems like angina and heart attacks. Figures released by the CPCB show that as of November 1, 1999 (Real Diwali was on November 7th), the amount of sulphur dioxide in the atmosphere almost doubled, increased rapidly and reached its peak on the actual day of the festival, that is November 7th and 8th 1999. Even the amount of carbon monoxide increases to 2,000 micrograms per cubic metre. The acceptable limit for sulphur dioxide at this time of the year is 20 micrograms per cubic metre and 2,000 for carbon monoxide. The figures are almost four times the acceptable limits, and with every passing Diwali, these figures have shown further increases. People need to change the way they celebrate this festival, in particular since vehicular pollution is also on the increase. The CPCB chairperson, D.K. Biswas states that government has been monitoring the level of pollutants during Diwali for the last six years after receiving reports that a growing number of people were being admitted to hospitals with respiratory and bronchial ailments during the festival period. Some scientists say that the problem is compounded by the fact that Diwali falls during the winter months and that the sudden drop in temperatures at this time of the year are in large part responsible for trapping pollutants in the atmosphere, thereby giving rise to treacherous smog that makes life impossible for those with respiratory problems.

Festival Baths

Millions of people bathe in big rivers during the festival season to cleanse their sins. In the process, however, rivers are polluted.

Noise Pollution

Crackers and other fireworks also create noise pollution. They generally generate a noise level of more than 100 decibels (impulse).

Trees Suffer Silently in "Smoky" Diwali

If there was a way trees and birds could express themselves, Diwali would definitely evoke SOS messages from them. For trees and other vegetation life the day after Diwali is burdened with thick layers of sulphur dust and suspended particulate matter. This makes it difficult from them to carry out even basic functions like breathing. Layers of particulate matter block the stomata [pores on leaves] and thereby obstruct the photosynthesis process. In simple words, trees are prevented from releasing oxygen and moisture into the air.

Diwali also spells trouble for birds. Survival in nests becomes unsafe. On the one hand, they have to cope with the loud blasts and on the other hand they have to guard against the obnoxious smoke. Over the years, air pollution has deprived the city of Delhi of at least 100 rare species of birds.

November 7, 1999 Diwali Festival: An Awakening

During the last two years, the Delhi government has taken to fighting Diwali-related environmental problems on a war footing. The Environment Department enlisted the help of NGOs to spread the message against the use of crackers. Play posters and appeals in city schools helped to disseminate the message to children, among the major consumers of crackers. Advertisements on television and radio also sent the message home. In addition, it is hoped that social workers will take up the challenge and make people realize the gravity of pollution. If the fight against Diwali pollution continues, the festival may regain its glory as the festival of lights, rather than the festival of noise and pollution.

The 1999 Diwali was indeed grateful of Delhi's children as the city breathed free and easy. A clear sky greeted the city on the morning of Monday November 8, 1999 and a perceptible decrease in the air pollution confirmed that the millennium's last Diwali was less messy and irritating. Sources in the Delhi Government's Department of Environment confirmed that the air pollution barometer slipped by between 30 and 50 per cent in many places in the city. Noise pollution levels also showed a decline in various areas.

For 15 million Oriyans in the ten districts devastated by the October 1999 super cyclone, however, the Diwali festival of lights remained a period of darkness since the cyclone polluted the total environment of the state and it will take years to recover.

III
THE POLITICAL WILL

The cyclone's dance of death and destruction in Orissa prompted artist Jatin Das to speak out. To speak not only of the devastation wrought by nature but also of that brought on by politicians, the bureaucracy, and the Oriyans themselves over the years. In Orissa, with the exception of handicrafts, no other cottage industry or other small scale industry has been encouraged. Politicians and bureaucrats only talk about big industries. With money pouring into the state for cyclones relief, Das would like to see it used for reconstruction of houses, providing clothing, and generating employment, among other things, since Orissa can, he says, no longer afford to sit cross-legged.

Environmental protection needs total participation of the people and one cannot wait for government to act. Laws are not effective in the absence of efficient machinery for enforcement, and judicial delays are proverbial in India. The present political and development processes are a catalyst for collective environmental decadence in a society which lays more emphasis on the accumulation of power and wealth rather than on restraint and morality. Indeed, one of the basic questions today is whether rulers and political parties have a high level of seriousness and a sense of urgency with regard to a policy of environmental security. The obvious answer is "no". The saddest aspect of the current situation is that politics takes precedence over human considerations. Most present day leaders are easily tempted to use political power for personal gains and self-aggrandizement. Environmental security takes a backseat.

The herculean task of a mass-awakening and mass movement is required to save us from mass destruction. Today, we live in the age of information. A poet like T.S. Eliott would wonder where we lost the wisdom we had in knowledge and whether we have lost knowledge in information. Nevertheless, the fact remains that we are in the information age. The "wake up call" for our hearts and minds should stir us to take immediate steps to protect our environment from various pollutants since tomorrow will be too late. Environmental security in this county cannot be jeopardized by socio-cultural facts which impinge upon the quality of life of the people in India.

REFERENCES

Aiyar, Swaminathan Antlesaria (1999), Crowding Out Justice, *The Times of India*, Sunday, November 7, New Delhi; p. 12.

Correa, Charles (1995), New Landscape on Planning for Cities, *The Times of India*, February 22, New Delhi.

Chandra, Praful (1999), "Orissa? Is it in Bihar or Bengal", *The Times of India*, Sunday, November 7, New Delhi, p. 1.

Gangrade, K.D. (1997), Environmental Crisis: A Challenge to Modern Civilization for Secularization of Environment Stewardship in *Environmental Stewardship and Sustainable Development*, Edited by Jain, R.B., Friedrich Ebert Stiftung, New Delhi, pp. 85-106.

Gangrade, K.D. (1999), *Gandhi—Since 50 years of Azadi*, Gandhi Smriti and Darashan Samiti, New Delhi, pp. 68-120.

Gupta Rahul (1999), A Cleaner Diwali in Delhi at last, *The Times of India*, Tuesday, November 9, New Delhi, p. 1.

Indiresan, P. V. (1993) Managing the Environment: Urban Dimensions, *Indian Association of Social Science Institution (IASSI) Quarterly*, Vol. 11, No. 3 & 4, January-June, pp. 1-14.

Khosroo, T. N. (1997), Gandhian Environmentalism: An Unfinished Task, *Indian Association of Social Science Institution (IASSI) Quarterly*, Vol. 16, No. 1, July-September, pp. 1-16.

Malik, Iqbal (1999), Diwali then and now, *The Times of India*, Sunday, November 7, New Delhi, p. 6.

Puri, R. K. (1995), Darker Side of Development—Toilet Facilities, *The Hindustan Times*, Thursday, April, p. 16.

Sengupta, Arjun (1999), Delivering the Right of Development ESCR and NGOs, *Economic and Political Weekly*, Vol. XXXIV, No. 41, October 9-15, Mumbai, pp. 2920-2922.

Shiv Shankar, Rahul (1999), Seasons of Joy, Noise, Asthma, *The Times of India*, Friday, November 5, New Delhi, p. 3.

Vittal, N. (1993), Urban Environment Management—The Telecom Option for Connectivity, *Indian Association of Social Science Institution (IASSI) Quarterly*, Vol. 11, No. 3 & 4, January-June, pp. 63-77.

7

Bhoodan and Gramdan
Revolution through Love

The greatest achievement of Indian democracy since Independence has been that the former Vice-President Kocheril Raman Narayanan was elected President of India. He is the first *Dalit* to rise to the highest office of the country. Of course, when asked how he felt to be the first *Dalit* President, Mr. Narayanan said, "I am just the President." This fulfils, in the Golden Jubilee year of freedom, one of Gandhi's dreams to see one of the *Dalits* occupying the highest position in the country.

In 1947 the dismemberment of the Indian subcontinent compelled more than 15 million people to move. Some 8.5 million people migrated from India to Pakistan and 6.5 million the other way round. It was perhaps the largest refugee flow in history. Fifty years on as partition sufferers and survivors come under the media glare in India, the "refugee" is once again a thorny subject. Einstein was a refugee, and so is our the then Prime Minister, Inder Kumar Gujral. This is the second triumph of Gandhian democracy.

But if Gandhi was alive in flesh and blood to him all these achievements would appear mere cosmetic. To him the achievement of national independence was only the first stage in Indian revolution. The second—and more important—stage was to be a non-violent social revolution. He said: "The Congress has won political freedom, but it has yet to win economic freedom, social and moral freedom. These freedoms are harder than the political only because they are constructive, less exciting and not spectacular."[1]

He wanted Congress to transform itself into a voluntary organization of Lok Sevaks (servants of the people) with workers going amongst the villagers to help them achieve true *Swaraj*, full self-reliant independence—economic as well as political. His idea of *Sarvodaya* (the welfare of all) envisaged a reconstructed Indian village society with people using simple hand-tools in agriculture and industry, engaged im production for local use rather than profit. It was to be a society of equals, a kind of communitarians, wherein each individual would place the common welfare above their own selfish interests, and the principle of "from each according to their ability, to each according to their need" would be paramount. This vision of a society of small, largely self-sufficient village communities, a just and non-violent political, social and economic order, was far removed from the modern industrial society that Nehru and many of the other Congress leaders eagerly anticipated.[2]

Over the next five decades India succeeded in increasing her foodgrain production, improving technological capabilities, and maintaining formal democracy. However, during the same period poverty, inequality, landlessness and unemployment increased. Of all reforms we have seriously failed in implementing land reforms. These reforms were soon introduced after independence in order to increase agricultural productivity and ensure redistributive justice.

The British conquest of India had led to the disintegration of the village community by the introduction of land revenue system and commercialization of agriculture. The new land system meant untold exploitation of Indian peasantry.

Following Gandhi's death in January 1948, those of his co-workers who were committed to his model of a Sarvodaya society established an organization known as Sarva Seva Sangh.

The third conference of the Sangh was held at Hyderabad in 1951. After the conference, Gandhi's spiritual heir, Vinoba Bhave, travelled to the Telengana district of Andhra Pradesh where a violent struggle was taking place between the landless peasants and their feudal landlords. Vinoba had joined Gandhi at the age of twenty, and soon afterwards Gandhi had said: "He has come not like others to be blessed, but to bless; not to receive, but to give." That was in 1917, when Vinoba was twenty-two. Ever since, Gandhi had regarded him, though much younger than himself, as a teacher rather than a pupil. He had chosen him as the first person to court arrest during the Quit India movement.

Birth of Bhoodan Movement

Vinoba reached Pochempelli village on the morning of April 18, 1951. Forty Harijan families had come to him in the afternoon to tell why did they support the communists. Communists were the only people who were ready to give them land, so what else could they do? Couldn't Vinoba ask the government to help them?" And Vinoba replied: "Of what use is government help until we can help ourselves?" He said: "My aim is to change hearts, not governments... The government is only a bucket. The people are the well. If there is not water in the well, how can there be any in the bucket? I go to the source of water, the people themselves." If the people are converted, he believed, then the government will automatically change. His methods of conversion? Not legal sanctions nor threats of retaliation and revenge, but power of self-denial and gentleness (*tapas,* as the Indian culture calls it.)[3]

So he had put the problem of these forty poor families before the village to see what the village could do. "Ram Chandra, one of the big landlords of the village, took a piece of paper and signed away 100 acres of land. Vinoba asked the forty Harijan families to decide how they would like to divide the land and whether they wished to farm it individually or together. The Harijans told him that they would farm the land collectively. The various caste groups among them—washermen, leather workers, weavers already lived together as communities, eight families to a group, the houses of each community being built behind one wall with a common veranda in the front. It would only need a small extension of this system for them to farm together with each group responsible for the whole. Also, they said they did not need more than 80 acres to start with—two acres each. The surplus 20 acres could be used elsewhere.[4] Thus the Bhoodan Movement was born.

Gramdan

Vinoba was quite consciously searching for an answer to the problems of India's landless which would serve as an alternative to a violent revolution. He embarked on a series of *Padayatras* (walking tours) throughout India, appealing to the conscience of the landlords, begging for land for the landless, achieving social revolution through individual acts of charity. He reached Mangroth on April 24, 1952. He made his usual appeal. In response, Diwan Shatrughana Singh, headman of the village gave him all that he had—houses, trees, barns, wells, clothing and every single acre of land. "Do with them what you like," he said, "There is nothing in the whole earth I can call my own. All belongs to God." Vinoba handed over the gift to a village committee and a fortnight later the village held a public meeting at which every family except for one small holder and one Chamar (leather curer), was present and decided to follow the example of their headman. There was new problem, however, the second largest landlord lived outside Mangroth in the nearby village. He had not been present in the meeting. The villagers approached him, pointing out that since all Mangroth landless labourers would now be able to cultivate their own plots, he would find it difficult to obtain labour there for tilling of his Mangroth land. The landlord agreed to hand over to the village committee his plots of land—much to the chagrin of his own village, where he had not given a single acre.

Vinoba had never believed in the mathematical equality of human beings. "We are equals," he says, "just as the five fingers of the hand are equal. Equal in our usefulness and importance, but not always in our size or strength or capacity." Now that the 800 acres of Mangroth land had all been vested in the village community, they were redistributed again to the villagers on the basis of each family's capacity and need. Diwan Singh, who had given all of his 100 acres to the community received back 40 acres, since he was known to be the most efficient farmer in the village. While at the end came the potters, shoe-makers and silver-smiths who had a trade already, and they received only small plots. All the land, however, whether given to a Harijan or to Diwan Singh, was to be held in trust for the village, which could review and change the distribution whenever the need arose. Thus the Gramdan was the second stage of Bhoodan.

Total Revolution

To Vinoba the movement is either the first step towards a total revolution of society, a revolution through love, or else it is nothing. So great was the enthusiasm that a target of 50 million acres was to be reached by the end of 1957, which was designated as the "Year of the Land Revolution." In fact, a total of 4.2 million acres of land had been donated by the end of the year. By that time, however, the movement was calling not for the individuals' surrender of a proportion of their land and but for the complete surrender of property rights in favour of the village community. This was the call for Gramdan—gift of the village—the pooling of all the village land vesting its ownership in the community.[5]

Whereas in Bhoodan village the basic structure was similar to a normal Indian village except for there being fairer distribution of land, in a Gramdan village (in theory at least the landless ceased to be recipient of) individual acts of charity and became equal member of the village community which owned the land in common.[6]

According to G. Ostergaard and M. Curry the substitution of Gramdan for Bhoodan represented a move from a basically individualistic to socialist programme.[7]

"Number One Thief"

On 25 December 1956, Vinoba came to Gandhi Niketan Ashram of J.C. Kumarappa during his Bhoodan *padayatra* in Tamil Nadu. He had a lively discussion with his old colleague in his hut. In the course of dialogue, Kumarappa told Vinoboa that he was a "number one thief in India." Vinoba was taken aback by this unexpected charge from his bosom friend and asked for clarification. Kumarappa calmly told him that he was merely referring to his hoarding the lands, obtained through the Bhoodan without proper arrangements of their distribution. Vinoba immediately understood the truth behind his statement and thereafter expedited the distribution of lands to the needy.[8]

Weakening of the Movement

The early 1960s witnessed the weakening of the pace of movement to a considerable extent. So a new approach was developed in the form of a "sulabh" (simplified) Gramdan which represents a concession to the principles of land ownership. The late 1960s witnessed the promulgation of the concept of block-*dan*, district-*dan*, and state-*dan*, Vinoba's fertile imagination has widened the concept of *dan* (gift) further into other forms, like *shramdan* (gift of labour) *sampatidan* (gift of money), *buddhidan* (dedication of one's mental abilities to the realization of Sarvodaya ideals), and *jeevandan* (dedication of one's life to the cause). By this time, Vinoba formulated the concept of Shanti Sena and as a result the programme of action of the movement was turned to be a three-fold one which emphasizes Gramdan as revolutionary aspect, Khadi as a constructive economic programme, and Shanti Sena as the non-violent political force devoted to peace work.[9]

Under the revised Gramdan scheme the private use of land was to continue, whilst the formal ownership of the land was vested in the village community as organized in the village Gram Sabha or village assembly. In other words, the land owners would continue to retain possession of the land for cultivation purposes and could also pass on in inheritance. In addition, land owners were required to donate at least five per cent of their holdings to the Gram Sabha for distribution to the landless. Also a village fund was to be established into which every family would contribute a portion of their income equivalent to one-fortieth of their agricultural produce. The common affairs of the village were to be managed by the Gram Sabha, membership of which would be open to all adult members of the village. Disputes between villagers would not be taken to the courts but would be settled in the village itself by a special committee set up for the purpose. A village was to be declared a Gramdan village when at least 75 per cent of its residents had expressed their approval and sufficient number of land owners were involved so that at least 51 per cent of the total land in the village would be covered in the Gramdan scheme.[10]

This revolutionary character of Gramdan made it difficult to promote. Nevertheless, in the wake of Vinoba's *padayatras* throughout the country, village after village declared itself for Gramdan. By 1971, it was claimed that 168,108 villages had declared for Gramdan, over one quarter of the total number of villages in India. However, the majority of these were mere "declarations of intent." Only in about 5,000 cases had the land titles actually been transferred to the village assembly and the village officially registered as a Gramdan village whilst, according to Osotergaard and Curry, little more than 500 of these villages would have revealed to an observer signs of development and social reconstruction.[11]

Basically what had happened is that villages would declare themselves for Gramdan in a wave of enthusiasm following a visit from the saintly Vinoba or one of his lieutenants like Jayaprakash Narayan. The leaders would then move on to the next village or location leaving the local Sarvodaya workers on their own to implement the declaration of intent. This clearly showed that the movement lacked the resources, both finance and trained and committed personnel, to do the follow-up work effectively. Out of the 4.2 million acres of Bhoodan land, 1.85 million were uncultivable or legally disputed and of the remaining only just over half had actually been distributed by 1969-70, to the landless through the various Bhoodan boards which had been formed to allocate the land to the landless. Out of the 168,108 Gramdan villages, only a few thousand had been officially registered.[12]

Dependency Culture

Furthermore, even when land was distributed it was found that in many cases the allottees were not in a position to benefit from the gift. They lacked the finances and other resources to reclaim land that was often unirrigated and need of levelling. They lacked the means to acquire the necessary implements, seeds and fertilizers and draught-power to start cultivation. In addition, they lacked the experience and self-confidence to manage their own land. Theirs had always been a life of complete and utter dependency on the local land owners. Indeed, in many cases they were too poor to contribute their own labour to the development of their land, as they were so dependent for their day-to-day survival on the wages received as day labourers from local land-owners.[13]

During the late 1950s and 1960s, various attempts were made to deal with this situation. Bhoodan cooperatives were formed, government loans were obtained for irrigation and land reclamation purposes, and development agencies intervened to offer funds for specific projects. On the whole, these efforts had only a marginal impact. Many of the schemes omitted crucial inputs—finance might be made available for irrigation but not for the purchase of draught animals and seeds. Other schemes concentrated on the economic development of the land at the cost of the necessary social and educational work among the villagers, with the result that project crumbled once the sponsoring agency had withdrawn.[14]

Lesson Drawn

Lesson drawn from these experiences by certain key figures involved in the Gandhian constructive work movement was that full development of the Bhoodan and Gramdan lands required their concentration upon the promotion of the necessary qualities of self-confidence and self-reliance and the capacities for self-management and cooperative endeavour amongst the allottees in addition to the provision of the physical and technical inputs required for the full utilization of the newly acquired land. They were still a long way from achieving Gandhi's goal of Gram-Swaraj: self-sufficient, self-supporting and self-ruling communities. Of course, the gap between the ultimate ideal and the actual situation in the villages is often great. The material conditions of those that possess land has frequently increased disproportionately compared with the lot of the landless.

Tardy Land Reforms

It is a pity that land reforms in Independent India have been very tardy in the absence of a "political will." Even today 5 per cent of the people possess 25 per cent of the land and 20 per cent are owners of 60 per cent of the land; the rest 75 per cent have to content with only 15 per cent of the land. It was reported in *The Times of India* of March 7,1997 that in a reply to a Parliament question the Minister of State for Rural Areas and Employment said that nearly 14 per cent of India's agricultural land is owned by less than one per cent of the country's big land-owners.

The reasons for tardy implementation are absence of pressure from below because the poor peasants and agricultural workers are passive, unorganized and inarticulate; lukewarm and often apathetic attitude of the bureaucracy, absence of up-to-date land records and legal hurdles in the way of land reforms.

Distribution of Surplus Land

The progress of distribution of surplus land was palpably slow. Between March 1985 and June 1992—a span of 7 years—only 0.711 million acres could be distributed. The area declared surplus so far is less than two per cent of the cultivated area.[15]

Collapse of the Movement

In the minds of many people the movement was identified with the Congress party. This was the greatest reason for its failure besides other reasons already mentioned. When Vinoba started the Bhoodan Movement, the government and the Congress embraced it whole-heartedly by giving all support to it. But when it entered the second phase of Gramdan, the response was passive, for they were afraid of its revolutionary character. From the very beginning itself, the opposition parties were very critical and they were skeptical towards the movement due to the active involvement of the Congress and the government in it. Slowly the movement failed considerably to get the necessary political rapport and also the much needed governmental enactment.[16]

The constructive programme had been relegated to a subordinate position both by the Congress and by the government with the advent of Independence. Slowly, there emerged two confronting ideas among the constructive workers. One view was that constructive work should scrupulously keep itself away from all politics. Another line of thinking was that the government should be given unconditional support. According to Shankarrao Deo : "A non-violent revolutionary should keep aloof from power politics, but never from politics as such or from political power."[17] There was much confusion aroused as a result of identifying the Congress with Gandhism.

Stephen Murphy, an Australian Gandhian scholar, describes the situation in the following words: "Mother India is suffering, horribly, back-broken under Himalayan mountains of poverty and filth, corruption and vice, political and self-seeking, apathy and inertia, sheer hopelessness and despair, violence and untruth. Mother India is weeping at how disfigured she had become, despite the precious democratic jewel in her crown."[18]

This was the fate of Bhoodan movement as it was hijacked by crook politicians and to some extent untrained workers.

When Jayaprakash Narayan (JP) was confronting the political corruption and government high-handedness, Vinoba suggested to the executive of the Sarva Seva Sangh which met to discuss the issue, "I hold the view that a violent movement is always bad and therefore, it should never be organized. But under the present circumstances, even a non-violent movement against the government... We should confine ourselves to peaceful constructive work. Otherwise the country will be in jeopardy."[19] JP and the majority of constructive workers were not ready to heed the advice of Vinoba. So he urged those in the movement to either withdraw the movement or quit the Sarva Seva Sangh. But the pro-movement leaders decided to silence only the central-level workers, consisting of only 300 Lok Sevaks out of a total of 3,000 of them.[20] The Sarvodaya meeting which discussed this issue ended in sheer confusion.[21] This situation pained Vinoba too much and finally, he took the decision of dissociating himself from the Sarva Seva Sangh.[22] This sounded the final death-knell to the movement. The Sarvodaya workers who had worked substantially in the Bhoodan movement split into three—the majority went along with JP to follow his agitation, a minority opposed JP's agitational approach, who were sympathizers of the Congress and the government, and a considerable number of those who opted out from the ugly scene of confrontation kept themselves silent and idle.

The corruption has become an integral part of our society that the then Prime Minister Inder Kumar Gujral virtually admitted his helplessness in doing anything about politicians named in corruption cases who steadfastly refused to relinquish the public offices they occupy.[23] That is to say, people lose faith in their leaders and workers, which adversely affected the movement.

It is so often the fate of other movements in India. The great man imposes himself by sheer force of personality. His authority is like the spring of a watch and while he is alive everything goes like clock-work. Then the spring breaks. There is no substitute; the watch stops and goes rusty. So it is with Gandhi or Vinoba; once the old man's guiding influence is withdrawn his work will fall apart. X will start quarrelling with Y, B will refuse to accept the directives of Z—all of them good, admirable men, but being Indians, no respecters of institutions and able to accept control at the hands of a saint. Alas. Saints like Gandhi or Vinoba have no successors.[24]

The movement has become so insignificant that text books do not mention contribution of Bhoodan and Gramdan as a historical fact in their chapters on land reforms. People's memories are so short that a very few professionals and knowledgeable Gandhians are able to recall the contribution of Vinoba. His goal was to usher in a three-fold revolution. Firstly, I want to change the people's heart. Secondly, I want to create a change in their lives. Thirdly, I want to change the social structure...We do not aim at doing mere acts of kindness, but creating a kingdom of kindness.

NOTES

1. Quoted in Kantowsky, D., *Sarvodaya : The Other Development*, New Delhi : Vikas, 1980, p. 2.
2. Rigby, Andrews, "Practical Utopianism: A Gandhian Approach to Rural Community Development in India," *Community Development Journal*, Vol. 20, No.l [January 1985], pp. 2-10.
3. Tennyson Hallam, *Vinoba Bhave's Revolution of Love—Saint on the March*, W.D. Willis, Bombay, 1961, pp. 53-66.
4. *Ibid.*
5. Rigby, Andrews, "Practical Utopianism," p.3.
6. *Ibid.*, pp.3-4.
7. Ostergaad, G. and Curry, M., *The Gentle Anarchists*, Oxford; Clarendon Press, 1976, p. 10.
8. Muniandi, K., "Kumarappa, the Man," *Gandhi Marg*, Vol.14, No. 2 [July-September, 1992, 322.
9. Pulickan, Jacob, "The Gandhian Movement in India," *Gandhi Marg*, Vol. 18, No. l (April-June), pp. 66-80.
10. Rigby, Andrews, "Practical Utopianism," p. 4.
11. Ostergaard, G. and Curry, M., *The Gentle Anarchists*, p. 14.
12. *Ibid.*, pp. 10-12 and 15.
13. Rigby, Andrews, "Practical Utopianism," pp. 4-5.
14. Report of the Task Force on and Reforms headed by P.S. Appu, quoted in *Indian Economy* by Datt Ruddar and Surendra Ram, S. Chand and Co. Ltd., New Delhi, 37 edition 1997, pp. 480-81.
15. *Ibid.*
16. Ostergaard, G. and Curry, M., *The Gentle Anarchists*, p.10.
17. Shankarrao Deo, "Congress and Constructive Workers," *Harijan*, March 6, 1949.
18. Stephen Murphy, *Why Gandhi is Relevant in Modern India*? New Delhi: Gandhi Peace Foundation, 1991, p. 7.
19. *People's Action*, April 1974, p. 16.
20. *The Hindustan Times*, 25 March 1975.
21. *The Statesman*, 30 May 1975.
22. *The Times of India*, 14 May 1975.
23. *The Times of India*, 19 July, 1997.
24. Tennyson Hallam, *Vinoba Bhave's Revolution of Love*, p.13.

8

Communication Skills and Community Development

I
INTRODUCTION

If social workers and social work profession have to move forward to meet the challenges of the difficult decades that lie ahead, we must have social workers who are enlightened and perceptive communicators, articulate and with minds of their own, trained to cope with the demands of an increasingly complicated programme of community development and able to interact with the politicians, administrators, scientists and eminent persons in other walks of life. They must be prepared to face tricky national and international problems which may and do have little or nothing to do with being a social worker.

Community Development can be defined as an end product of a 'complex interaction' between technology and man. An effective communication provides the much acceded 'flexibility' in production adjustment and sharing information in a multifaceted yet closely knit environment. Communication assists both "decentralization" and "higher order of integration". Communication can be classified into two categories, first, direct interaction between persons and secondly, through mass media. But researches on acceptance of new practices have shown that people accept new practices when the impersonal means of communication is supported by personal communication. That is people generally consult members of the family, kinship, relatives, neighbours and friends.

The progress of social change would be faster and smoother and development goals can be realized more speedily and effectively if the active involvement and enthusiasm of the members of the community can be generated, guided and channelled through appropriate modalities of communication.

Serious differences, even conflicts are inevitable in the process of transition from tradition to modernity in most of the third world countries. The chapter by drawing data mostly from the field work at the grassroots stresses the need for greater flow of easy communication, sympathy and understanding to tide over the difficulties of the present transitional period through which the larger Indian society is passing in the midst of many stresses and strains from within and powerful influences from outside.

The community development worker's skill lies in getting the community to adopt *consensus model* rather than *conflict model* to achieve the developmental goals of the community. He may develop skills in himself to use traditional and modern means of communication for the dissemination of the correct and right information. However, in our anxiety to catch up with the western world, we should not blindly follow the methods used by them specially when the mass medias are not free. They are under the control of government. Harry Skomia said that use of Television specially for election purposes was very dangerous. He says that in the USA instead of the consent of the governed, it appears that the governing of consent, the manufacturing of public opinion prevail more and more and that the candidates are no longer elected, they are merchandised. The same warning is given by Anthony Smith, a BBC producer who said that Britain had become a case of advanced telecracy. The worker must enhance his skills to prevent misuse of particularly Radio and Television which have become a very powerful source of communication media.

The survival of a policy and implementation of a programme is dependent if people assume responsibility themselves, share their ideas and experiences so that they can work together to achieve the goal identified by them. The communicator or leader by defining clear goals and strategies and then communicating them to his people (followers) and training them to take responsibility for reading those goals, the leader (worker) can create a secure working climate that fosters flexibility and innovation. Thus, the leader has to be a good listener, communicator and educator—an emotionally expressive and inspiring person who can create the right atmosphere rather than make all the decisions himself. Informing, persuading and inspiring are all part of communicating. A good leader or worker spends more time communicating than doing anything else. The leader has to be truly certain that every person in community, as far as possible, has truly understood and absorbed it. Message, to be powerful, must be simple and direct. In India, TV has emerged a potent and big medium in recent years.

The independent press has far more credibility than government TV which time and again, proved to be partisan and sacrificed objectivity in the presentation of news and views and which are more commercially oriented in its quest for maximizing advertising revenues. But in the ultimate analysis, both the print medium and TV have their own distinctive and definite roles to play and have to complement each other.

II
PRIME FACTORS IN COMMUNICATION

In fact, modern mass media is basically a "one-way informational street", where the receiver remains at the inoperative end. He is passive. He has no means to 'respond' or 'react' in actual sense of the terms, to the transmission of message or communication, to participate in the process of creation of understanding. Modern mass media in global dimension is a mind management industry, where communication is tailored in a particular fashion or design. Here receivers, minds are systematically controlled and conditioned to that particular design by repeating the same message to the audio-visual senses of the receiver, through different devices or means. He communication degenerates into a mere transmission o information, and its "socially interactive and participator vulgarises itself to a task of conditioning the receiver' unconditionally accept the message.

Acceptance of any new practice requires effe communication. The social worker working at the g identify the local leaders who would be able influence people to change and adopt innova provide direct link between the outside lea people.

The introduction and adoption of any innovation or new practice will require the following five stages : (i) idea; (ii) awareness; (iii) trial and error; (iv) evaluation; (v) adoption or acceptance. These stages will depend on the following nine factor's to make communication effective and to enable people to accept change, (i) credibility of the communicator; (ii) content of programme or message; (iii) channel of communication; (iv) participation of politicians and bureaucrats in development; (v) understanding and involvement of peer groups; (vi) ultimate decision to plan and implement should rest on the people; (vii) awareness of resources; (viii) accessibility and availability of resources; and (ix) adoption or acceptance. The stages and the factors may not follow the sequential order given above. The dynamism of the community and of the communicator or worker will decide; the procedure to be followed to reach the ultimate goal. This adoption matrix as given below illustrates the points graphically.

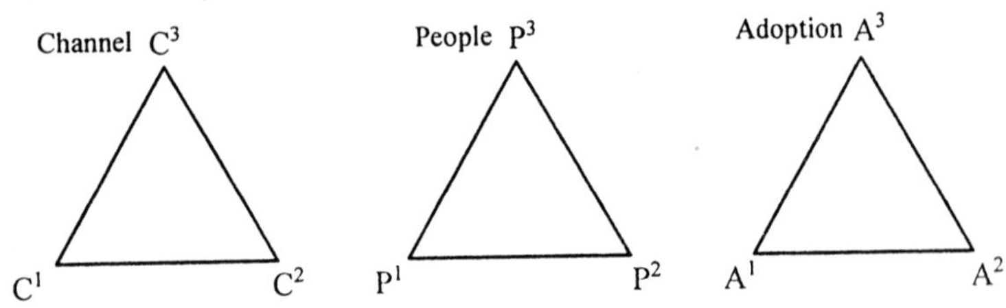

Fig. 1

Formula of Effective Communication:

$$EC = C^3 + P^3 + A^3 = \text{Adoption or Acceptance}$$

Legend

EC= Effective Communication

C^1 = Credibility	P^1 = Peer Group	A^1 = Awareness
C^2 = Content	P^2 = Politician	A^2 = Accessibility
C^3 = Channel	P^3 = People	A^3 = Adoption or Acceptance

Social Structure and Communication in Rural Areas

I should like to give in brief my experience of working in three villages of Delhi. It is found that heads of the households are kingpins and good means of communication with the rest of the family members. Once they are convinced of the usefulness and utility of the project, it is not difficult to get the cooperation and support from other members of the family. The ideal of mutual inter-dependence is further extended from family to lineage or kinship groups. A group of families tracing their descend through the male line is commonly referred to as *Kunba* by the villagers. A small *Kunba* may consist of as many as fifteen or more people. These units within the village are grouped and locally known as *thollas* or *panas*. An individual belonging to a particular lineage or kinship group or *Kunba* is expected to keep all the obligations, rights and duties towards its members. This is very much evident at the time of rituals, ceremonies, etc. The members belonging to the same lineage are also expected to help each other in their economic and political needs.

The lineage system has definite rules to govern the behaviour of its members. A senior member of the lineage, that is, *Karta*, from among the members of the constituent lineages of the senior branch, is the head and leader of the lineage group. He attains his position by his age and as a matter of hereditary rights. His position is much more than that of the head of the family. He solves the intra-*Kunba* problems and also leads and represents the whole of *Kunba* in dealing with other *Kunbas* and other castes in the village. He also represents in the village meetings interest of his members at various levels. The spatial propinquity of the members of the same *Kunba* makes it possible to have intimate and close relationships among the various members of *Kunba*. The leaders of the lineage or *Kunbas* serve as an effective channel of communication for the different constituent families consisting of a *Kunba*. These *Kunbas* are further grouped into sub-groups or factions based on minimal (one or two generations) and maximal (three, four or more generations) lineages. The leaders of the sub-groups are called as the secondary leaders, while those of the whole faction as the primary leaders. The primary leadership comes in the hierarchical pattern as a matter of right and by heredity. But in some cases leadership acrues to one or the others, often the richest of the allied household to which the extended family spreads. In organising the villagers for work I found this method of identifying the village leaders who were effective communicators much more rewarding. I was able to get to know the felt needs of the village from them and canalise the programme through them. The decisions of the primary and secondary leaders were mostly binding on all the households of their constituent groups. The self-help action projects and the election process in the village made it abundantly clear that the leaders generally took the decisions on behalf of their constituents and their decisions were largely accepted and honoured by the members.

The inter-group alliances also followed the lineage group line. With the shifting and changing of the loyalties by the leaders the heads of constituent household would also change or shift their loyalties as desired by leaders. To avoid conflict and misunderstanding the primary leaders did consult or talk to the secondary leaders before taking a final decision on any matter affecting their respective faction or group. Whenever this process was ignored or neglected conflicts cropped-up and divided the groups into various factions.

The family, lineage and kinship group merges into caste which forms a bigger group. Caste is a closed group. It is all pervasive. It is the responsibility and duty of an individual to uphold the caste rules, and the deviants are punished. The principle of seniority in age, inherited privilege, and economic power determine the position of individuals or a group of individuals as the caste leaders. The members of the dominant caste wield a great power and influence in the village. In fact each head of the household, of the Jats or the Rajputs considers himself a leader by birth.

Unity among the leaders brought about by various situations among the dominant castes helped in Anandpur and Chandpur villages to complete a number of action projects. Bharatpur village could not accomplish much as the leaders of the dominant caste remained divided. The conflict amongst the leaders and their shifting alliances had helped the Scheduled Castes, especially the Chamars, to rise to power and pose a threat to the higher castes in the field of politics. The Chamars rose to power because their leaders had political linkages with party bosses at the higher levels and their improved economic position.

It is no doubt the election based on adult franchise has equipped an adult with a power to vote for the candidate of his choice. But very rarely does the adult exercise his independent choice in casting vote at the grassroots level. In practice, the villagers, with the few exceptions, are bound by family, lineage, kinship and caste considerations. Usually these represent the views of the male head of household or joint family.

This was well capitalised by the leaders and candidates who were contesting the elections. Heads of large and important households were the special targets of the candidates and their supporters to woo them as their decision would decide the fate of the contestants. In counting the potential strength on one side or the other reference was constantly made to the number of votes that a household could "give". Once the support of heads of household was assured to a candidate or a faction he might be also requested by that side to bring his wife back to the village from a visit to her parents in time for elections or to delay the departure of his son or other adult members from the village until after the polling. In other words, it was assumed that the head of the household controlled the votes of his household members.

Caste and religion played a very important and crucial role in election campaigns in the villages, the leaders made all efforts to get the support of the various caste members in favour of their respective candidates to ensure victory. Each faction sought to attract the votes of various castes by making the contestants caste by caste to divide the votes. Every imaginable means were used to gain support. Heads of families of lower castes who hoped to acquire title deeds to some of their land as a result of land reforms were promised that their rights would be protected and proved by the land-owners if they voted for the candidate nominated by them. Or, if they proved politically obstinate, they were told that their claims would be opposed. Such promise of help and hindrance were most effective, for the lower castes, mostly illiterate and fearful of officialdom, depended on the support of the literate and experienced high caste persons in these matters. Moreover, threats of reprisals were received fearfully for low caste individuals, dependent on high-caste people for timely loans of money and seed and for other needs. Indeed, for many dependent low-caste members the problem became one of giving no offence or the least offence.

A fact that receives confirmation from the analysis of the action projects and elections in these villages is that the individual villager has not come of his own in our village democracy as faction leaders make commitment, on their behalf in all matters and their commitments are binding on the members. It is, therefore, essential to communicate with these leaders and use them as communicators.

The villagers accept the leadership of outsiders, because of their knowledge; influence, political and official position. The villagers sought the help of their influential outside caste men to resolve their conflict.

The social workers who worked as a catalyst and organized the village communities to meet their needs from the resources available within and without the communities need to accept challenging tasks and work in villages. They emphasized more on the process of building the communities rather than on achieving the physical targets. They had no ready-made programmes. Their programmes, were initiated at the instance of the villagers. On the other hand, the block officials, who were also supposed to be catalyst, came with ready made programmes and were eager only to achieve targets rather than to initiate the process which will make these communities self-sustaining and self-reliant in the long run.

Outside leaders, as stated earlier, are bearer of new ideas and specialized skills. Their status in regard to village structure is uncertain, they may unwittingly compete with established leaders in one or the other field of activity. They may be equated by the village community as the representatives of governmental organizations who come to the village community to collect taxes, impose levies and effect a series of interventions regarded by the community as recurrent inevitable misfortunes. The first task of the outside leader is to win personal acceptance. Once he impresses on the villagers that he is a "neutral" person, i.e. as one who does not in anyway pose a threat to community, he is in a position to play an active role. This role is not easy. On the one hand, the outside leader is the representative of an organization which has a particular goal, and in which he occupies a specific status with certain duties determined by the organization. On the other hand, his activities in carrying out these duties must win the acceptance of the community. He has two sets of obligations. One set towards the organization and the other towards the community which involves adding to its well-being. He cannot determine the cooperation but can achieve this only by influencing the members in bringing about the desired changes.

An outside leader as a catalyst begins his work without enjoying a clear-cut leadership status within the community and without recognition and/or acceptance by the community and without as defined by his organization within the community, his leadership will be informal. Generally, he has to create new groups and gain a position of prestige and influence within established groups. His leadership functions are primarily those associated with setting group goals, providing the groups with an ideology and serving as a resource person to the groups. In doing so he avoids competing with established community leaders since this threatens the community solidarity. Sometimes, this cannot be avoided, for few village communities are free of longstanding factions, which may either try to use the community worker or with which he may unwittingly get closely involved. One way to overcome this problem is to promote projects desired by the whole community and to help involve the whole community to participate and achieve them.

Long established factions may be united on such projects, with the skilful worker bringing about a truce, for the joint consideration and carrying out other activities. It is true that by and large the power positions at the village level are still determined by caste kinship and economic status. However, it is worth noting that higher castes are losing their power and the lower castes are coming up. Education has created new awakening and the youth are asserting themselves as well as finding the place in the panchayat. The idea of a positive, constructive type of leadership in the public interest and acceptance of innovation is only gradually emerging, with the ushering in of democratic decentralization and adult suffrage. The existence of factions, the persistence of kinship loyalties, the absence of village-wide leadership, and the limited identification with larger groups, present serious bottlenecks in the way of development programmes.

III
MEDIA AND MESSAGE

Communication makes the community and its development possible. Communication is the integrating process or force and community is the end result of this process. In this sense communication becomes the core value in so far as community development is concerned.

Communication gives the isolated community access to new ideas, improved technology and additional resources. Effective communication at the individual level, by helping to get the isolated individuals into people with similar knowledge, values and goals, this would make possible formation of social groups and communities who would be able to think collectively and act together.

Community development worker, making use of his communication knowledge and skills, helps the group members, identify their most-pressing problems and reach agreement on solution they find workable and to which they are willing to devote their efforts and resources. Community development is assisting people to take greater control over social, economic and political factors determining their development. In this sense community development is much more than mere mobilisation of people for building such visible objects like schools, roads, wells etc. Greater control is achieved through increased participation in community development goals and activities. People cannot participate in things they do not understand. Understanding develops through inter and intra group communication interactions. These communication interactions take place at various stages of identifying the problem, setting priority, planning and making decisions to undertake solution of problem, decide the procedure and mechanism of implementing the decisions and shouldering the responsibility for monitoring and evaluating the results of mutually agreed upon community development activities. In simple terms, it means need of communication skills related to planning processes, implementing processes and monitoring as well evaluating processes. At each of these stages three types of communication skills are required : These are (i) communication for motivational change, (ii) technical communication, and (iii) administrative communication. These skills are discussed here in reverse order.

Skills Related to Administrative Communication

Administrative communication involves need of specific planning, monitoring of implementation, supervision, management, logistics and use of reports and records for improving community development, programme planning and performance. Communication skills for bringing about effective coordination between social groups and various organisations are very critical. Coordination is achieved through the difficult and often frustrating process of negotiation between people, making heavy demand on human relation skills of community workers. Thus skills in effective human relations and interaction become necessary for every successful community development worker. Coordination relates very closely to team work and communication skills for strengthening team spirit, therefore, are equally important for effective community development work.

Another very critical area of administrative communication is ensuring free and fearless feedback communication from the workers and community members. This is perhaps the most neglected aspect of administrative communication. Representations from workers and complaints from community members are not taken kindly by the establishment. This attitude in course of time leads to disintegration of the community. Therefore, the community development workers must have the skill for ensuring free flow of feedback information for processing it usefully and for making use of it in strengthening community development process.

Skills Related to Communication Technology

Community development invariably involves introducing alternative, improved and appropriate technology into the communities for their development. This requires the community development workers to be very thorough with communication skills necessary for and transferring technology to the simple, tradition bound and illiterate rural communities. Communication skills for implementing such a process of technology transfer is a category by itself and community development workers need to be trained in this aspect of communication. Some of the communication skills of relevance here are skills of effective demonstration, knowledge of concerned technology, repeated practice or use of technology and use of audio-visual aids and electronic media. Community development workers must have necessary skills using the ever increasing list of such media. Social workers will have to have skills for proper and appropriate use of the following *mass media:*

Newspapers

News,
Feature studies,
Effective articles,
Editorials,
Letters to the Editor
Columns, Photographs,
Cartoons.

Radio and Television

News, Dramas,
Songs, Talks, Interviews,
Panel discussions,
Documentaries,
Spot announcements,
Question and answer shows,
Quiz shows, Television films.

Film strips and Slides

Informational,
Motivational,
Instructional,
Advertising.

Demonstration and Teaching Materials

Flip charts,
Models, Wall charts,
Texts and Manuals,
Flash cards, Tapes.

Magazines and Periodicals

Feature stories,
Fiction,
Technical articles,
Humurous anecdotes,
Cartoons,
Special issues Columns,
Advertisements.

Films

Full length films,
Short documentaries,
Short motivational films,
Spot films,
News reels,
Instruction films for training.

Printing Materials

Posters, Bulletins,
Leaflets, Folders,
Pamphlets and booklets,
Books, Calendars.

Outdoor Billboards and Permanent Signs

Lighted, Unlighted,
Exhibitions,
Songs, dramas and
dance troupes.

There is almost a revolution in mass media and electronic and it will be desirable for community development workers to be responsible about this and have skills for appropriate use of as many media as possible and relevant in this work situation. Transference of technology requires training. Here community development workers will be required to have instructional skills of participatory nature.

Let us discuss in some detailed role of journalists in the newspapers.

Role of Journalists

T.N. Ninan says: "Virtually all successful newspapers all over the world are published by companies. The companies by definition used to make profits. And where the share-holders are demanding, they need to get return on capital that compares with other avenues for investment. But even as they pursue profits, publishers try to insulate their journalists from financial pressures by separating Church and State, and put a Chinese wall between the two. The tension between these two purposes would not exist if either of the two conditions ...fied. The first condition is that journalists simply write the tune dictated by the piper. But whereas managing a company is a trade activity, while journalism is a profession. The difference between the two is that the latter has a value system which its practitioners swear by and usually uphold. This is true of doctors, lawyers, professional social workers, etc. whereas in management the only thing matters is profit and how to maximize it without breaking the law. In most cases publishers have given up the business of having an independent editor. In more and more cases the publisher or the person who owns/controls the shares has become the editor: *The Statesman*, *The Telegraph*, *Deccan Herald*, etc. The difference between Church and State is artificial and journalists have to take orders like everyone else. As Rupert Murdoch said about Harold Evans when he was editor of *The Times* : "He thinks it is his paper; it is mine." From this follows the further dictum that freedom of press is not the responsibility of the editor, it is the freedom of the proprietor.

The whole gamut of Gandhiji's writings clearly indicates that print media occupied an important place in his communication.

Motivational Communication

Community development takes place when people change their behaviour and adopt improved practices and technology. To get community people motivated to accept new ideas and practices appears to be a most exacting task. Communication activities are aimed at influencing human behaviour making use of persuasive communication skills mainly geared to the motivation which is considered to be basic to behavioural change. Such motivational communication skills perform the following tasks :

1. Making people better informed at the community as well as individual level.
2. Creating conviction and favourable attitudes among individuals towards community development programmes and activities.
3. Getting community and societal mood and atmosphere favourable to community development programmes.

Providing information would be based on understanding community members who generally differ in so far as their information needs are concerned. Management of information involves such skills as assessing the information needs of clients, designating the information contents, choosing the channels for providing this information and assessing the impact of the information in terms of desired community development goals. People can be convinced or educated in different ways. Procuring information is one such way. There are other mechanisms and skills, such as, personal contacts, lectures, adult education, group discussions, debates, exhibitions, self-learning material and mass media etc.

But among all these, personal communication has been proved to be most effective in bringing about changes in human behaviour and overall community development. Researches have shown that people accept new practices when impersonal sources of communication is supported by personal face to face communication among community members. It has been found that for making changes in behaviour people generally are guided by the opinion and advice of members of the family, kinship group, relatives, neighbours and friends. Thus for effective motivational communication the workers must be very skilful in face to face communication. He needs to be a good listener, communicator and persuasive educator all combined in one.

IV
CONCLUSION

In his famous work, *The Rhetoric*, Aristotle mentioned three elements in the process of communication—the communicator, the message and the receiver. The objective of communication according to him was to "influence or persuade the receiver in a manner that is considered appropriate by the communicator". By and large, this is still the basic approach to what has come to be called the western model of communication. Harold Lasswell's famous formulation of the five questions : Who ? Says what ? On which channel? To whom? With what effect ? What appeals to constitute the western model today only adds emphasis to the channel of communication and its effect on the receiver of the message. Both these elements are ascribed to development and expansion in the media.

There are two significant developments to be noted. First, the functions of communication are, today, much wider. Besides information and motivation, they include socialisation which implies stimulation of people's active involvement in public issues whether they relate to the functioning of the political system, programmes of economic development or to dissemination of social ethics and preservation of the heritage of the past. In other words communication is linked to people's needs, both material and non-material.

Secondly, the media of mass communication, particularly the electronic media, radio and TV tend to claim a much higher degree of attention than verbal media or others which are culture-specific. Also, the objective of socialisation is not universally emphasised. In the western model it is almost neglected. The cultural ethos is of no great relevance in this model. That is why it has been characterised as "communicator-based, undirectional and manipulative".

Are philosophy, culture and tradition relevant in the process of communication today ? If so, how far can they be integrated with the modern media of communication? Answers to these questions will determine whether there can be an Asian communication theory or model. Since the theory is concerned not only with the process but with the selection and functions of the media the subject is of vital interest. It does not need to be emphasized that communication today covers almost the entire spectrum of human behaviour. Prof. Godwin C. Chu, on the basis of "some soul searching" at the East West Centre, agrees that western theories and research have not been very productive because apart from the distinctive experience the priorities in Asian countries are different, often specific to a country.

In India the subject has been totally neglected. The policy planners have been preoccupied with the adoption and expansion of modern media of communication. The message, if any, is selective and the methodology borrowed or transplanted. Even the training institutions are, primarily concerned with western concepts. The theory as well as the syllabi taught are largely inspired by American writings. With the investment of resources in the media how can the message be meaningful and accepted by the people ? This has made it highly commercialised oriented rather than people oriented or centred.

Communication whether formal or informal, whether based on grassroots initiative or state control mass media is riot likely to change the indigenous social structure very far specially not where the economy is stagnating and opportunities for innovation are absent.

The goal of community development as an end in itself has been sidelined by means of an ineffective means of communication.

Consequences of planned development have been, very dismal. The rich have become richer and poor poorer by the western model of development adopted by us which has been rejected in the West itself. If we also reject this model, I feel no tears would be shed in our country. Man centred model advocated and practised by Gandhi in which the Talisma given by him to planners and development workers is as follows:

> Recall the face of the poorest and the most helpless person whom you may have seen, and ask yourself if the step you contemplate is going to be of any use to the person. Will he or she be able to gain anything by it? Will it restore control over life and destiny? In other words, will it lead to *swaraj*, self-rule, for the hungry and also spiritually starved millions of our people? Then you will find your doubts and your self melting away.

Let us not be under wrong illusion and boast that "I have done this work and I can take credit for it". The worker must in all humility reduce himself to zero. Gandhi in his autobiography (My Experiments with Truth) has rightly concluded in the following words : "To see the universal and all pervading spirit of Truth face to face *one* must be able to love the lowliest of creation as one-self—I must reduce myself to zero. So long as man does not of his own free will put himself last among the fellow-creatures, there is no salvation for him. *Ahimsa* is the farthest limit of humility.

The Gandhian model of development; therefore, requires active involvement and participation of man building his own destiny. This is possible if some of us belonging to so called rich and middle class voluntarily instead of drifting towards consumerism are willing to sacrifice and share our pleasures in the interest of down-trodden of our society. Schumacher as follower of Gandhian philosophy in his book. Small is Beautiful said, "Perhaps by being much less greedy and envious ourselves; perhaps by resisting the temptation of letting luxuries become needs and perhaps by even scrutinising our needs to see if they can be simplified and reduced. If we do not have the strength to do any of this, could we perhaps stop applauding the type of economic progress which palpably lacks the basis of permanence and gives modest support to those, who unafraid of being denounced as cranks work of non-violence, as conservationists, ecologists, protectors of wild life, promoters of organic agriculture, distributionists, cottage producers and so forth. For India time is running out and it must adopt strategies and methods to transform socio-eonomic life of people to suit Indian ingenuity and culture. Integrated approach to development sets forth a strategy of working with people—a strategy in which participation by all people is both the means and end itself.

Ambedkar in one of his speeches said : "Power is one thing and wisdom and prudence quite a different thing". In deciding the destinies of people the dignities of the leaders or men of parties ought to count nothing...Let us prove by our conduct that "we have not only the power but also the wisdom to carry with us all sections of the country and to make them march on that road which bounds and leads us to unity." He exhorted people : "your salvation lies in your own hands through your own efforts."

There is lot to be said in favour of the statement of Clarke. He said : "Every problem has not one, but many technological solutions". Unfortunately, 90 per cent of the solutions are worse than the problem. Wisdom lies in finding the vital 10 per cent. Today, everyone seems hypnotised by the threats of energy and material shortages. Yet in absolute terms, it is judicious to talk of such things. We are surrounded by energy and live on a planet whose crust we have barely scratched. The only real shortages are of intelligence, foresight and simple humane decency. Community participation is the lynchpin of the desired social change.

Gandhi as Communicator

Gandhi was the great communicator. Realising the impact of communication on the people that Gandhi had wielded. Sir J.H. Holmes wrote, as early as in 1920s : "This man holds absolutely in his hands today the destinies of his people. When Gandhi speaks, India speaks. When Gandhi acts, it is India that acts. When Gandhi is arrested, it is the India that outraged and humiliated. More truly, I believe than any other man who has ever lived, this great Indian is the incarnation of a people's soul." He further commented: "He holds today the centre of world's attention. That position of primacy held so proudly by Woodrow Wilson in 1918 and 1919, and by Nicolas Lenin in 1920 and 1921, is now occupied by a little oriented who has never held any official position who seeks neither glory nor power." The only leader who measures to this test in India was Loknayak Jayaprakash Narayan. The best quality the communicator must possess is to practice what he preaches.

REFERENCES

Ambedkar, B.R. Quoted by M.L. Shahare, in *Dr. Bhimrao Ambedkar—His Life and Work*, NCERT, New Delhi, 1988.

Balwant, S., Communication and Media Role of Books, *FIP News*, Vol. II, No. I, May, 1989, pp. 27-29.

Chawla, N.S. Media and Message, Review of the Book Communication Theory, The Asian Perspective. Edited by Wimal Dinsanayake (The Asian Mass Communication Research and Information Centre, 39, Newton Road, Singapore, 1130) in *Sunday Review of Times of India*, Sunday, January 15, 1989, p. 8.

Clarke, Arther C., "Looking at the Future" in Development, *International Development Review*. 22 (2 & 3), 1980, Society of International Development, Rome.

Gangrade, K.D. *Social Work and Development*, Northern Book Centre, 1986, pp. 118-22.

Holmes, H.S., P.C.,Bridge, and E.F. James, *Mahatma Gandhi: The World Significance* (Kolkata: C.C. Baisk, The Research Home, year not given) pp. 67.

Holmes, H.S., *et al. Ibid.* , p.4.

Munnilal Vishwakarma: *Samajik Nyay Ki Prapti: Manjil Abhi Dur Hai* (in Hindi) *Kurukshetra*, Vol. 35, October, 1990.

Nivan, T.N., Identity Crisis, *The Hindustan Times*, February 19 and 20, 2003, New Delhi, pp. 16 and 18.

Pasricha, Ashu, Gandhi the Communicator, *Gandhi Marg*, Vol. XXIV, No. 3, October-December, 2002, pp. 315-326.

Schumacher, E.F., *Small is Beautiful: A Study of Economics as if people matter*, Blond and Brings Ltd., London and Tiptree Elochester Essex 1973, Indian reprint—Radha Krishna, Daryaganj, New Delhi: 1978.

9

Fifty Years of Freedom

Achievements and Failures

Friedrick Max Muller was very much fond of India. He said: "If I were to look over the whole world to find out the country most richly endowed with all the wealth, power, and beauty that nature can bestow in some parts a very paradise on earth—I should point to India. If I were asked under what sky the human mind has most fully developed some of its choicest gifts, has most deeply pondered on the greatest problems of life, and has found solutions to some of them which will deserve the attention even of those who have studied Plato and Kant—I should point to India. And if I were to ask myself from what literature we, here in Europe, who have been nurtured almost exclusively on the thoughts of Greeks and Romans, and of one Semitic race, the Jewish, may draw that corrective which is most wanted in order to make our inner life more perfect, more comprehensive, more universal, in fact more truly human, a life not for this life only, but transfigured and eternal life again I should point to India."

Such was the past glory of India. However, for ce remained under foreign bondage and the latest was Britis over India for two centuries. They made India ir August 15, 1947 based on two-nation theory.

Achievements

India's achievements since Independence a Constitution; (ii) Integration of the co sation on the basis of language; (iii) F

Sheel and neutrality and initiating Non-Aligned Movement; and (iv) Establishment of Planning Commission.

Failures

(i) Failure to maintain law and order; (ii) Failure to bring unbounded economic potential of the country to fruition; (iii) Failure to make human investment; and (iv) Failure to provide moral leadership.

National Flag

On the midnight of August 15, 1947, the National Flag was hoisted atop the ramparts of the Red Fort by the country's first Prime Minister Jawaharlal Nehru. The flag had three colours. It has a saffron on the top, a white band in the middle and a green one at the bottom with a wheel in navy blue on the white. The colours are not to have any communal significance. The colour saffron represents courage and sacrifice, white represents peace and truth, and green represents faith and chivalry. The wheel represents the hope of the masses. All citizens of India including leaders are expected to honour and abide by the significance of our flag.

Nehru on this auspicious occasion made his famous speech wherein he referred to India's "tryst with destiny" and her "awakening to life and freedom."

The greatest achievement of Indian democracy despite ups and downs is that it has more or less survived unfractured for fifty years. Nine hundred and fifty million people live together as one political entity under conditions of freedom. Never before in history, and nowhere else in the world today, has one-sixth of the human race existed as a single free nation.

Unity in Diversity

The achievement is all the more creditable, no other democracy has had such diversity in unity, such a mosaic of humanity. There are twelve great living religions in the world and all twelve flourish in India. We have sixteen major languages written in different alphabets and derive from different roots; and for good measure, our people whom you can never call taciturn express themselves in 250 dialects. English, though not included in the major languages listed in the Constitution, continues to be the only link language for the whole

Constitution

Indian Constitution in its Preamble proclaims India to be a sovereign, democratic, secular, socialistic republic and ensures to secure all its citizens: justice, liberty, equality and fraternity. But Dr. Ambedkar, chairman and chief architect of the Constitution said: "On the 26th January, 1950, we are going to enter into a life of contradictions. In politics, we shall have equality, and in social and economic life we will have inequality. In politics, we will be recognizing the principle of one man one vote and one vote one value. In social and economic life, we shall by reason of social and economic structure, continue to deny the principle of one man one value. How long shall we continue to deny equality in our social and economic life? If we continue to deny it for long, we will put our political democracy in peril. We must remove this contradiction at the earliest possible moment or else those who suffer from inequality will blow up the structure of political democracy which this Constituent Assembly has so laboriously built up."

In 1950, we started as a republic with three estimable advantages. First, we had 5,000 years of civilization behind us, a civilization which had reached "the summit of human thought." We inherited great skills and many splendorous intelligence, since the genes had evolved over five luminous millennia. We had a superb entrepreneurial spirit, honed over centuries of obstacles. We had an unlimited reservoir of skilled labour, and abundance of capital available for investment in new projects. The trader's instinct is innate in Indian gene. An Indian can buy from Jew and sell to a Scot, and yet make a profit. Secondly, whereas before 1858 India was never united as political entity. In that year a united political accident of British rule welded us into one country, one nation, and when Independence came, we had been a unified nationality for almost a century under one head of State. Thirdly, our Founding Fathers, after three long years of laborious and painful toil, gave us a Constitution which was described "sublime" by the former Chief Justice of India, Meharchand Mahajan.

It is the longest written Constitution in the world. The substance of the Universal Declaration of Human Rights adopted by the United Nations on December 10, 1948 is embodied as Fundamental Rights in our Constitution. The right to equality before the law is guaranteed to citizens and non-citizens alike. In one respect our Constitutional law is more secular than that of the UK. Religion is no bar to the holding of public office whatsoever in the State. In another respect our Constitution may claim to be more progressive than that of the USA. Equality of the sexes is a guaranteed right in India, whereas the recent attempt to incorporate a similar right in the US Constitution has so far been unsuccessful.

The right to carry on any occupation, trade, or business is again, a guaranteed right. The concept of "socialism" did not figure in the Constitution as originally enacted. On the contrary, the Constitution provided in the Directive Principles of State Policy that the State shall endeavour to secure that "the ownership and control of the material resources of the community are so distributed as best to subserve the common good" and that "the operation of the economic system does not result in the concentration of wealth and means of production to the common detriment. These words rule out State ownership, the Monolithic State which is the hallmark of communism, euphemistically called socialism.

India is the only country in the world where, in the States which are governed by the communist party, human rights are fully respected and that is because the Bill of Rights firmly ingrained in our Constitution. We can proudly say that our Constitution gave us a flying start and equipped us adequately to meet the challenges of the future. Unfortunately, over the years we dissipated every advantage we started with, like a compulsive gambler bent upon squandering an invaluable legacy. India today is only a "caricature" of the noble democracy which Gandhi-Nehru and others strove to life and freedom in 1947.

Decline in our March

The moral crisis is writ large on the entire political scene. In the 1950s (grandfather's generation) we had many eminent men in public life who were every inch a gentleman. In the 1960s (father or mother's generation) we had many public figures who were every alternate inch a gentleman. Unfortunately (son's generation) we have an unacceptable large number of politicians who are no inch a gentleman. The noble process of our Constitution has been trivialized by the power-holders, the power-seekers and the power-brokers in our cities. Elections have been reduced to horse race by the contesting politicians—the difference being that the horse is highly trained. We must shed the divisive tendencies which split the votes on caste and sub-caste lines, and which are so devastating to our unity as a nation. It is said "One Indian is an intelligent human being; two Indians are a political group; three Indians are two political groups." When Jayaprakash Narayan talked of "Total Revolution," he meant a total transformation of the spirit, which would enable the people to control the government instead of being dominated and dragooned by the government.

Integration of States

Sardar Vallabhbhai Patel aimed at integration in two ways not only territorial integration but the integration of the different communities by developing a sense of national identity. There were 554 Indian Princely States which composed two-thirds of India, while only one-third was British India. He brought all of them together, while continuing to remain on terms of mutual affection and respect with the former rulers. He sought to forge communal integration. He made different communities give up their claim for separate electorates. Even the spokesman of the Parsis had in mind a separate electorate. But Sardar merely smiled at the ridiculous idea and the matter was dropped. The Parsis were a microscopic minority, but the Muslims, Sikhs and Christians were in substantial numbers. Even in those days the Sikhs demanded Khalistan. Sardar Patel dealt with the problem with great understanding. He went to the heart of Sikh hinterland. He talked to the Sikhs in Amritsar and impressed upon them how we have to live together as brothers and sisters.

In December 1949, the Congress Working Committee directed that a separate Andhra State should be created forthwith. In spite of this directive, Sardar Patel took no action on the contrary, he openly criticised this directive of his own party. At a public meeting in Trivandrum in May 1950 he said :

> "Some people say they want provinces on a linguistic basis like Andhra, Tamil and Kerala. What will be its effect in the North or in the West nobody cares to consider. We should cease to think in terms of different States or provinces. Instead we should think that we are Indians and should develop a sense of unity."

The pressure of the people would not be arrested and based on the State Reorganization Committee the map of India was re-drawn on the basis of linguistic States. This has given rise to regionalism and regional parties. India is today governed by a coalition of 13 regional parties.

Foreign Policy and NAM

Indian foreign policy is based on the *Panch Sheel* or Five Principles. These are: (*i*) Mutual respect for territorial integrity and sovereignty; (*ii*) Non-aggression; (*iii*) Non-interference in international affairs; (*iv*) Equality and mutual benefit; and (*v*) Peaceful coexistence.

What does neutrality—or as we prefer to call it, non-aligned—mean and why does India follow this path? In the world situation we are confronted with two alternatives. One is that peace is maintained by building military might and by an armament race. The other is that it can be preserved by Gandhian non-violence or peaceful means. The relevance of NAM has not disappeared despite world becoming uni-polar and with the termination of Cold War. Its leaders are acutely conscious of their state in the world as a whole. They know that outside pressure impinge on them, and cannot be avoided. They feel that they can contribute much to international sanity and cooperation. India does not propose to join any camp or alliance. But we wish to cooperate with all in the quest of peace and security and human betterment.

A meeting of NAM Foreign Ministers held in New Delhi in April 1997 solemnly adopted a resolution that as far as the issue of expanding the UN Security Council and eliminating or diluting the Veto power of its permanent members is concerned, the NAM is firmly against the "Germany and Japan first" formula for Security Council's expansion. Of course, there is no guarantee that smaller countries will not eventually give in to the discreet charms of 'Yen-DM' diplomacy.

At a time when there is a concerted effort to impose unipolar *modus vivendi* on the world, when the discourse on development, disarmament, and sovereignty is pulled in one direction by the big powers it is important that an alternative articulation be sounded from time to time. Indeed, the Movement's future relevance lies precisely in providing its members room to manoeuvre in a world that is out to be made unidimensional.

Planning Commission

India adopted planning as a way and method to deal with the complicated problems of change and transform socio-economic life of the people. Thus, came the Five-Year Plan, a model of human patience, skill and endeavour; a documented account of the national resources both human and material; and suggestions for their optimum utilization. A constructive revolution had begun as part of a serious development effort at national as well as state levels.

Success and Failures of Plans

Plans have given India skilled manpower and advance technology base with its vast market size. It is well placed for accelerated economic growth with the adoption of New Economic Policy since 1991. The recent UN Economic and Social Survey has warned us that high economic growth could not have rapid "trickle down effect" on poor. India provided a substantial Rs. 6,440 crore for poverty alleviation in its 1996-97 budget but it was not effective enough as design, organization, financing and targeting of such programmes needed to be sharpened further.

It is a pity that even after fifty years of Independence and eight Five Year Plans we have not been able to provide Basic Human Needs to people. As per 1991 census the total literacy rate is 52.11 per cent. There are only 27 per cent villages and 21 per cent cities having safe drinking water. The housing conditions of 36 per cent of cities and 73 per cent villages are appalling. In 1991 per capita availability of food was 510 grams which has come down to 474.2 grams by 1994.

Till 9 March 1997,18 per cent Indians were below the poverty line. But on 10 March 1997, the new calculation of the Planning Commission made it 36 per cent. There are experts who feel that planning has lost its relevance in 'free-market economy.'

A multitude of populist schemes and welfare measures are all part of the game politicians play in a democracy. By doing so, they are promoting their own selfish interests and by no means serving any public cause.

Tryst *vs.* Destitution

There is no need to elaborate our failures as the assessment in the previous paras clearly demonstrate our achievements and failures. The outside world sees India as a bumbling, self-destructive giant. That after half a century of freedom, India should be fifty year old with the mental age of seven. Indeed, euphoria about the emerging market in India had started waning.

Law and order has become so worse that the police which is expected to protect has taken to crime. In the capital city of Delhi in 1996, 169 police officials were involved in various crimes—12 were charged with murder, 13 with extortion or robbery, six with rape, 30 with corruption and the rest with other crimes.

On the eve of Indian Independence, Prime Minister Jawaharlal Nehru recalled the pledge of a 'tryst with destiny' and redeeming it, and hoped that the newly independent nation would progress on the path of freedom. Responding to this clarion call, the Indian Government designed programmes aimed at 'richer and more varied life' for its people. Over the next five decades India succeeded in increasing her grain production, improving technological capabilities, and maintaining formal democracy. However, during the same period poverty, inequality, landlessness and unemployment increased. India's failure to adequately address the problems of inequality, poverty, justice, and human rights seems to reflect more of a 'tryst with destitution.'

Among the tributes received in New Delhi within hours of Mahatma Gandhi's assassination on 30 January, 1948 was one by Sarojini Naidu who said: "May the soul of my master, my leader, my father, rest not in peace. Not in peace—my father—do not rest. Keep us to our pledge. Give us strength to fulfil our promise to your heirs, your descendants, guardians of your dreams, fulfillers of India's destiny."

Five decades of our effort to eradicate poverty can be put in a cartoonist version as follows: "In the first decade I was told I was poor. In the second decade they told me I was not poor but needy. In the third decade they informed me that to be called needy was a self-defeating term and I became deprived which was again changed to under-privileged in the fourth decade. This was later changed to disadvantaged as I reached in the fifth decade. I have no rupee yet but a rich vocabulary."

In 50 years of our Independence the tri-colour fluttering all over the country is black, red and scarlet symbolising black money, red tape and corruption.

To sum up, the aim of democracy is to make life better for the voters and people and not legislators.

10

Gandhi's Constructive Work Programme

A Critique

The future lies in India, its path of democracy as well as the spiritualism that lies at its core through constructive work programme. Life should be about experiences rather than explanations.

Man works on a material which grows into a finished product and at the same time, in the process of making the finished product, man grows spiritually. The product of the work is useless when compared to the reaction of 'work' on 'man'. Work is not merely for producing things; it is the means of 'educating and spiritualizing man'. It means developing 'self-discipline' and 'self-control'. When the material manifestation is overemphasized, work is missing.

To feel that our standard of living will come *down* if we relieve the suffering of others by sharing and caring, is to bring ourselves down to worse than the animal level. In 1947, India, the land of Mahatma Gandhi was a moral beacon to the world. Today it is a moral cesspool, where criminals sit in the legislatures and corruption has become a way of life. During the same period (1947) India was in economic terms, at the very forefront of developing nations. Today, it remains desperately poor, having been overtaken by one country after another. If people are asked what they are most ashamed of after 50 years of independence, many will point to the political class. The main reason for our downfall and decline is neglect of constructive work programme as evolved by Gandhi. This should become the beacon light for the twenty-first century.

I
CONSTRUCTIVE WORK NEEDED FOR THOUSAND YEARS

India achieved political independence on 15th August, 1947. But it still has to attain economic and social freedom. This is possible by adopting Gandhi's twenty-point constructive programme. Gandhi himself came to believe that his constructive programme or constructive work, was generally even more important. In fact, he stated: "In placing civil disobedience before constructive work, I was wrong."[1] Civil Disobedience, he explains, "is but a minor part of *Satyagraha*... Civil Disobedience is not absolutely necessary to win freedom through purely non-violent efforts, if the cooperation of the whole nation is secured in the constructive programme."[2]

Gandhi felt that *Satyagrahis* must prepare for non-violence through constructive work which is "an expression of non-violence". Moreover, constructive work is "the basis for non-violence of the brave", because it is "whole and indivisible" and contributes to wholeness and indivisibility both in *satyagrahis* and society itself. A concrete feeling for the starving millions" leads *Satyagrahis* to concrete action to end their oppression.

He realized in 1939 that the origin of *Satyagraha* was constructive work, and he believed that the future of India "for thousand years"[3] was constructive work. As Ved Mehta asserts: "Between 1924 and 1940 Gandhi had devoted himself mostly to the social, economic, and spiritual regeneration of the country which he came to believe would be achieved not by constitutional concessions and reforms, political debates and resolutions, but by the efforts of the people themselves. As the years passed by, he put more and more emphasis on what he originally conceived as "spiritual-socialism" the positive counterpart of non-cooperation and civil disobedience and eventually called the constructive programme. For, Gandhi, the constructive programme was really another form of *satyagraha*, which was the only road to economic development for a poor country like India."[4]

The Gandhian thought and principles and proxis are not meant for any particular country or region. They are meant for the whole human society. The indications of the age, the worldwide inquisitiveness and the future needs and aspirations—all point to the necessity that attempt should not be to limit Gandhi within national walls. Gandhi's strategy was that social transformation should begin with the millions of "non-persons" and "half-persons", "marginalized Indian Humanity", living on the outskirts of organized society and below the margins of subsistence within the society.[5]

How to make them acquire manhood and identity, was the all-consuming passion of Gandhi. Gandhi believed that "no social order, be it international or national or any lesser unity of human organization, can be considered 'normal' unless the creative energies of these "non-persons" and "half-persons" are not harnessed fully by making them participate in socio-economic life on the basis of freedom, honour, dignity and equality."[6]

According to a report of the National Commission for Women (Based on data given by the Ministry of Women and Child Development, Government of India), a woman is molested every 26 minutes. A rape takes place every 54 minutes. Every 48 minutes a woman is kidnapped or abducted. And every 10 minutes a woman is burnt to death over dowry. But these statistics do not include the cases of sexual abuse by members of the family or people known to the victim. *This amounts a whopping 87.4 per cent of minor girls* and women. The victims rarely report such crimes to the police. A woman having an identity of her own is a concept alien to Indian culture (See, R.D. Sharma, Violent Imbalance, *The Hindustan Times*, May 3, 2001, New Delhi, p. 10).

The imbalance is further reflected in the sex-ratio between male and female as per the findings of the 2001 census. The sex-ratio in the 0.6 age group has declined sharply from 945 females per 1000 males in 1991 to 927 females in 2001 except in the States of Kerala, Tripura, Mizoram, Sikkim and Lakshwadeep. This decline has been particularly sharp in the Union Territories of Daman and Diu (from 969 to 709) and Dadra and Nagar Haveli (from 952 to 811).

This decline is sharp in some economically prosperous States like Punjab, Haryana, Maharashtra and Gujarat. Punjab with the highest per capita income has the lowest sex-ratio of 793 females per 1000 males in 0.6 age group. (See, *The Times of India,* May 5, 2001, New Delhi, p.1)

Girl Child is condemned in the womb. It is the writing on the wall, often with a not so-hidden subtext, which sends out the first dubious signal. In Delhi's neighbourhood, in UP, Punjab and Haryana, apart from the gaudy hand written advertisements of sex clinics promising vitality and vigour to married couples, there are the sly messages hung on trees and electricity poles: 'Spend Rs. 1000 today save Rs. one lakh tomorrow'. Behind this coded message stands a flourishing underground profit making industry of sex determination tests, seducing the typically Indian male-centric mindset towards organized female foeticide. Amnlocentesis on Sex determination test of the unborn child is illegal in India. But that does not deter the quacks and unscrupulous doctors as long as the parents are willing to pay huge sums to abort the female foetus.

Earlier, as in Tamil Nadu, many female children were murdered immediately after their birth, often without the consent of the mother. Now, in the changed political economy of both values and technology, female infanticide has given way to female foeticide. This is specially so in the several prosperous states with high per capita incomes. Indeed, the sex test industry has thrived to such an extent that male-female sex ratio in the age group of 0-6 has fallen to dangerously low proportions. This trend might lead to serious biological sexual and emotional distortions in the social fabric (Condemned in the Womb, see *The Hindustan Times*, May 7, 2001, p. 10).

Gandhi was very clear in his mind. He included raising the status of women as one of the points in his constructive work programmes. He made all efforts to bring them in the mainstream of the Indian society. Let the cardinal principles propounded in the Internet Humour (*The Times of India*, May 7, 2001, p. 14) that "don't walk in front of me, I may not follow, don't walk behind me, I may not lead: walk beside me, and just be my friend."

Women are not to be messed around with. After all half the population is female. But when it comes to sacrifices for them the heart-burn starts. Politics, a male fiefdom, has strong reservations about letting them in. Even in Kerala, where women are an emancipated lot, a quick glance at the candidates list for the May 10, 2001 Assembly Elections, exposes their double standards. The three major parties, the Congress, the CPI(M) and the BJP have failed to give women a lift.

The Sonia Gandhi led Congress has given nine seats to women from its quota of 88.

The Marxists have marked out 10 (ten) seats out of 75, though it has given three seats to Muslim women.

The *BJP is* not far behind: 11 (eleven) out of 111.

And the Muslim League, true to its orthodox style, has completely shunned women in a State where women outnumber men. Such disdain, is indeed ironic (see Baba Ramesh, No Fair Play in Politics. Parties keep women candidates at Bay, *The Hindustan Times*, April 28, 2001, New Delhi, p. 9).

The Women and Child Development's (WCD) official documents and the Standing Committee's Report both show that little has changed over the years. Virtually repeating what they have been saying every year, both the government and the Parliament Committee point to the slackness in the implementation of the programmes with the budgets for the schemes lying unspent.

The Centre, on its part, puts the onus on the state governments for the under-utilization of the funds. The committee has been particularly harsh in its indictment of the functioning of the Balika Samridhi Yojana launched in 1997 for the specific purpose of improving the status of the girl child. The scheme has, however, been floundered as the allocation of Rs. 27 crore in 2000-2001 was reduced to Rs. 21 crore, and the revised estimates with only Rs. 13.43 crore being utilised till last March. The achievement level of the physical target is also very discouraging. Only 2.70 lakh beneficiaries have been reported against a target of 12 lakh beneficiaries.

The Committee was shocked to learn that though Rs.169 crore have been released to all the States since 1997, the fund utilization position is as low as Rs. 49 crore, 31.41 per cent of the total allocation. All the States except Punjab, Mizoram, Tripura and Dadra and Nagar Haveli, have been found to be defaulters (see Anita Katyal, Drive To Boost Status of Girl Child on Cards, *The Times of India*, May 7, 2001, New Delhi, p.1).

In the global context, the process of transformation meant struggle against imperialism and colonialism. In the national context, it meant struggle in defence of the "Outcastes" (viz., the Scheduled Castes, the tribals, the leprosy patients) and the under-privileged and the weakest (viz., the landless, the artisans, the unemployed and so on). The dominant section of society condemned them for centuries to eke out an existence in the wilderness or below the margins of subsistence.

Gandhi's constructive programme is a comprehensive instrument of reconstruction which specially included the needs of the non-persons, the outcastes, the half-persons, the castaways and the lowliest and the poorest section of human population. He realized that the normal mode of organization were either too good or too advanced or too inadequate to be used effectively by them (viz. half-persons or non-persons). The institutions and organizations or alternative structures have to emerge from the ground work to meet the needs of poor people. It is in this sense that it can be said that the constructive programme was conceived as a means as well as an end for the creation of new civilization. The core of the programme is the synthesis between the material and moral advancement of human society.

II
THE PRESENT SCENARIO

It has been a fact that in India those who are socially oppressed are also economically marginalised. As per 1991 census, about 76 per cent of the Scheduled Caste workers are agricultural workers. Out of the total SC agricultural workers, about 50 per cent are agricultural labourers and only about 33 per cent are cultivators. Among the cultivators, as high as 73 per cent are marginal farmers with an average of less than 2.50 acres of land. Despite their exploitation in villages, the *Dalits* have, for long, not been able to challenge the village system and oppressive social structure because most of them fully depend on the caste Hindus (for their livelihood).

In spite of 50 years of Independence, 23.8 per cent of rich farmers are in possession of 71 per cent of cultivable land of the country. ·As per 1992 National Sample Survey, there are 11 per cent households in rural India which are completely landless and 31 per cent households have less than 0.2 hectares of land. Thus, a very large number of villages have been denied the very source of their livelihood. The Planning Commission had estimated that people living below poverty line were 54.9 per cent in 1973-74 and in 1993-94, 36 per cent. In other words, in 20 years reduction in people living below poverty line was only at the rate of one per cent. This speaks volumes about our developmental activities.

Serious and sustained threats to the survival of the environment and well-being of human kind pose the greatest problem and challenge to the twenty-first century. USA has about 5 per cent of population of the world, but is guzzling a large amount of resources. From resource-consumption point of view, its population is actually 20 per cent of the world; though India has 16 per cent of the world population, but from actual resource-consumption point of view it represents less than 4 per cent of the world population.

Tiny tots in Indian metropolis are non-smokers but are exposed to baffling air pollution levels equivalent to smoking four packets of cigarettes daily. In order of risk magnitude, the World Resource Institute (WRI) and World Health Organisation (WHO) study ranked the top 10 polluted cities as Mexico City, Beijing, Sanghai, Tehran, Calcutta, Mumbai, Delhi, Tianjin, Manila and Sao Paulo.[7]

A recent study covering over 300 households in Gujarat showed that well over 50 per cent of the *women* respondents had suffered some form of *abuse* at the hands of their husbands and *other members of the households*. The Gujarat study is a *pattern of* what is happening all over the country in an atmosphere of heightened violence against women. RAHI, a Delhi based women's support organization, after an extensive survey found that 76 per cent of Indian women were subjected to some form of sexual abuse, half of them by persons known to them. The youngest respondents were around 15 years old and the oldest 66.[8]

When women seek to hit back or seek justice, they face overwhelming odds. Prito brought her rapists to get justice after a long and. bitter battle lasting over two years. During this time both she and her husband were financially ruined and socially ostracised. Yet, worse was in store for Prito when the offender jumped jail and chopped off her leg. Today, equipped with a prosthetic leg, she has not lost her spirit. She would rather have died, she says, then not have fought the case but for the conviction of the rapists. Prito's example is symptomatic of the increasing brutal attacks on women. There were 1,15,723 brutal attacks recorded in 1996 alone. WHO (World Health Organisation) says: "One out of five women in the world has been physically or sexually abused by a man at some time in her life."[9]

The disparity between the poor and rich in the world is widening in recent years. In the past 30 years, the share of the poorest 20 per cent of the world's people in global income declined from 2.3 per cent to 1.4 per cent while the share of the richest 20 per cent rose from 70 per cent to 85 per cent, leading the ratio of the shares of the richest and the poorest to go up from 30 : 1 to 60 : 1. Growth, which can be a means to human development, inf act, departs from this role and in some clearly identifiable instances become the source of human misery and frustration.[10]

The United Nations Development Programme (UNDP), 1996 speaks of five such possibilities:

1. *Jobless Growth* is the pattern of growth that results in increase in income for some accompanied by loss of jobs, or in some instances being pushed down to jobs of lower earnings for others,
2. *Ruthless growth is* the process which makes some rich while leaving others in ever deepening poverty,
3. *Voiceless growth* is the experience in material welfare which however deprives people of their right for social and economic participation,
4. *Rootless growth* results in the withering of the cultural identities of people, and
5. *Futureless growth* is one where the present generation squanders resources needed by future generations. In some, the development experience of the past has had diverse impact, enriching some, excluding others and marginalising yet others against the pious hope that it will open to all people, opportunities for a richer and more varied life.[11]

A number of examples can be cited that there is perhaps no other hope for the strife torn world, not only in the 21st century but for all centuries to come, but to accept the Gandhian paradigm for establishing a qualitatively better sustainable social order, nationally and globally. Let us enter the dawn of the twenty-first century realising the need of constructive programmes and resolving to do what we can to improve the quality of human life.[12]

There is a greater awareness of the Gandhian model of development internationally. Ironically an undeniable fact is that now there are more research formations, groups and centres devoted to the study and examination of Gandhian thought in other countries than in India.[13]

The thought of Gandhi is the thought of the future. The coming century may be described as a century of Gandhi, and the world today has accepted Gandhi as a model to solve the problems of the present century. Gandhi gave to the world new and revolutionary concepts such as *Satyagraha* (Truth Force), *Sarvodaya* (Welfare of all), and *Shanti Sena* (peace-brigade). In the coming years particularly in the twenty-first century, these Gandhian concepts are bound to gain greater relevance... In fact, Gandhi is more relevant today than ever before. We have to choose between Atom and *Ahimsa*, Non-violence and Non-existence, and between *Sarvodaya* and *Sarvanasha* (total annihilation).[14]

III
REJECT MODERN CIVILIZATION

Gandhi rejected modern civilization. The civilization which India has evolved is not to be beaten in the world. Nothing can equal the seeds sown by our ancestors. Rome went, Greece shared the same fate; the might of the Pharaohs was broken; Japan has become westernized; of China nothing can be said; but India is still, somehow or the other, sound at the foundation. The people of Europe learned their lessons from the writings of the men of Greece or Rome, which exist no longer in their former glory. In trying to learn from them, the Europeans imagine that they will avoid mistakes of Greece and Rome. Such is their pitiable condition. In the midst of all this, India remains immovable and that is her glory. It is a charge against India that her people are so uncivilized, ignorant and stolid, that it is not possible to induce them to adopt any changes. It is a charge really against our merit. What we have tested and found true on the anvil of experience, we did not change. Many thrust their advice upon India, and she remains steady. This is her beauty; it is the sheet anchor of our hope.[15]

Civilization is that mode of conduct which points out to man the path of duty. Performance of duty and observance of morality are convertible terms. To observe morality is to attain mastery over our mind and our passions. So doing, we know ourselves... Our ancestors set a limit to our indulgences. They saw that happiness was largely a mental condition. A man is not necessarily happy because he is rich, or unhappy because he is poor... They saw that our real happiness and health consisted in a proper use of our hands and feet. They further reasoned that large cities were useless encumberance and that people would not be happy in them, that there would be gangs of thieves and robbers, prostitution and vice flourishing in them and the poor men would be robbed by rich men. They were therefore, satisfied with small villages. They saw that kings and their swords were inferior to the sword of ethics, and they, therefore, held the sovereigns of the earth to be inferior to the *Rishis* and the *Fakirs*. A nation with a constitution like this is fit to teach others than to learn from others... In parts of the world, and under no civilization, have all men attained perfection. The tendency of Indian civilization is to elevate the moral *being*, that of the western civilization is to propagate immorality. The latter is Godless, the former is based on a belief in God. So understanding and so believing, it behaves every lover of India to cling to the old civilization even as a child clings to the mother's breast.[16]

Gandhi argued that the process of its regeneration required *Atma Shuddhi* or purification of the national soul by means of a sustained *tapasya*..Thanks to its Karma over the past few centuries, its soul had lost its *Sattvic* tendencies and acquired *tamasic* ones and needed to mount a massive national *yagna* or "moral revolution".[17] Unlike a social or political revolution, a moral revolution could not be undertaken over the heads of its intended beneficiaries but entailed personal commitment and intense soul searching on the part of every Indian.[18]

The programme of national *Atma Shuddhi* had to be so designed that each of them was able to participate in it and purify himself.[19] Gandhi thought that his *satyagraha* and constructive programme achieved this objective and that it would serve as a tool for a Gandhian revolution. Under Parliamentary and Revolutionary struggles, *satyagraha* required every Indian to suffer and make sacrifice for his country. And the constructive programme required him to follow a way of life involving identification with an active service of his fellowmen.[20] No doubt, constructive programme would be the heart of a Gandhian revolution in the centuries to come.

Imagine all the hundred crores of people busying themselves with the whole of the constructive programme which is designed to build up the nation from the very bottom upward. If the constructive programme could be successfully worked out, the end would be the "Independence" we want. The word "Independence" here does not mean political freedom alone. It is, in fact, Swaraj of Gandhi's conception. Vinoba Bhave carried this logic further when he said our aim is to create an "Independent People's Power" (*Lok Shakti*) which is different from "State-Power" (*Raj Shakti*) and is against the forces of violence prevailing in the society.

The Gandhian Constructive Programme never failed to furnish a vital, moral and spiritual background to secular activities contained in it. All those engaged in the constructive programme developed in a larger or smaller measure a missionary zeal and at whatever point they worked, they felt the inspiration that their work is necessary in a great programme of national reconstruction. They are soldiers of great and grand army of Gandhi. They are the builders of the new society and they are the torch bearers of new civilisation. That is the spirit and vision of the Gandhian Constructive Programme.[21]

IV
GANDHIAN MODEL OF MASS MOBILIZATION

Gandhi was convinced that whatever the final form of the new model, at least the process and tactics leading to his objective must be based on the direct, intimate and massive involvement and participation of common people at all levels. During the early stages of his career, in the last decade of the nineteenth century and in the first one and a half decades in Africa and India—the two ghettoes of modern civilisation—Gandhi introduced a number of programmes, touching social, political, educational, economic and cultural aspects of man's life. Gandhi from 1915 to 1945, was able to formulate a compact programme of total transformation of society. This programme has been described as the constructive programme. In its final form in 1945, it covered the following items :

1. Communal Harmony
2. Removal of Untouchability
3. Prohibition
4. *Khadi*
5. Other Village Industries
6. Village Sanitation

7. New or Basic Education
8. Adult Education
9. Women
10. Education in Health and Hygiene
11. Provincial Language
12. National Language
13. Economic Equality
14. *Kisan* (Peasants)
15. Labour
16. *Adivasis* (Tribals)
17. Leprosy
18. Students
19. Improving of cattle
20. Nature cure

Gandhi felt the constructive programme in its entirety is to enable masses to emerge out of unfreedom into freedom and out of economic and social deprivation into self-reliance and out of state of alienation into cooperative living. Through this programme, he explored the possibility of building up a powerfree, non-authoritarian, non-exploitative society by changing the present set up. In 1948, there were ten national level constructive work organisations having about 2,500 cadre workers and lakhs of ordinary workers all over India. *There* had come into existence a body of experience and experiments in the field of education, social action and community building and techniques. After his passing away, the constructive programme was taken up by his followers through two agencies Sarva Seva Sangh (SSS) and Gandhi Smarak Nidhi (or Gandhi Memorial Trust)... After Gandhi's death on 30th January, 1948, his constructive work followers met at Sevagram in March 1948. Two things happened in the meeting (*i*) fellowship or brotherhood under the name Sarvodaya Samaj was started; (*ii*) a coordination organization named *Sarva Seva Sangh* for all the constructive work with which Gandhi himself had been conducting experiments, was formed.[22]

It must be noted that since Independence, constructive work has been undertaken not only by those who were directly influenced by Gandhi's thought but also by a large number of agencies, groups and individuals. There are thousands of constructive work organisations having lakhs of workers spread all over India. Gandhi wanted the cadre of workers composing the institutions to take for themselves minimum means for their own sustenance. Unfortunately, the structure of these institutions continue to remain pyramidical, even though Gandhi during the last few years of his life spoke about their operating in oceanic circles. The structure is intended to bring about equality among those constituting the institution. The motivation of the workers greatly counts in the proper functioning of the institutional approach. *Swadeshi*, Non-possession, Detachment, Voluntary Poverty etc. are to be the guide in the way of life of the workers.

There has been some awareness among the leaders of the movement during the recent years for decentralization of the activities of the institutions and education of the workers. While there is a tendency towards specialization which is good in itself, there is a great need for integration of the institutions with other activities of the constructive programmes. There is the problem of effective and proper special training of workers and middle rung leadership. There is need for more effective means of coordination and exchange of ideas and experience and information.

This is not a purely administrative or managerial task. Crucial to the successful realization of Gandhi's original objective is the urgency of two-fold action (*i*) Reiterating and reaffirming the essential purpose of constructive work, viz. to bring about socio-economic changes and reconstruction of social and human relations based on freedom, equality and respect for the individual personality and ultimately building a non-violent, non-exploitative social and economic order for a society based on the ideals of Sarvodaya. (*ii*) Evolving such practical ways as will enable us all to ensure that the principles and fundamental revolutionary intention which lay behind Gandhi's programme get woven into our routines of work and thus his ideals remain in command.

V
IMPACT OF CONSTRUCTIVE WORKERS ON POLICIES

It is a pity that the constructive workers at present are not pulling their full weight either in shaping or the implementation of national policies and programmes. It is the Central and State Governments, little influenced by constructive workers, which are shaping national policies. These policies and programmes are rarely in conformity with those laid down in the Gandhian Constructive Programme.[23]

Constructive workers are not yet able to affect the situation for the reason that they have not fully realized their own unity of purpose and organization. So long as Gandhi lived, he was the point of unity among all constructive workers and he was the authoritative link between them and political leaders. After Gandhi, the constructive workers have had to discover some other effective points of unity. They have not yet succeeded in doing this.[24]

The Gandhian constructive workers who could have acted like a watchdog and catalyst must equally share the responsibility for the state of affairs obtaining in the country today. The Gandhian constructive workers who were the symbols of idealism, dedication and incorruptible lifestyle in the 50s and 60s have now allowed themselves to be marginalised because of their own weaknesses for power. It is history now how many of them strayed into the practical field which proved to be a fatal blow to the Gandhian movement in this country. Today, they are a spent and demoralised force.[25]

Everything is not lost, for the Gandhian constructive workers. There is still tremendous goodwill for many of them and probably they should consider the following:

> They should stop politicking and singly and jointly undertake extensive tour of the country spreading the message of peace and non-violence as Mahatma Gandhi would have done had he been in our midst today. The Gandhian constructive worker has to realise that the enemy within is to be fought vigorously and seriously. The threat from this is far more serious, for if we can fight this enemy all extraneous problems will get resolved on their own.[26]

VI
CONCLUSION : LAMP AND MIRROR

The future of India is inextricably connected with the future of villages. There are increasing problems. With courage and conviction and with abiding faith in the teachings of Gandhi, we have to tackle the problems of poverty, ignorance, malnutrition, insanitary conditions, population explosion, and the caste system. In every village, there should be a body of workers (not servants) of the nation engaged in constructive work to achieve social, moral and economic freedom. It should be organised democratically from the bottom upwards. Five adult workers should form a unit. Two contiguous panchayats should elect a leader. Fifty-first grade leaders should elect a second grade leader and so on till they cover the entire country.[27]

In this way, Panchayati Raj institutions can play a vital role in the constructive work and service. In the centuries to come, we may encourage 'service worship', instead of 'leader worship' so as to make the upcoming centuries as 'constructive service'.[28]

Late Sh. C. Subramaniam told an interesting parable from the days when he was a Minister in Madras (Chennai). The State Government got a directive from Delhi to spend an equal amount of money for fisheries development in each block, when he pointed out that several blocks did not even get drinking water, what to speak of pisciculture potential. He was told that the Delhi directives could not be violated under any circumstances. This was a parable of cautions as the tendency to dictate from Delhi was still very much in vogue. [*Community Development and Panchayati Raj*, Report of Seminar, (ed.) R. Sudarshan, India International Centre, New Delhi, 1990].

Salvation of present and future crisis can be resolved by adopting fully constructive programme as evolved by Gandhi. It would help us to lead from darkness to light. Constructive work should become both a lamp and a mirror. As a lamp it will guide us, and as a mirror it will show us what we are. Both lamp and mirror will enable us to continuously introspect our behaviour and conduct so that we will not become a notoriously divisive lot.

The greatest tragedy of India is that there is no national commitment to a positive and productive work culture backed by an equally positive and productive political ethos.

A young Gandhian, when asked by a newspaper reporter to react to the news, "Gandhi is dead" said : "Impossible, the sun can never go down on Gandhi. If he goes, truth and nonviolence go". That is right! Millions of Gandhi's followers will continue to live on and carry forward the torch lighted by Gandhi. The master cannot be easily consigned to history. On the contrary his death has brought alive more memories of the legendary movements and his ability to motivate, mobilise and organise people for action. He was much more than the leader ever to walk not only on the Indian soil, but in any part of the whole world as a celebrated human being. He was the crucible of all human values, integrity, chivalry, dedication and fraternity. He had internalized human values. His constructive work programme is an answer to the ailing world society.

Gene Sharp, an outstanding scholar on Gandhi says : "The constructive programme is an attempt to build the beginnings of the new social order while the old society still exists. The non-violent revolutionary which Gandhi claimed to be thus begins to build the new even when the struggling old one does not need to wait for the capture of the State machinery to begin. The constructive programme has been described as the scaffolding upon which the structure of the new society will be built".[29]

He believed that constructive work also served as a preparation and training for the individuals for participation in non-violent action. By doing constructive work the non-violent volunteer would become trained and disciplined. New recruit would be trained, tested, and strengthened, and would develop, discipline in the course of the hard everyday work involved in the constructive programme.[30]

Gandhi felt training was necessary for civil disobedience, just as it was for violent revolt. Training for violent revolt meant learning the use of military weapons; training for civil disobedience meant the constructive programme. Gandhi said: "My handling of civil disobedience without the constructive programme would be like a paralysed hand attempting to lift a spoon." He recognized that previous constructive programme would not always be needed for local specific direct action where the common grievances are tangible and limited to a specific locality. However, Gandhi was convinced that such work was necessary whenever one sought to achieve such large and vague aims as "independent" or "a new society".[31]

The essence of man's life is work and more work. Without work there will be no lustre in life nor any means to achieve fulfilment. The golden principle is the harder the person drives himself to work the more he is at peace with himself, with the environment and the world.

Gandhi viewed that the outward political forms and structures are a reflection of and dependent upon certain other qualities of the society. He was convinced that if freedom is to be genuine and lasting, change must be made on a deeper level than simply the constitutional or the institutional reforms at the top of the society. In this context we can see why Gandhi emphasised the moral improvement of the Indian people and the constructive programme as politically relevant. This combined programme of moral improvement, resistance and constructive work would, in Gandhi's view, lead to genuine self-rule.

He further said: "If my argument is sound, any violence done to the rulers would be violence done to ourselves. It would be suicide. And since I do not want to commit suicide, nor encourage my neighbours to do so, I become non-violent myself and invite my neighbours to do likewise". Moreover, violence may destroy one or more bad rulers, but like Ravana's heads, others will pop up in their place as the root lies elsewhere. It lies in us. If we reform ourselves, the rulers will automatically do so. The responsibility is more on us than the rulers or politicians. The rulers (politicians) will be powerless to do evil if *we are* good. Hence, Gandhiji's incessant emphasis on reform from within.

Laotse was born in China in BC 604. He wrote his famous book *The Tao the Ching* (The book of the Way and Its Power) some *2,500* years ago, in about *5,000* words. It embodies the first path breaking philosophy of China, which resulted in the formation of its first powerful religion, Taoism. Goethe had said that in this world there are so few voices and so many echoes; this book is a real voice, and the voice indeed of ancient China. Laotse thought that all Governments were unwise. The message of the book is: "If things go their natural way, the result is harmony, but if man forces himself upon nature, the result is disharmony. (B.G. Tandon, Meditations, *The Hindustan Times*, May 25, 2001, New Delhi, p. 2). The constructive work of Gandhi will maintain the balance.

NOTES AND REFERENCES

1. M.K. Gandhi, *Non-violence in Peace and War* (Ahmedabad, Navajivan Publishing House, 1949), Vol. I, p. 291, cited in Richard L. Johnson, in his article Gandhian Constructive Work in the City of Joy: Novel and Film, in *Gandhi Marg,* Vol. 17, No. 2, July-September, 1997, p. 147.
2. M.K., Gandhi, cited in Nirmal Kumar Bose, *Studies in Gandhism* (Calcutta; Indian Associated Publishing Company, 1947), second edition, p.178.

3. Constructive work...began my work in South Africa...I did not know that I was training them for civil disobedience. I did not know myself that I was so training myself. *Vide* M.K. Gandhi, *Non-violent Resistance* (Satyagraha), New York: Schocken, 1983), p. 101. The "thousand years", quote occurs on the same page.
4. Ved Mehta, *Mahatma Gandhi and His Apostles* (New Haven: Yale University Press, 1993), p. 5.
5. Dev Dutt, *Report* to *Gandhi,* Gandhi Smarak Nidhi, Rajghat, New Delhi-110002, 1982, p. 12.
6. *Ibid.*
7. *The Times of India*, Metro Kids Smoke Equivalent to Four Packs Daily, Saturday, November 28, 1998, p. 1.
8. Lalita Panickar, Taking a Beating from Cradle to Grave, *The Times of India,* Wednesday, November 25, 1998, p.10.
9. *Ibid.*
10. C.T. Kurien, Development and Marginalisation : Global and National Scenario, in *The Indian Journal* of *Social Work,* Special Issue, On Towards People Centred Development (Part 1), edited by Marlipesac, Anjali Monteiro and Late Narayan, Vol. 59, Issue I, January 1998, pp. 36-37.
11. *Ibid.*
12. T.K.N. Unnithan, Mahatma Gandhi's Nonviolence and the Twenty-first Century, Annamalai University, 1996, p. 2. quoted by S. Narayanaswamy in his article, Constructive Programmes Towards the twenty-first Century, *Gandhi Marg,* Vol. 19, No. 3, October-December, 1997, pp. 341-352, specially pp. 341-342.
13. N. Radhakrishnan, *The Gandhian Pill* : *Medicine for Machine Man,* Gandhi Smriti and Darshan Samiti, 1995, New Delhi, Unpublished Paper, p. 6.
14. S. Narayanaswamy, Relevance of Gandhian Constructive Programme Today, *Gandhi, Marg,* Vol. 18, No. 3, October-December, 1996, pp. 303-315.
15. M.K. Gandhi, *Hind Swaraj,* Navajivan Publishing House, Ahmedabad, Seventh Reprint, 1984, pp. 54-57.
16. *Ibid.*
17. S. Narayanaswamy, Constructive Programme Towards the Twenty First Century, *Gandhi Marg,* Vol. IX, No.3, October-December, 1997, pp. 343-344.
18. *Harijan,* 4 April, 1936.
19. Bhikhu Parikh, *Colonialism, Tradition and Reform: An Analysis of Gandhi's Political Discourse,* Sage Publications, New Delhi, 1989, p.78.
20. G. Ramchandran, Rural Realities, quoted by S. Narayan, *Ibid.* p. 344.
21. K. Arunachalam, Intro to Report to Gandhi, by Dev Dutt, Gandhi Smarak Nidhi, New Delhi, 1982, pp.1-10.

22. S. Narayanaswamy, Relevance of Gandhian Constructive Programmes Today, *Gandhi Marg,* No. 3, October-December, 1996, pp. 306.
23. *Ibid.*
24. N. Radhakrishnan, The Linkage between Education and Constructive Work Towards a Culture of Peace, *Journal of Gandhi Smriti and Darshan Samiti,* Vol. 2, No. 2 & 3, July 1996, pp. 69-81 specially 70.
25. *Ibid.*
26. Gopinath Dhawan, *The Political Philosophy of Mahatma Gandhi,* p. 177.
27. S. Narayanaswamy, p. 350.
28. Sharp Gene, *Gandhi as a Political Strategist,* Gandhi Media Centre, New Delhi, 1999, p. 81.
29. *Ibid.,* p. 86.
30. *Ibid.*
31. Arora, S.C., Meditation Work and be the best, *The Hindustan Times,* May 22, 2001, New Delhi, p.2.

11

Dalit and Development
A Neglected Dimension of Social Work

Development has become a key word for social work educators and practitioners. It has also become a pan of social work curricula in the institutions of Social Work. But the gap between the haves and have-nots has not been reduced. The benefits of development have bypassed many poor people. The task appears to be very formidable for social workers to tackle the challenge of poverty. Can social workers aim at "No-poverty Society" in an enequitous world as is revealed by the following data ?

High Degree of Inequality

The richest 20 per cent of the world's population receive more than 150 times the income of the poorest 20 per cent. Twenty per cent of the world's population has 83 per cent of the world's income and, hence, five times the purchasing power of the poor 80 per cent. People in industrial countries make up about one-fifth of world population but consume 10 times more commercial energy than people in developing countries, and they account for 71 per cent of the carbon monoxide emissions and 68 per cent of world's industrial waste.

Western Model

Industrial or western countries have roughly four-fifths of the world's income and consume 70 per cent of the world's energy and 75 per cent of its metals. Hence, it is clear that the present life of the majority of people in industrial countries cannot serve as a model for other countries specially Asian which are predominantly rural and based on agriculture.

The world economy, despite being supported by amazing advances in science and technology, has performed very badly from the point of removing poverty and injustice. Without removing poverty or reducing it to insignificant level, the existing trend in world economy has inflicted massive damage on the environment, endangered the future of various forms of life, including human kind. Given the serious distortions that exist in the global economy, the words "growth" and "development" acquire entirely different connotations of growing injustice and environmental ruin. This kind of growth without basic reforms can bring grave perils.

Late Professor Sukharnoy Chakarvarty had pointed out many years ago, the fact that world income has increased several fold in the last half a century but it has in no way reduced international disparities or poverty in the third world or in their own countries. His dictum was that in India privatisation cannot promote development and especially poverty removal. On the other hand Prof. Jagdish Bhagwati's assertion is that it can.

The economic deprivation is at significant level in the rich countries. In both the USA and the European Union, nearly 15 per cent of the people live below poverty line. In the European Union 44 million people (some 28 per cent of workforce) receive less than half the average income of their country. In the USA real earnings fell by three per cent in the 1980s, and between 1987 and 1990 real benefits per pensioner declined by 40 per cent.

Results of Wrong Development

Unfortunately, since the beginning of the process of industrialisation in Europe to the end of the 19th century, development is defined in terms of shifting from agriculture to industry and latter to service activities. Developing countries have followed blindly this model of development. The successive decades of wrong development following the Western model has in the 1990s brought to India the following results: (i) This has left us a beggar country. (ii) The disparity rate, the difference between the wealth of the poor and the rich (the ratio between wealth of the 50 per cent of upper level and lowest 25 per cent is around 3,000 times which is amongst the highest in the world, (iii) The rate of unemployment has reached alarming proportion in both the educated class and dumb millions of the masses. In both the cases, the percentage of unemployed in the former and the forced idleness amongst the latter has risen with time. (iv) Environmentally India is more degraded now than what it was when it became free. The forest cover has shrunk, the water level of the sub-soil has diminished due to intensive agriculture practices motivated by cash crops, and urban growth caters to the need of the affluent class. The pollution of air, water, and soil has increased at a rate that could not be coped with. (v) Urbanisation has led to an increase in city populations by three times. The bigger the city the greater has been the rate of growth of its population. These maladies would not have manifested themselves if the Gandhi-Kumarappa model had been adopted.

It was Prof. J.K. Galbraith, who said that if economists are winning applause and avoiding acrimony, government should be deeply alarmed. Economists, he said, need to understand that what is good for the poorest people is best for economic performance but worst for gaining applause.

Gandhi in the context of India had aptly said : "If India is not to perish, we have to begin with the lower rung of ladder. If that was rotten, all work done at the top or at the intermediate rungs is bound to fall" (*Harijan*, 13 April, 1935, p. 68). He further said about the problem of city and village. "The blood of the villages is the cement with which the edifice of the city is built. I want this blood that is being today inflating the arteries of the city to run once again in the blood vessels of the villages" (*Harijan,* 23 April, 1946 p. 198). He did not talk simply in terms of the city-village dichotomy. In addition to referring to the village exploitation and role of the city, he spoke of alienation, of city dweller. He referred to village as a community.

Rural Development

The so called third world comprises of 141 nations and has a large population living in villages, numbering about 3 billion. That is, 60 per cent of the world's population is living in villages and out of this

85 per cent or 2.5 billion live in Asia and Africa. The living standard of villages is far below that of the cities as the national income of these countries is much less than that of the affluent countries. The United Nations data show that in these countries the urban population consists of 35 to 65 per cent of rural migrants. The affluent nations being basically urban and the poor nations rural, rural development is a critical factor to be tackled which bring about a less exploitative society and more satisfying system of all round or total development or *Sarvodaya.*

The term *Sarvodaya* literally means "the rise or welfare of all". It consists of two Sanskrit component words, *sarva* and *udaya*, which means "all" and "rise" respectively. It aims at a complete transformation of the present social structure through quiet, constructive, social work carried on primarily at the village level and in slum area, with a view to initiating a nonviolent revolution and establishing a more just social order. *Sarvodaya* draws its inspiration as much from the ancient religious traditions as from the modern, national secular, humanitarianism or revolutionary idealism. It looks upon service to society as the *raison d'etre* of man's life on earth. In this sense *Sarvodaya* is all social work and nothing else. The concept is not new as we find it in the *Ishavasyopanishad* which speaks of perfect roan who sees "the self in all beings and all beings in the self." The *Bhagavad Gita* also describes devotees as "persons who rejoice in the welfare of all beings", a traditional invocatory verse which was included by Gandhi in his daily prayer embodied the same idea:

> "May all be happy May be free from disease. May all meet good fortune. May none have sorrow or misery of his lot."

The ideology of *Sarvodaya* is not a product of intellectual theorisation. It grew out of the activities, experiences and inner conviction of great soul, i.e. Gandhiji who wanted to do away with all kinds of social disabilities, injustices and inequalities.

Unequal Distribution of Land

The land which is a main stay in Indian villages has been unequally distributed amongst villagers. This has made many *Dalits* landless labourers. About one-fourth of land is in the possession of five per cent of farmers in India. Sixty per cent in the hands of twenty per cent of peasants and rest fifteen per cent in the hands of three-fourth of the people. This is despite the fact of claims made by various state governments about land reforms in India.

In one of my studies I found that the land was given to the *dalits* but the documents of land-deeds were still in possession of the original owners. Their plea was that landless labourers did not have proper arrangements to keep the papers. They continued to treat the *dalits* as labourers instead of owners despite land being transferred to them.

People Centred Model

Prof. K.K. Jacob in his edited book titled Social Development Perspectives emphasises in his introduction that the basic thrust of the volume has been participatory model in which people or masses are in the centre of development. This model has been found to be more acceptable and has both theoretical and practical validity. It is the one in which development comes as a result of participation and organisation of the people, where people come together, empower themselves and sort out their problems themselves. It is the model that holds the key to the people's efforts and which is the key to the success of social development efforts. This has been the message of Gandhiji as well as recent *Human Resource Development Reports* (1994): that unless people are kept in the centre "development and peace" as well as "human security" will continue to elude us. In terms of priority rural development must get first priority.

Size of Poverty

According to a UN face sheet, of 5.6 billion people in the world, more than a billion live in a state of poverty. Around 550 million people go to bed hungry each night. Among the poverty stricken, women suffer the most (represented by 70 per cent) followed closely by the elderly.

In India, infant mortality rates are close to 100 per 1000 while in Africa it is 145. The biggest concentration of poor people are in rural areas of Africa and Asia. In India as per 1991 census about 74 per cent Indians live in over half a million villages. Most of them are settlements consisting of less than 1000 persons where agriculture is the primary source of their livelihood. Pressure of population on land is increasing with 16 per cent of the world population depending on only 2.4 per cent of the world land area. As per the latest UNDP report (1994) on Human Development Index (HDI).

India is placed among the least developed countries and it ranks 134 out of 173 countries.

Gains

Poverty has begun to swell even in developed countries. In the US and Western Europe nearly 15 per cent of the population live below poverty line. The world, however, is not such a dismal place to live in. There have been signs of social progress—average life expectancy in developing countries has increased from 40 years in 1950 to 63 years in 1990; from 1960 to 1990 education spending in the developing world has risen from 2.2 per cent to 3.4 per cent of GNP, female literacy doubled from 36 per cent in the least developed countries between 1970 and 1990.

The spectacular achievements in some industrialised countries stand side by side with increasing poverty in less developed regions. Trends that have contributed to the widening gap of economic growth and creation of new jobs include : a preference for capital intensive than labour-intensive production methods, increased use of labour saving technologies, growing efforts of labour unions to protect jobs of members and tendency to reduce permanent labour force and employ more temporary workers of the world's labour force of 2.8 billion people, an estimated 30 per cent are not productively employed. Some 700 million are under-employed.

Some of the solutions proposed by the Expert Group Meeting on expansion of productive employment include: creating opportunities, encouraging investments, enabling growth, ensuring that growth creates jobs, adapting outward export oriented industrialisation, supporting the service sector, improving labour markets, investing in education, protecting vulnerable groups, bringing a quality job balance, and protecting to workers rights.

New Economic Policy (NEP) and the Poor

There is a premise that developments do not help people but are products of a conspiracy between greedy technocrats, will bureaucrats and corrupt politicians in close league with degenerate industrialists to rob the poor. The elite *versus* people syndrome keeps intruding into the debate of NEP. The goal of economic reform is eventually to benefit the poor.

Two Worlds

But stark reality of India is that it lives in two worlds. One, of 250 millions and odd who clamour for washing machine, Kentucky chicken and Uncle potato chips. The other, the vast majority, finds it hard to buy food grains from the ration shops even though the government godowns are stocked with 31 millions tonnes of food grains.

According to leading economist Prof. Kirit Parekh, the per capita net availability of total food grains declined from 510 gm a day in 1991 to 465 gm a day in 1993, in spite of bumper agriculture production and mounting stocks of food grains. Liberal values must extend to social and administrative areas that most affect the 74 per cent of people who live in rural areas and are barely touched by the liberalisation of industry or imports.

The government claims that it has turned the economy around, boasting exchange reserves by 20 billion and ushering in prosperity through boundless of foreign investment. In the past three years, the poor have been doubly hit by inflation which, as is well known, is disparity enhancing. Thus, the consumer price index for agricultural labour has risen at the rate of 13 to 17 per cent a year, compared to the 9-11 per cent for whole sale prices.

Prof. Amrtya Sen has recently said that foreign investment can never be a substitute in a large country like ours for high domestic saving and investment rates, and that development will lose all meaning if growth is not accompanied by a wise social policy and vigorous pro-poor intervention. Trickle down economics always makes for bad politics. But trickle down politics or the permise that the under-privileged will follow the powerful in making political choices in favour of elitist policies—is a total disaster.

Ideology and Reality

The principal tension of our time is between ideology and reality. While ideological commitment of our economic structures has indeed shown appreciable convergence. G.K. Chesterton had declared that both capitalism and communism were against private enterprise. The hallmark of both is the stultifying reality of large organisation—the State in one case, corporate giants in other—suppressing individual enterprise. Chesterton gave a beautiful analogy of the pocket under the two systems. Capitalism thrived on the virtues of the pirate: the pockets are so full that a little picking would not matter. Communism sought to deal with the pocket by abolishing pockets. Chesterton's solution was distribution, akin to the middle path proposed by Mr. Narasimha Rao, the then Prime Minister of India.

At Devos, Switzerland in 1992 Mr. Rao told global tycoons: You look at the 150-200 million well to do Indians as targets of your investment and as consumers of your goods. You are welcome. But look at 750 million Indians who need basic necessities of life and means of livelihood. If your coming can sub-serve this objective of India and ensure adequate return to you: our policy will achieve the basic objectives of reforms.

Policy Made to Stand on its Head

Economic policy can never be divorced from politics. Classical economist from Ricardo and Mill to Marshall rightly name the science as political economy to differentiate it from pure economics. Both politically and economically, the economic reforms were not, and were not seen to be beneficial to the large mass of semi-urban and rural people. It is meaningless to tell the average income carrier who has to buy rice at Rs. 15 a kg. and pay Rs.20. and above for a kg. of *dal* that the country is flush with foreign reserves and the Moodys have given India high credit rating. In a recent article in *The Hindu*, former President R. Venkataraman says: "As a first step, free and 'unfettered competition in the domestic market must be ensured". That means globalisation must succeed and not precede liberalisation. This is essentially what is wrong with the reforms. Instead of trying out privatisation at home, assessing its impact, analysing the problems it creates and solving them and modifying the programme, the reform policy has been made to stand on its head.

Structural Adjustment Policy (SAP)

SAP conceptually has two parts: (*i*) Stabilisation, and (*ii*) Structural reform. Stabilisation is a short affair spread over a year or two.

Structural reform, on the other hand is more time consuming. It is designed to pave the way for lasting growth in the economy. In reality, stabilisation is aimed at two things slowing down of inflation and elimination of deficit.

According to Prof. R.R. Jain, the macro-economic policy reforms introduced since 1991 have miserably failed. They have made the rich-richer and the poor-poorer. The image of the Congress today across the entire nation is that of a party which is pro-rich, pro-corrupt and pro-industrialists and pro-multinationals. The poor masses, the weaker sections and the working classes are feeling utterly neglected in the present scenario of privatisation and liberalisation unleashed by pro-multinational economic reforms. (Yogeshwar Davar, *The Hindustan Times,* Tuesday Dec. 20, 1994, letter to the Editor, p. 13).

Today and Not Tomorrow

Fiscal discipline as a part of reform hits the poor because it is easy to reduce expenditure on social services. It is easy to cut down expenditure on education and public health, as was really the case in both 1991-92 and 1992-93. The experience of all countries that launched programmes of reform show that the poor are affected in the transition period adversely. And there is no example of a country with a democratic set up that has carried out reforms successfully. But as already indicated the reforms hit the poor most for whom today is more relevant than tomorrow's gains from reforms.

From among these poor Scheduled Castes (*Dalit*) and Scheduled Tribes would be the greatest sufferer. Schools of Social Work may make special studies about the impact of reforms on these groups and suggest appropriate measures to alleviate them from sufferings.

Liberalisation Ruining Tribals (Scheduled Tribles)

Dr. B.D. Sharma, the former Scheduled Castes and Scheduled Tribes Commissioner, said that economic liberalisation is destroying the culture and livelihood of tribals. He warned that the tribals would be forced to defy the "legal and institutional framework" in their struggle for survival. The state, after failing to fulfil the constitutional obligations towards tribals, is now displacing them on the pretext of development. He lamented that neither the State nor the Supreme Court adequately acknowledged that constitutional provisions on tribals have been violated with the liberalisation, the sense of guilt in the administration over its failure to deliver is also vanishing. "Globalisation is a convenient pretext." But the tribals, he said, had no use of even for truck loads of money. The basic question is : "do we recognise the rights of tribals to control their resources as they have for centuries?" The state's laws against exploitation by moneylenders and others were "mice traps", while now rogues (big industries including multinationals) are allowed to enter and trample the tribals. Prof. S.C. Dube, a noted sociologist, is of the opinion that a blurred elite perception of development had meant that weaker and vulnerable sections were ignored. "Build *dams*. Tribals be dammed." If that is the philosophy of development then be prepared for the consequences. (*The Times of India,* Thursday, January 5, 1995, New Delhi, 3).

Employment vs. Education Market : Representation in Central Services

Forty-seven years of planned economy and social expenditure have helped the *dalits* to attain a literacy (not education) level of 37 per cent. The economic share of this vulnerable group has dipped from 50 per cent in 1947 to 30 per cent in 1990.

Before 1935, Muslims and Kayasthas, with a representation of 35 to 40 per cent respectively dominated the bureaucracy. Their share gradually declined and stood one per cent and two per cent in 1990.

On the other hand representation of the Brahmins as a single ethnic group has risen from three per cent to 75 per cent in 1990.

As far as the Scheduled Castes and the Scheduled Tribes are concerned, despite the mandatory 22.5 per cent reservation 2.99 per cent of the senior Grade A level posts in 1972, 5.49 per cent in 1982 and 9.7 per cent in 1992 while none reaching the Secretary or Additional Secretary rank in the Centre till 1990-91.

The following table gives share of the Scheduled Castes and Scheduled Tribes in jobs by now.

Table 11.1 : Time Limit for Reservations : The Case of Scheduled Castes and Scheduled Tribes

Category jobs (central)	Total jobs (percentage)	Filled up so far (percentage)	Time required to reach present percentage	Time required to reach the due percentage at this speed
Class-I	.22.5	4.95	38 years	172.7 years
Class-II	22.5	8.54	38 years	100.0 years
Class-III	22.5	13.44	38 years	63.6 years
Class-IV	22.5	19.46	38 years	43.6 years

Source : K.C. Yadav and R.S. Yadav, *Gandhi Marg*, Vol. XVI, No.: April-June, 1994, p.65.

The basic reason for this gap is that adequate conditions have not been created to impart education to Scheduled Castes and Scheduled Tribes and to retain them in the education stream.

Wrong Assumption

The Constitution made a wrong assumption that this group will need reservation only for a period of ten years. The assumption at that time made was on the basis that all the Scheduled Castes and Scheduled Tribes children were already in educational institutions in 1950. To get class IV position, passing of 8th standard was made essential and desirable. Those who qualified upto this standard preferred to take employment rather than to pursue studies further. Most of them got married which prevented them to proceed further for higher studies. A very microscopic children went upto B.A. which was essential qualification for class I job. Many Scheduled Castes and Scheduled Tribes found employment market more lucrative than the education. The aspiration level of the students and their corresponding parents was very low as has been revealed to me in my empirical studies and fieldwork observations. The Scheduled Castes and Scheduled Tribes must be given facilities of hostels, books and substantial scholarships to encourage them to take to liberal and technical education. They should be made eligible for profession and higher jobs.

Twenty per cent of the rural population does not have access to even a primary school. "Access" implies that the school is within a kilometre, and to cover even that distance may be too much *for* the busy girl child. Education for Scheduled Castes and Scheduled Tribes has been like an obstacle race. Even entry at the first stage is extremely difficult. For girls belonging to this group has been made extremely difficult. Parents are not interested in education of girls and schools are extremely reluctant to encourage Scheduled Castes and Scheduled Tribes boys to study. The drop-out rate among those who enter school is very high.

Exploitation of women by their own families and groups is very high. Society also makes them victim of atrocities as already discussed. The Panchayat Raj introduced in 1993-94 will empower women of this group as reservation for them and women in general has been made in these institutions. Let us see the case of Delhi about the place of backward women in politics which is governed by Bhartiya Janata Party.

Role of Backward Women in Politics

Despite the much proclaimed policy of the BJP about women and the backward sections they were being neglected both in respect of Government and organisation at the state level.

Women constitute nearly 45 per cent of the city's population. Out of the 49 BJP MLAs in Delhi only one is a woman Ms. Purnima Sethi from Kalkaji. Yet, when the six member Council of Ministers team was formed, the lone woman MLA although she has been vocal party member, was not given a berth. Nor was she made to head any of the government corporations.

In the state unit of the party headed by Prof. O.P. Kohli, M.P., the 16 member office bearers committee comprises only one woman. The situation was marginally better in the case of Scheduled Castes (SC) The party had eight SC MLAs four from East Delhi including Gyan Chand, Balbir Singh, Fateh Singh and Inderraj Singh, two from outer Delhi to include Chand Ram and Swaroop Chand Rajan as well as two from Karol Bagh including S.P. Ratawal and Motilal Sodhi. While Mr. Ratawal was Minister of Social Welfare but not even one of them was in the 16-member team of the office-bearers of the State. The lone representative to their lot in the Pradesh Estimates Committee (PEC) was a party MP from Karol Bagh.

Among the OBCs, the BJP had six MLAs. Interestingly, the Delhi Government had announced the priority being given to SCs and

OBCs. Chief Minister, Madan Lal Khurana, had announced that apart from the 22.5 per cent reservation in government jobs for SCs there would be 27 per cent recent reservation for the OBCs thereby allowing for a 49 per cent reservation for the SCs, STs and OBCs.

A senior office-bearer of the BJP unit pointed out that around 22 per cent of the *Dalit* population were SC and though no definite figures were available an estimated 20 odd per cent were OBCs. Party leaders felt that with this high percentage ratio in the population these sections ought to have greater representation in the State Unit.

Reservation Continues and Conversion of Ambedkar to Buddhism

The special provision made under Article 330 for the representation of Scheduled Castes through reserved seats was to cease to have effect on the expiry of ten years. It is a different matter that the major political parties, competing for *Dalit* vote, have joined hands to extend the period of reservation from time to time. The second significance feature is that according to an explanation to Article 25 which guarantees freedom of religion and provides for legislation for the throwing open of Hindu religious institutions of a public character to all classes and sections of Hindus. When Ambedkar embraced Buddhism along with many of the followers on October 14, 1956, less than two months before his death, he only moved from one to another family of Indian religions.

And Ambedkar found it necessary to reinterpret the Buddhist movement even as Gandhi freely interpreted the Hindu scriptures. Gandhi accepted the scheme of the four Varnas or collections of castes for the purpose of following the family occupation, but he rejected the notion of high band low castes. He affirmed the right of members of all castes (not only Brahmins) to acquire learning and said: "If we must talk in terms of Varna, there is only one Varna today for all, whether men or women; we are still *Shudras*. We must all serve". Ambedkar similarly advanced his novel interpretation of the circumstances of Gautam's renunciation of the world, and of Buddhist belief in *Karma* and rebirth.

Another fact which must be disconcerting to advocates of an alliance between *Dalits* and other Backward classes is that Ambedkar was not attracted by the idea of *Dalits* joining other non-Brahmin castes in an anti-Brahmin front. He was too well aware that the immediate oppressors of the SCs were often, landlords belonging to the lower castes of the fourth Varna.

To sum up, there has been considerable economic and social discrimination against the untouchables. There has been bar on temple entry and social exclusion. *Dalits*' access to water resources has not substantially improved, equality of opportunity remains a distant dream, land redistribution a joke and the fulfilment of reservation quotas a mirage. All special provisions—under Articles 15 (4), 16 (4), 17, 23, 330, 332 and 335 of the PCR Act and the latest Prevention of Atrocities Act of 1989 have failed to produce a minimal acceptable level of amelioration in the condition of *Dalits*.

Caste System is the Villain

The economic aspects underlying caste rivalries and violence have often been ignored while discussing the failure to eradicate casteism-from Indian society. The Naxalites are the only ones to have accepted the underlying reality, which might explain their popularity amongst the tribals and *dalits* of parts of Andhra Pradesh and Maharashtra. Mr. V.P. Singh too may have economic restructuring in mind when *he* tabled the Mandal report. But his transparent attempt at political populism failed because he did not see basic contradiction in putting the *Dalits* and the other backward classes on the same platform. After all many of the atrocities on the *Dalits* have been committed by the dominant peasant OBCs. (Bhargava, Arati, Concern over neglect of Women, *The Hindustan Times*, Saturday, Dec. 1993).

In fact, reservation policies are guided more by political expediency than a sincere wish to uplift the backward and lower castes. With the national reservation scenario resembling an auction sale, the prices for the backward caste or class 'vote bank' are paid in the form of quota percentage, in the educational and employment field. If one state announces the quota percentage of 67 per cent, another makes it 73 and third is 80. There is also fierce competition over the inclusion of more and more castes and communities in the SCs, STs and OBC groups.

The political dominance of a caste or the numerical strength of a community have become the determining factor about their being in the SC or ST or OBC category. Not surprisingly in two decades the official number of backward castes have doubled in Tamil Nadu and increased nine times in Karnataka.

Mistake of Mahatma Gandhi

Mahatma Gandhi too erred in emphasising the moral regeneration of Hindu society when he spoke of removing untouchability. In effect, he sought to keep *Dalits* within the Hindu fold in the hope that untouchability was merely a temporary, if grotesque, distortion of Hinduism. His romanticised version of Hinduism ignored the hard facts of an essentially hierarchical social structure. It is this structure that sustains untouchability.

Role of Social Worker

In this critical situation the role of social worker is essentially working in the community as a whole, rather than with any of its particular sub-groups. The role can be divided into two types, manifest and latent. Manifest roles are those which can be easily identified by the worker and community alike, such as facilitator, whereas latent roles are those which are interwoven in the manifest roles by the particular view of development which guides the worker's intervention, e.g. facilitator as alienator/dealienator. Social worker's role is basically two-fold that of catalyst to set ideas motion, and that of facilitator to help structure the development process as and when people required. Translated into concrete terms, the role of the worker is to help people form their own organisation in order to be able to tackle their problems.

The role involves various tasks, first, worker should positively discriminate to work amongst those who have benefited least, or not at all from government programmes. That is, worker should work with the poor and an oppressed who has least access to aid. Secondly, it is important that the worker works with groups as opposed to individuals because it is only as groups that people can have the bargaining power necessary to achieve their goals. Thirdly, the task of the worker is to initiate the process of conscientization—of critical awareness—by getting people to formulate and articulate their desires about issues important to them. It is most important that these are their issues and not those preconceived by the worker. The worker should encourage people to analyse their situation, thus activating some of their invate critical abilities.

Radical Changes Needed in Social Work Education

The problem of eradication of untouchability is very complex and intricate. The approach so far except with the conception of Gandhi is disintegrating Hindu society rather than integrating one. A powerful campaign of education needs to be launched to *educate people* at all levels. The policies that have already been put into practice since the beginning of the Indian Constitution and those that need to be implemented must be explained to the people through a deliberate campaign to build up political support for them. A powerful educational programme is needed for this purpose. Consideration of what needs to be done in this direction must deal with two sets of issues. (*i*) This concerns the "targets" of such an educational programme. (*ii*) The second relates to the content of that programme. The primary objective of process of education has to be the elimination of poverty and social injustice. Its (education) critical role must be to create congenial climate of opinion that will be absorbed by the common man in his thought and action.

Macro-level

Social work as a discipline and profession has not made much significant contribution at the macro-level. Some of the individuals who have occupied prestigious position may be attributed to their personal traits and contribution made by them.

Social Work education has celebrated Golden Jubilee and has now attained the age of about 58 years, an age by which a government servant or people in the organised sector retires. Similarly Social Work education has to develop new visions based on two Review Reports and Curriculum to meet new challenges. Some changes have been made based on the meetings and discussions with the authorities of the UGC and Tata Institute of Social Sciences.

The maturity acquired over a period of six decades should be used to consolidate and innovate in research teaching and fieldwork rather than continue to look to western models and institutions. The proceeding of the three seminars so ably edited by Dr. K.K. Jacob, Principal (Retd.) of Udaipur School of Social Work would prove immensely useful in bringing out radical changes in Social Work education and practice. The latest is Social Work Education in India (1994). It contains papers contributed by eminent professionals and educators of long standing. Prof. S.N. Ranade suggests that "social workers and educators have a special role and stake in helping to build up *peace-movement.* Such a movement cannot succeed unless policy makers are made to realise that real defence and security lie in ensuring the well being of the people, and not suppressing their discontent". "Welfarism must be seen in terms of human rights. Both environment and human rights must envelop all mankind, and social work must become part of the movement for the protection of both." Dr. P.T. Thomas also advocates that the issue of peace must be recognised as a human relations skill, namely *conflict resolution.* Prof. Gokan writes that the major purpose of an academic curriculam is to develop rational minds, and also develop research skills. She further says Social Work Education belong to humanistic category of curriculum which is aimed at making education a "dyanamic personal process" related to "growth integrity and autonomy".

However, we should not forget that learner is the focus of any academic programme. The learner's characteristic may range from motivation for a career in a helping profession to jobs available. Interest, desire to change realities, helping people, newness of the profession, and availability of jobs are probably some of the factors for enrollment.

The thrust as viewed by the Second Review Committee for Social Work Education in India is to support communities, groups and individuals to meet challenges. These present themselves as problems with their basis in exploitation and injustice, resulting in inequalities and the existence of poverty. The deteriorating ecological environment, illiteracy, lack of access to opportunity, social conflict and dire poverty of disadvantaged groups need to be addressed. Viewed from a distance all this appears a struggle of the masses to meet 'needs' coupled with an experience of many "wants". The curriculum activity for any educational programme for a profession that has such diverse concerns is a serious challenge to those involved in developing a paradigm for the same.

I shall not like to duplicate the various efforts already made by various committees and groups to revamp and change programme of Social Work Education to suit its contemporary need. I shall like to identify following areas for emphasis in Social Work Education :

(1) Peace Movements and Peace Studies;
(2) Resolution of Conflicts;
(3) Social Legislation and Social Action;
(4) Policies, Programmes and Strategies for Development of Scheduled Castes and Scheduled Tribes and other Backward Classes;
(5) Social Movements with particular reference to upliftment of Backward Classes;
(6) Anti-Poverty Programmes and their impact on Poor and Welfare Programmes;
(7) Sarvodaya (Gandhian Model) *vs* Vestern Model of Development;
(8) Panchayati Raj System to build participatory democracy from grassroots upward; and
(9) Communication and its effective use in educating people.

The other topics can be included depending on local needs and ethos. I should like to caution that we too often use the experiences of the poor and oppressed as a means to enhance our career opportunities as workers or researcher rathers than improving the life circumstances of people with whom we work or who become the subject of our research and study.

Factors Responsible for Insignificant Contribution

Schools of Social Work as true of all higher educational institutions have not been able to make any significant contribution in improving the lot of poor relate to the problem of location, gender, inter-generation, class-dualism, management, educational level of parents and international typology.

Location

On the location question, following the model of industrial countries, all schools like all higher education institutions are located in urban areas, whereas 74 per cent of people live in rural areas. The Tata Institute of Social Sciences deserves to be congratulated for opening a rural campus. Some of the Schools of Social Work (specially Delhi School of Social Work) had rural camp as a compulsory part of training which had been discontinued. They had also discontinued placement in villages or rural areas which had been a unique feature of the school despite the specialisation offered by a student.

Gender

The gender inequality in higher education is very much evident. The schools giving specialisation in Personnel Management and Labour Welfare attracted all the boys till the admission was based on free choice. Because this was the only field which had professional degree in Social Work as a statutory requirement as per Factory's Act of 1948 to appoint Labour Welfare Officer. The position has now changed with Tata Institute of Social Sciences giving an independent course and degree in Personnel Management. The University of Andhra has also begun to give a separate degree in Personnel Management. This has made it possible for more women students to get admitted to Schools of Social Work. The competition in spite of 70 Schools of Social Work is tough. On an average at the nation level out of six students one gets admitted in any School of Social Work.

Intergenerational

On intergenerational inequality the most vivid expression of this is seen in financial provision made for new *or* younger schools of social work. The Tata Institution of Social Sciences, which has become a deemed university gets substantial financial resources from the University Grants Commission, though the Institute has complained that it does not get enough funds to meet its requirements. The Departments located in the Central Universities are better off than the departments of the State Universities. The departments which are located in colleges are worse off due to absence of funds and regulatory mechanism. All kinds of Schools of Social Work take birth which compromise with the training as a result quality of profession suffers.

Intergenerational or Hereditary Affairs

On class based inequality, the earlier treatment of this intergenerational inequality showed that higher education policy has to be countered from re-inforcing and directing a system in which children of the well-to-do minority who are survivors of the primary education stage tends to take advantage of education and have a ready access to higher education. This has been by and large hereditary and mostly a middle class phenomenon.

For about three to five per cent of the population—say about 40 million people—education would run in the family, with everyone, no matter how capable or incapable, going through high school to a college, then to university, and finally, ending up with a job. For the remaining, educationally deprived 95 per cent, even literacy is a struggle, leave aside education. Can social workers take challenge to keep the *Dalit* in the education stream to fill the reserved posts? This would need persuasion to parents, providing of access to schools, developing hostel facilities, awarding fellowships, supplying free books, giving mid-day meals, arranging coaching classes, and providing vocational and entrepreneurial training.

The question that arises as to whether this dualism (privileged and unprivileged) is inherent in higher education, and whether various measures being tried to bring about a certain degree of uniformity in standards are capable of realisation in a basically inegalitarian society?

Management

The whole system is based on top down process. The inequality between the teachers and the taught which is both historical in this country, going back to the *guru-shishya* tradition built into all forms of higher education, is gradually breaking down, its vertical hierarchical dominance being questioned by horizontal egalitarian interaction. With the rate at which knowledge and information is exploding higher education is being forced gradually to lose its top down nature and become a system of learning how to learn, in which there are no hierarchical superiors and mendicants, no teacher and taught, because all are learning all the time.

Education Level

The equity issues as related to levels of education raises difficult and somewhat emotional issues in this country. On the one hand as per the Indian Constitution in 1950 as a part of Directive Principles, we said that we shall endeavour to provide within a period of ten years from the commencement of Constitution, free and compulsory education for all children until they complete the age of fourteen years. The target date, however, was shifted from 1960 to 1972, then to 1976 and later 1990. But now it has been clanged to 2000. The target date keeps on changing.

International Typology

The international inequity typology is not really as theoretical as it sounds, in the light of the brain drain from India and other developing countries to the industrialised ones, which reinforces their science and technology competence leaving the other group of (drained) countries—with lower educational and scientific levels. The question is whether this is built into the system of higher education under which the poor countries help the rich countries to grow richer through contributing to their science and technology...a kind of reverse foreign aid from developing countries to the industrialized ones, adding further to the net flow of resources from poor to the rich countries.

A good number of Social Workers till 1980s migrated to USA, Canada, Australia and other western countries for jobs and green pastures. These countries considered the training in India was suitable for the professionally qualified persons to serve in their countries as programme of training was almost designed and shaped on western models. Even books and teaching material was also drawn from mostly produced in the USA.

Activism vs. Careerism

Barring Medha Patkar and Pandurang Hegde most of the Professional Social Workers are interested in careers rather than jobs requiring change of social structure and social action. They were as careerist bound by rules and regulations of the agency *or* organisation they joined. They had to surrender their autonomy and freedom. They were not to take social action programmes requiring radical change and reconstruction of society.

Absence of Professional Body

In the absence of vibrant professional body they are neither able to influence policies nor programmes. The Schools of Social Work must take lead in forming such bodies at local, state and national levels.

Communication

Social workers have to move forward to meet the challenges of the difficult decades that lie ahead. They have to be enlightened and perceptive communicators, articulate and with minds of their own. They should be able to cope with the demands of increasingly complicated policies and programmes of development. They should be able to interact with the politicians, administrators, scientists and eminent persons in other walks of life as well as with common people.

The progress of social change would be faster and smoother and development goals can be realised more speedily and effectively if the social workers are able to involve and enthuse poor people to participate in policy formulation and implementation of programmes meant for them through appropriate modalities of communication.

The process of communication involves (*i*) *the communicator*, (*ii*) the *message* and (*iii*) the *receiver*. The object of the communication according to the communicator is to influence or persuade the receiver to accept change. People cannot participate in things they do not understand. Understanding develops through inter and intra-group communication interactions. These communication interactions take place at various stages of identifying the problems, setting priority, planning for making decisions to undertake solutions of problems. Three types of communications are needed. These are : (1) Communication for motivational change, (2) Technical communication, and (3) Administrative skills. Motivational communication skills perform the following tasks : (a) making people better informed at the community as well as individual levels; (b) creating conviction and favourable attitudes among individuals towards community programmes *and* activities; and (c) getting community and societal mood and atmosphere favourable to development programme. Management of information involves such skills as assessing the information needs of community, designating the information on contents, choosing the channels for providing this information and assessing the impact of the information in terms of desired development goals. Personal communication (face to face) has been found most effective to bring about changes in Human Behaviour.

Technological Related Communication

Development invariably involves introducing alternative, improved and appropriate technology into the community for its development. This requires the social workers to be very thorough with communication skills and for transforming technology to the simple, tradition bound and illiterate communities.

Skills Related to Administrative Communication

Administrative communication involves need of specific planning, monitoring of implementation, supervision, management, logistics and use of reports and records for improving development programme, planning and programme. Communication skills for bringing about effective coordination between social groups and various organisations are very critical.

Audio-Visual Unit

Tata Institute of Social Sciences has an Audio-visual Unit which has prepared very useful material for teaching and communicating with people. The other schools can use the material gainfully.

But by and large very few schools use the modern means of communication either in teaching or in their work. The mass media such as press is very scantly used by social workers. There was a time when Tata Institute of Social Sciences had a TISS Press. This was giving weekly articles to the press. *Indian Express*, New Delhi also for some time carried full page articles on Community Welfare and Rural Scene. The mass-media must be used to make people specially *Dalits* aware and conscious of their rights and duties.

Conclusion

Dalit have not got their due share in Hindu Society. They continue to feel deprived and exploited group. The problem is not new. Human communities through wit history have had their hewers of wood and drawers of water, men whose lives were spent in a struggle for barest necessities of survival in the margins of society. One of the basic tasks and the ultimate criterion for the success of a community has always been its ability to incorporate its marginal members to give them opportunity to appropriate the life and values of the community and find personal in them. Social Work today is a conscious attempt to accelerate and guide the process of social integration. Social work as we know is both a continuation and a transformation of the integrative process. There are three types of changes : developmental, transitional and transformational. *These* generate different reactions and require different processes and leadership (or Social Worker).

Development change, simply, is an improvement upon the current way of operating. *The* aim is to do more and to do things better. Enhancing communication skills, enhancing technical expertise, building teams and expanding opportunities fall into this category. Developmental change is the least threatening to survive.

> Transitional change is an implementation of known new state and require rearranging or dismantling old social structure. Transitions usually occur over a set period of time. Transformational change is more profound and traumatic. It is somewhat out of direct control and it produces a future state that is largely unknown until it evolves. This type of change occurs when an organisation (or society) reaches a plateau in its life cycle and fall prey to unwilling demands from the environment.

Special skills are needed to be developed in social workers to deal with transformational change skills in managing ambiguity and conflict in leading derived group towards a moving target and cearly communicating a change strategy and a vision. Transformational times are not just difficult on the bottom line, they also wreck havock on the larger society. This is the most challenging task to be performed by the social worker to empower *dalits*. Training must provide and militate learner (Social worker) to be successful in coping with the challenges of change while at the same time serving the community as a whole. Training the learners (Social Work students) to lead their marginal group through is a challenging task and only those Social Work Educators, who are fully equipped with knowledge, skills and more importantly an attitude of openness and determination will succeed in imparting right education. Follow-up programmes must be introduced to ensure that concepts learned in the Schools are applied during real situations.

In the final analysis we may conclude that very few have recognised that the essential foundation for stimulating development lies not in super imposition of technologies for the development of material culture: rather, the first step must be the discovery of an effective method of working with people. Social Work Education provides an answer to this dilemma.

Salvation of social work profession lies in moving towards rural and tribal areas and giving *dalits* a top priority in their work. This is because the man belonging to the fourth State (or poor) or the common man of India or for that matter of the third world of today as well as of tomorrow and day after belong to rural and Tribal India. To restore vitality to the Indian Society and build up the future prosperity of the common man it is necessary to strengthen and develop *dalits*. Only then, and in that process, the well being of the Indian people will be realised.

Social work is both palliative as well responsible for changing institutions. It helps individuals in the framework of existing conditions as well as to help change social institutions. It recognizes the multiple causation of problems and realises that the cause lie neither exclusively in the individual nor in the societal structure. It becomes clear that profession which works towards social justice in a wide sense must feel responsible for amelioration and social change.

In the absence of a professional body, social worker has shied away from being given or taking, social responsibility at the National level. This has been mainly due to ego-centric behaviour of some of the senior members of the profession. As somebody has very correctly remarked that divided we cannot stand and united we fall. The change therefore should begin from within to influence the policies at various levels to change the plight of *dalits*.

REFERENCES

Adiseshiah, Malcom, S., Issues in Development of Higher Education: The Indian Context, *Social Change*. Vol. 20, No. 4, December, 1990, pp. 3-9.

Ambedkar, B.R., *Poona Pact,* (Jullunder N.D), pp.120-127.

Ambedkar, B.R., "What Congress and Gandhi have done to the Untouchables, in Dr. Babasaheb Ambedkar: *Writings and Speeches*. Bombay, Vol. 9, 1990.

Bagal, Baburao, Dalit Literature is but Human Literature in Arjun Dangle (ed) *Poisoned Bread,* translation from Modern Marathi Dalit Literature, Orient Longman, New Delhi, 1992.

Benemen, G.D., *Caste and other Inequalities,* New Delhi, 1979.

Bhargava Arati, Concern over neglect of Women, Backwards, *The Hindustan Times,* Saturday, Dec., 1993, p.57.

Bidwai, Praful, Abolishing Untouchability, *The Times of India,* Wednesday, Feb. 19, 1992.

Biersteker, Thomas, J. Reducing the Role of the State in the Economy: A Conceptual Exploration of IMF and World Bank, Prescription, *International Studies Quarterly,* Vol. 34, 1990.

Dasgupta, Sugala. *Social Work and Social Change,* Extending Horizons Books, Parter Saigent Publisher, Boston U.S.A., 1968.

Dasgupta, Tapan, Will Rao Resort to Populism? *Times of India,* 11th December, 1924, New Delhi, p.20.

Dharmpal *Bhartiya China Manas and Kala,* (Translated from Hindi by Jitendra Bajaj) Centre for Policy Studies, Madras, 1993. pp. 42-43.

Gandhi, M.K., *Young India*, January 22, 1925.

Gandhi, M.K., *My Religion,* Navjivan Publishing House, 1955, pp.128-57.

Gharye, G.S., *Caste and Class in India,* Popular Prakashan Bombay, 1950.

Gangrade, K.D. Role of Education in Contemporary India, *IASSI Quarterly,* Vol. 12, July-December, 1993, Ncs : 1 and 2.

Gore, M.S., *The Social Context of an Ideology Ambedkar's Political and Social Thought,* Sage Publications, New Delhi, 1993.

Jacob, K.K., *Work Education in India*, H. Publications, Delhi, 1994.

Jain, R., Bond Bongartz Heinz, *Structural Adjustment Public Policy and Bureaucracy in Developing Societies,* Har Anand Publications, New Delhi, 1994.

Omvedt, Gail, *Dalits and the Democratic Revolution Dr. Ambedekar and the Dalit Movement in Colonial India*, Sage Publications, New Delhi, 1994. pp. 324-325.

Pyarelal, *The Epic Past,* Navjivan Publishing House, Ahmedabad, 1932.

Raghavan, G.N.S. To each bis Ambedkar I & U, *The Hindustan Times,* Tuesday, July 5, and Wednesday, July 6, 1994, New Delhi.

Sabnis, Shripal, in Barbara Joshi, (Ed.) *Untouchable Voices of Delhi Liberation Movement,* Zed Books, London, 1986.

Satpathy, Archana, Reservation Bids Letters to the Editor, *The Times of India,* Friday, December 23rd, 1994.

Sardesai, Rajdeep, Atrocities on *Dalits, The Times of India,* Monday, September, 9, 1991, New Delhi.

Shrikant, L.M., Scheduled Castes and their Welfare, *Encyclopaedia of Social Work in India,* Vol.11, Publication Division, Government of India, New Delhi, 1968.

Sinha, Arun, Class War in Bhojpur, *Economic and Political Weekly,* 7th January 1978.

Sunder, *The Rum,* Dalit Sahitya Academy, Bangalore, 1987.

The Tmes of India, 6th December, 1993.

Yadav, K.C. and Singh Rajbir, *India's Unequal Citizens : A study of other Backward Classes,* New Delhi, 1994.

12

Conflicting Value System and Social Work

Management of Crisis in Indian Families

Introduction

There is a continuous dominance of western theories and concepts despite the fact that most of the Third World countries are politically free. In India the Ganga of education, specially of social work and psychiatry, has been so much contaminated and polluted by western thoughts, concepts and practices that it would require a herculean task to cleanse it. The impact of imperialism, particularly of American, has been so great that it has lost its properties of self-purification.

We Indians are very proud of our Nationalism. But what is taught in our courses of Social Work and Psychiatry is just stinking American material. While we serve unabashedly western material to our students we make only a peripheral grafting of our thoughts of great thinkers and activists of the Indian Nation. The graft naturally becomes artificial. It indeed hangs loose from the rest of the material and can be treated more as a ritual that could be discarded as something alien to the hard core of the syllabi one teaches. The material, in no way is related to the profession *per se* much less to its methods and practices in India. The aim of *this* chapter is to emphasize that enough recognition has not been given to the "family" or the "client" who is in need of help.

My intention is to illustrate from the two case studies, selected from the field of social work, that the family should be taken in a major way in Indian context in study, diagnosis, and treatment of the client. My contention is that it is not the individual but the family that should be considered as the unit of work. The whole burden of the case in conflicting value system, is to shift the emphasis from one-to-one relationship, of a client and a social worker to that of a family in Indian situation. The emphasis of the workers should be family centred rather than individual centred for the clients who are in need of help.

In the first case I have shown the intricate problems of "Joking relationships" among the peasant castes of Northern India by pointing out that in spite of the inroads made by urbanization, the attitude of the older generation towards the new generation has not changed much. A social worker is, no doubt, in a position to establish good rapport with the clients and to help them to think of new value systems. The worker has to work not with the clients alone but with others who are affecting the value system of the client.

The second case illustrates that the problem of family planning in India is not that of insertion of loops or sterilization. It is essentially a problem of combating the social values which are deterrent to family planning and having children is a sign of status and a barren woman is practically ostracized. The fatalistic attitudes of the people and the whole set-up of social relationships go against the ideas of family planning. This is particularly true of Indian villages, which are slow to change.

Thanks to Indian social structure and its resilience, the atomized individual like the Western counterpart, has not yet grown, resulting into breakdown of families and death of community life.

The love and care bestowed by the Indian family makes it essential on the part of professionals to adopt family-centred approach to understand, treat and prevent the psychological disorders and other problems. This approach will also be helpful in introducing innovations in Indian society.

The first case has graphically described the crisis and dilemmas faced by a sister-in-law about the advances made by her brother-in-law. She has preferred to fight out the situation rather than succumb to the traditional values. The second case has dealt with the crisis authoritarian structure of mother-in-law and daughter-in-law. The crisis specially refer to non-communication by the daughter-in-law to mother-in-law about the use of contraceptives to prevent unwanted pregnancies without the latter's knowledge, consent and approval.

The mother-in-law has been inflicting pregnancies on her daughter-in-law in the fond hope of having a male child to continue the family line.

The consensus model of give and take against the conflict model of clinging to ones values adopted by the social worker, has maintained and kept the harmonious relationships between the members of both the families and prevented them from breaking down. Actually an easy flow of communication, sympathy and understanding between the two generations could help them better accommodate their differences during a period of transition.

Before I take up the cases of two families, falling in the category of families in transition, I would like to describe some salient features of my study on inter-generational conflict in India. Both these cases have been selected from my study and work.

Findings

A study of inter-generational conflict of Indian youth conducted at the Delhi School of Social Work some years ago reveals interesting facts. The sample was drawn from 1000 post-graduate students of colleges on the Delhi University campus and their corresponding parents. The difference in general attitude between parents and students is sometimes attributed to the decline of authority of parents over their children. However, study shows that the generations tend to agree that the authority of the parents is not always flouted by the children. About 2 per cent students and 63 per cent parents feel that "sometimes" boys behave as if they were not under the control of their parents. This being so, what do the young feel about their obligations to their parents? Do they like for example, to give financial help to their parents? The answer from as many as 98 per cent of the students is yes, but the young are not as enthusiastic about this when it comes to helping the relatives or other immediate kinsmen financially.

The majority of the young (55 per cent) are a bit individualistic in the sense that they do not like the idea of living in joint families. But both the young (89 per cent) and old (80 per cent) agree that one should avoid having more than three children.

The authoritarian pattern of the Hindu family leaves very few areas of choice and decisions to the younger generation. Most decisions are taken without reference to the young members of the family. "This creates friction in the family and often leads to discontent and strained relationships between parents and their children. The study shows that 79 per cent parents want to choose bride/groom for their children with their consultation. But only 8 per cent students and 2 per cent parents want selection of spouse to be made with the mutual approval of the bride and bridegroom. However, 34 per cent students and 17 per cent parents consider parental approval necessary. It means that only 8 per cent of the students are individualistic enough to take the responsibility for selecting spouses for themselves, whereas 92 per cent seem to depend on parents in one way or the other. The parents seem to be very rigid as only 2 per cent like to yield to mutual choice proposal of their children.

It may be interesting to note that 48 per cent students and 22 per cent of parents approve the institution of love marriage. The approving of this institution by a significant section of students may mean that they want to break away from the traditional norms of society.

In other words, it may be said that unless we view the inter-generational conflict as an ongoing process of social change and continuous socialization we would get stuck up. For example, we should not take for granted, that the older generation has already spent its force and is not capable of further learning and changing. Since the evidence suggests that over the past years the younger generation has developed some value framework for its behaviour, modification of traditional values and behaviour may increasingly influence the values of parents in the direction of liberalism. It may become increasingly difficult for many parents to hold their children to a set of conservative values.

Over the years the values of parents and the adult community in general may become more liberal and the conflict between the two generations thereby may be reduced. But in the meantime, and certainly in the near future, it appears that parents and children will continue to live with somewhat different systems.

Parents will probably continue to hold to traditional values and assume that their children were conforming to those values until their action forces them to see the reality. The young generation will continue to develop its own modified value system and keep those values to themselves, and allow or encourage their parents to believe that they share the same traditional values. For many parents and their children, the inter-generational conflict will continue to be characterised by the parents playing the ostrich and the youth trying to keep the sand from blowing away.

According to inter-generational conflict the families can be divided into three categories:

(1) *Conformist families* in which both the generations conform to the traditional values and attitudes.
(2) *Modernist families* in which both the generations have been changed and have adopted modern values and attitudes.
(3) *Transitional families in* which students are comparatively modern and parents comparatively traditional.

In the first two categories of families there are likely to be less problems of inter-generational conflict since both the generations adhere to the same values and attitudes. In the traditional families, not only do the students and parents cherish different sets of values and attitudes but the parents also want to impose their own traditional values and views on their children. The authoritarian attitude of the parents creates a communication gap between the two generations resulting in lack of understanding between the two generations. These situations often become ripe for conflict.

CASE NO. 1

The most important features of the traditional Indian society are caste-system, the joint family system and the village community system. All the three systems are now losing their hold on the people due to inroads made by industrialization and urbanization in the country. This has given rise to problems of adjustment between the traditionalist and the modernist.

In the past the caste determined the behaviour and conduct of the individual, and anybody who violated the caste rules and regulations was either socially ostracized or punished. The joint family laid down the code of conduct for each member, and his relationship with others was also well marked. The deviants were not tolerated and were severely dealt with. Mostly woman was considered inferior to man. She was, in one sense, married to the entire family, including cognates and agnates of three generations up and down, besides her husband. She would first serve all the members of the family and the husband was the last to be served. There was plenty of social intercourse inside the huge joint families, and certain relations were marked out for persiflage, even obscene innuendoes.

In northern India in some of the peasant castes "joking relationships" are permitted among the certain categories of relatives, e.g., *devar* (younger brother) and *bhabhi* (wife of the elder brother) relationship. It is an accepted practice among the members of these castes to marry the woman with the other male member of the family in the event of death of her husband. Even the sex relations between the girl and her *devar* is not considered reprehensible, as he is a potential husband. Teasing of sexual nature often occurs between them and also finds a place in songs sung by women.

Indian women in the past were born for marriage. But today many Indian women do not consider marriage as the chief goal of existence and many prefer not to marry. Women have right to vote and most of them have been able to exercise their right to vote independently without getting influenced either by father, or husband, or any other relatives. Women now prefer nuclear families to joint families. The law prohibiting bigamy, the right to divorce, and the right to inherit property have helped them to raise their status. In the villages old notions still prevail, but even there the symptoms of change can be observed.

The present case deals with the problem of a client who was not willing to accept the traditional value system and objected to the demand of her *devar* for physical intimacy with her.

The case-record is drawn from the rural setting where the worker is working over a period of one year to organise the village women for cultural, recreational and craft activities.

The worker started her work in this village at the instance of the village Pradhan and a few other villagers. The village is a multi-caste village. There are 30 villagers who go to city for service. Some of them cummute everyday while a few of them stay in the city and visit the village only towards the week-ends or other holidays. The village has primary and secondary schools for boys and girls. But a few girls study beyond the primary stage. The main occupation of the villagers is agriculture and one of the peasant castes appropriates all the village land among its various families. Sugarcane and vegetables are the main commercial crops grown by the villagers in addition to wheat, bajra and maize. As the village is situated near a city some of the villagers have taken to milk selling to supplement their income. In the field both men and women work and no distinction is made on the basis of daughters or daughters-in-law. The numerical strength of the peasant caste is greater than any other caste accounting for 55 per cent of the total population of the village. The educational attainment of this caste is also higher than any other caste in the village. The worker in order to get the participation of the village women in the centre systematically planned home-visits and in a month was able to cover the whole of the village. These home-visits helped her to know some of the problems faced by the village women. The worker also prepared family cards. The following facts about the social history of the client are drawn from the family card of the client.

Social history of the client--The client, a married woman of 18 years of age, had come to live in her husband's house two years back. The client has studied up to the 5th standard. She is tall and slim. She is of fair complexion. She is a good looking and attractive woman. She dressed differently from other village women, but observes *purdah* and other traditional norms of paying respect to the mother-in-law and the father-in-law. Her husband is a healthy and handsome man and looks younger than his age. He is forty years of age. He is a non-matriculate. He works as a peon in the city and stays there. He comes only on week-ends or holidays. His younger brother, parents and wife live in the village. He has a good amount of land and by the village standards the family could be classed as economically average. His cash income helps the family to tide over difficulties at the time of crop failures or other contingencies like the death of a bullock or breakdown of any agriculture equipment.

The parents of the client live in another fringe village located near the city at a distance of about 16 miles from her husband's village. She has an elder married brother and an uncle. Uncle lives in the city. She has a loving and affectionate mother. She ranks second in the family. She received all the attention and love from her parents and other relatives in her native home. She was also allowed to have her own way by her parents and they did not interfere much in her work. She spent all her vacations at her uncle's house and attended sewing and knitting classes in the centre run for the women in the vicinity of her uncle's house. She had a number of women as her friends and she imbibed certain qualities and values from them.

Her parents allowed her much freedom because she was the only daughter. They loved her and were very fond of her, but wanted to get her married soon according to the custom prevalent in their caste. They did not allow her to study beyond the 5th standard and arranged her marriage with a boy who though otherwise suitable was slightly older than her. She moved to her husband's house after one year of her marriage.

The mother-in-law of the client is a very good person and likes her daughter-in-law and treats her well. Both of them maintain a good relationship. But the mother-in-law is old and follows the traditional customs and desires that her daughter-in-law should also follow the same.

The father-in-law is an old man. He does not interfere much in the domestic affairs and spends most of his time in the fields looking after the agriculture work. He is consulted occasionally by the members of the family in case of disputes in the family.

The brother-in-law is a young man. He has studied up to the 8th standard. He is a spoiled child of the family being the youngest member in the family. He was liked by all and was specially pampered by his mother. He likes the company of young girls.

Client refers her problem—The client one day came to the centre. She greeted the worker and sat near her. The client looked very worried and dejected and was not able to speak to the worker. The worker asked her how she was and how much progress she had made in her sewing classes. She told the worker that she was not able to make any progress as she was having a personal problem and was worried about the same. She did not find anybody with whom she could share the problem and take help to solve her problem. She had heard a lot about the worker from other women and wanted to talk to her long ago but she always found the worker surrounded by others. Even in the centre there were other women and she was much afraid and shy to talk to the worker in the presence of other members. But the problem had become acute and she could no longer bear it and she needed someone to talk to and seek guidance. The worker took the client in a quite corner of the centre. The worker began to talk to her and told her that she should feel confident and share her problem. The client withdrew into her shell, was silent for a minute, and said to the worker that she would tell her some other day.

The worker told her that if she did not feel like telling her anything that day she could tell her the following day. The worker asked her where her native village was and what her parents did? The client said that she came from a village situated at a distance of six miles from her husband's village and that her parents were agriculturists. At this point the client picked up the courage and acquainted her with her problem. The conversation that took place between the client and the worker is recorded below:

First Interview

Client : Miss, I have been married for the last one year and have been living in this village for more than six months. (While speaking she drew nearer to the worker and sat very close to her.) The people here are nice, and particularly my mother-in-law. I have a younger brother-in-law (husband's brother) with whom I have some problem. (Before she could hardly complete her sentence, tears began to roll down her eyes.) The worker consoled her and told her not to weep as sometimes younger people pick up quarrels to tease and not to hurt. "Our society allows joking relationships between *devar-bhabhi.*"

Client: (Sobered down and wiped her tears and continued) I do not mind relationships up to the joking stage, but he is taking too much liberty with me.

Worker: I am sorry to learn that he does not want to maintain a respectable distance from you. Tell me, sister, where is your husband?

Client: (with anger on the face) He is the main problem. He goes to work in the city and returns only on week-ends or holidays. I have to remain in the house with the other members of the household. But none of them bother about myself or my problems. Even though some time my mother-in-law sees my *devar* coming to my room she does not check him. I am fed up with life and sometimes, I wish to end my life instead of surrendering my honour to him.

Worker: Sister, even in your dream you should not think of ending your life. But you should stand up against your odds and struggle with the society. You should talk to your husband. You may also tell him that you feel very lonely in his absence and you would very much like him to come back to the village.

Client: (Felt very much relieved) I am really very much thankful for your suggestion and I shall speak to my husband when he comes back.

The client left the centre with a great sense of relief and was very anxious to talk to her husband. The worker told her that if she had any difficulty she should not feel shy to come to the centre again to talk over matters with the worker. In spite of this assurance the client did not come to the centre for a fortnight. The worker also could not pay a home visit as she was busy with other urgent work at the agency. The worker after completing her work made up her mind to follow up the cases she had taken in hand. She wanted to meet the client under reference. During one of her visits she went to the house of the client. At the house the worker was greeted by the mother-in-law and when the client also saw the worker she came from the kitchen and smiled at the worker. The worker saw that the client looked much pleased and was in good spirits. The client asked the worker to sit near her mother-in-law and went to the kitchen to bring a glass of milk for the worker. The worker had to take the glass of milk at the insistence of the mother-in-law and the client. The worker asked them as to why they had not been coming to the centre for many days past. Both of them said that they were busy with the harvest work and with cooking food for the men folk who stayed in the village during this season. The mother-in-law assured the worker that as soon as the work was over they would come to the centre regularly. She also told the worker that her elder son who was staying in the village would soon leave for the city. The worker noticed that this statement of the mother-in-law was not liked by the client and she looked very nervous. As the worker was bidding them goodbye, the client took the permission of her mother-in-law and came to the centre along with the worker. On reaching the centre the client immediately wanted to talk to the worker. The worker was also eager to know about the progress she had made in handling her problem. The following conversation took place between them at the centre.

Second Interview

Client : I acted on your advice and persuaded my husband to come back to the village everyday. He readily agreed to my request as he had to help the family in harvesting the crop. But now the harvesting season was over and he again intends to follow his usual routine. This would mean I would be faced with the old problem again. I am very much afraid of my *devar*. He may take undue advantage of the absence of my husband from the village.

Worker: Did you not suggest your husband to go by bus as the village was now on the bus route? This would not tire him much and would save botheration of either eating at hotels or cooking his food.

Client: I persuaded him to come home everyday. But he had refused to do so on the ground that it was too expensive. He also told me that I should adjust to the family and should not bother him much. I am unable to understand what he means by this statement. But I am not like others to stoop down to such a level.

Worker: I really sympathise with your situation and am glad that you are determined to stand up against it. If you feel that you face danger in the night, either you sleep with your mother-in-law or request her to be near the place where you sleep.

Client: Yes, I have more difficulties in the night. My brother-in-law approaches me stealthily and awakes me to have a relationship with me. I put him off saying that if he intended to play mischief I would cry and wake the rest of the members of the house. But he does not pay heed to this warning and continues to nag me. I do not allow him to touch my body. I get terribly afraid and do not get sleep in the night. I feel like running back to my parent's house. I have written to my parents to take me away during Dussehra and Diwali. In the meantime I would request my mother-in-law to be with me in the night.

The client went home. She succeeded in persuading her mother-in-law to be with her in the night. But this arrangement did not last for many days and the mother-in-law left her alone. The client one day complained to her mother-in-law about the behaviour of the *devar* and requested her to check him. The mother-in-law instead of correcting the son scolded her saying that she was a funny girl and instructed her not to object to the *devar* having jocking-relations with her. After all where would the men folk of the house go. They could not jump over the walls of the house and peep into other person's houses. This shocked the client and she lost all hopes she had in her mother-in-law. The mother-in-law also asked her to go to the field for work. This added another dimension to her problem. The brother-in-law found this a God sent opportunity and wanted to catch her in the sugar-cane field. One day she was virtually caught and managed to escape and run. He again tried to catch her but fell in a ditch. The client ran back home and was terribly upset and wanted to meet the worker badly. She came to the centre. The worker when she saw the client approaching the centre came out of the centre and warmly received her. The client sat near the worker. The other members had left the centre as it was time to close the centre. The client finding nobody in the centre and having received a very sympathetic response from the worker began to weep and in desperation she spoke the following words.

Third Interview

Client : Sister, today I would have lost my honour and would not have been able to show my face to anybody. But God protected me and I could get away from a giant. I am now very much upset and feel like ending my life. What is the use of living in a society where our relatives do not care and some of them are such that they would like to play with our honour?

The worker also was taken aback at the development of the case and for a moment she did not know what to do and could not utter a single word. However, she soon overcame her feelings and began to speak.

Worker: I know, how terribly upset you must be over this event. But still I would urge upon you not to think in terms of ending your life. Dussehra and Diwali we shall have soon, and your brother will come before Dussehra to take you to participate in the ceremonies in your home.

Client: Please, do something for me and at least stop my visits to the field. I am afraid to go to the field. If ever my brother-in-law finds me alone; I do not know what he will do to me.

Worker: I will come to your house and persuade your mother-in-law to send you to the centre to help me in making preparation for the annual day of the centre. I would also talk to your husband who is a member of youth club organized by the centre to stay in the village to organise inter-village tournaments at the centre. You should go to your house and I will come this evening to talk to your mother-in-law.

Client: I do not feel like going home but feel like running to my mother. But I am going home at your request and would expect you soon.

The worker closed the centre. She went to the house of the client. She found mother-in-law of the client sitting in the verandah busy doing something. The mother-in-law called the worker inside the house. The worker was offered a seat near the mother-in-law. The mother-in-law requested the worker for dinner, but she politely refused her saying that she would be late in returning to her home if she waited for the meals. She said that she had come to see her to inform her that the centre was going to celebrate the annual day soon and would like her and her daughter-in-law to participate in the annual day programme. The mother-in-law felt very happy and nodded her head. The worker said to her that she did not want only her cooperation but the cooperation of her daughter-in-law as well. She would like her to come to the centre everyday and prepare some articles for the exhibition to be arranged on that day, the mother-in-law said that these days daughters-in-law were real problems. She thought she had a good daughter-in-law but she now remained quiet all the time and did not allow other male members to talk to her. She was becoming a difficult woman. She would very much like to send her to the centre so that worker could help her to improve her.

The worker asked the mother-in-law about the "joking-relationship" prevalent in their caste. The mother-in-law said that it was natural to have "joking-relationship" between the *devar* and the *bhabhi* and it had the sanction of the society. She further said that there were a number of folk songs depicting the relationship between them. She went further and said to the surprise of the worker, that sometimes even an extramarital relationship between the *devar* and the *bhabhi* was permitted. She said that after all the children being to the household and the extra-marital relationships within the household were not taboo. The worker was really shocked to find such a value system prevalent in this village society. She herself came from a Brahmin family and in that caste one would shudder to think of such a relationship. In this caste even widow marriage is, not permitted. Here the problem was of conflicting value system. Both the client and the worker who were oriented to a different value system found it difficult to adjust to the traditional values still in vogue in this sub-culture. The worker was seen off at the door by the mother-in-law. The daughter-in-law could not take part in the conversation between the worker and the mother-in-law as she was busy cooking. But she also *come to* see the worker. The worker said to her that she should come to the centre from the following day and help in the preparation of annual day at the centre.

The client came to the centre and was very happy that the worker had succeeded in her mission. She began to take active interest in the activities of the centre and it seemed that she wanted to forget herself in the work. The worker also met the husband of the client in connection with the work of the centre and praised him for his nice wife. She was an asset to the centre and she had prepared a number of articles for the centre. The worker said these things to the husband to make him feel sympathetic towards his wife and take personal interest in her. He told the worker that he was happy that his wife had made some contribution to the activities of the centre. He also agreed to the request of the worker to stay in the village for a couple of days to help in the activities of the centre for the ensuing annual day.

The client seemed to be happy and was doing well. She was particularly happy that her husband was again staying back in the night. But in one of the casual talks with her he brought it out saying that he did not see much harm even if the *devar* had extra-marital relationships. This was an accepted pattern of behaviour in this society. The wife who had different value-system argued with him that this was an anti-social act and should not be permitted by the society. But she did not succeed.

In fact he went one step further and said that if his brother was to have relationship with her in his absence he would not see his brother's act as anti-social. He also told her that she should not worry much as she would soon become like other women of the caste. This was a challenge to her and she said to her husband whatever might happen she was not prepared to yield to the value-system prevalent in the caste. The husband did not take her words seriously.

The annual day was a grand success in the village. This had brought the worker into intimate contacts with a large number of women. She in her informal talks with some of the women with whom she had established good rapport asked about the relationships between *devar* and *bhabhi.* She was told by these women that all the male folk who were related by blood or fictional ties as the *devar-bhabhi* were allowed to have joking-relationships with the *bhabhi.* This made the worker realize that the problem was not one between the client and her family but that it was directed against the value system of the whole caste.

The client following the annual day went to her native home with her brother. She talked with her mother about her problem. Her mother avoided her but when continuosly goaded by the client said that it was the accepted practice in the caste which they belonged. The client told her mother that she would not like to follow such a value-system and would like to stand up against it. Her mother encouraged her to do so and advised her to take the help of her husband and prepare him to help her. She told her mother about the help she was getting from a worker of the centre. The mother was happy to know that there was somebody to help her daughter in the village. The client after spending a month in her native home returned to her husband's house. The next day she came to the centre. She looked cheerful and happy and talked to the worker as follows:

Fourth Interview

The client greeted the worker with a smile and said, "I returned from home yesterday after spending about a month with my mother and have been advised by her to seek assistance of my husband and your help to end the affairs with my younger brother-in-law and if possible set him right."

Worker: I am very happy to know that you had good time in your home. I agree with the suggestion of your mother to get the assistance of your husband in solving your problem and I am glad that you seem to be determined to fight the situation rather than fall a prey to it. I would however like you to continue your efforts to persuade your mother-in-law as well to see your point of view and seek her active assistance in the problem.

Client: My mother-in-law is old and wants to uphold the traditional values prevalent in the caste and wants me also to follow the same. I feel she is a very difficult woman to change and specially when I talk to her about my younger brother-in-law, she gets furious.

Worker: You should not lose faith in the goodness of human beings. If possible you should persuade her to tell your brother-in-law to remain at a reasonable distance from you.

Client: I assure you that I will make efforts to persuade both my husband and mother-in-law. But I want to tell you whatever may happen I would not like to yield.

Worker: I am really very happy about your determination and I would also continue my efforts with your mother-in-law and husband to make them conscious and aware of their changing responsibility.

The client left the centre.

The worker's and the client's efforts of working with the mother-in-law yielded some result and she began to keep a strict watch on her younger son and at times scolded him for his misbehaviour. The mother-in-law changed because the worker in one of her casual visits talked to her that a number of joint families in the village were breaking into nuclear families as the old and new generation were not able to live together due to different value-systems. The client also spoke to her mother-in-law that she was sick of her brother-in-law and if he did not mend his ways she would like to live separately with her husband in the village or city. The mother-in-law was aware of this problem as she had seen her own neighbours splitting into nuclear families. She told both of them that she would not like her house to break and would like all of them to live together and assured all help in solving the problem.

The client's husband saw the change in the attitude of his mother and on her advice began to visit the village quite often. This helped the client to solve her problem to a great deal and her brother-in-law also began to behave differently.

Analysis: The analysis of this case brings out clearly three important points: (i) that the problem arose in a joint family, (ii) that the solution of the problem thought by the client was to run away from it either by ending her life or returning to the native home, and (iii) the real problem was one of conflict of traditional and new value systems rather than between the members of the family.

The centre of the Indian family is woman and her main roles are daughter, daughter-in-law, wife, mother, mother-in-law. The last two roles belong to the old generation and they want to uphold the traditional values and want others also to follow the same. In the first three roles, as already stated, women have changed. They have different values and now understand their rights and duties. In their efforts to live by their values they find the mother-in-law, the father-in-law and even the husband a stumbling block.

Specially in the villages these people still follow the old system and have not changed their attitude much towards young women. Father-in-law and mother-in-law both consider themselves to be the heads of the household and want that they should be obeyed and respected by the members of the household and specially by the daughters-in-law. Many husbands consider themselves to be the sole monarch of their wives and want that they should obey them and satisfy their whims and desires. This is considered very essential by the society on the part of women if they wish to attain ultimate salvation.

The woman is willing to give due respect to all the three, but she is now not prepared to remain a slave in their hands. As a result of this conflict there develops a situation in which mother-in-law, father-in-law and husband form one group against the wife who alone forms the other group.

Whatever may be the solution of this situation, but one thing is clear that all the members of the family must change their ideas according to time and try to understand the new value system emerging as a consequence of new changes brought about in the society.

The worker here plays a supportive role and helps her client not to run away from the situation but to struggle with it and change the other members and their value system so that the desirable adjustment becomes possible. The worker is able to establish a good rapport with the client as she has been able to play successfully the role of a mother figure for the client. She also allows the client to visit her in the centre at anytime and does not strictly follow the time schedule as she knows that in the village the concept of time is different. The worker makes effective use of home-visits to understand and solve the problem of the client. The worker could sympathise with the client because she herself was oriented to the client's value-system. The worker and the client both had to stand against this value-system as the other members of the society still hold on to the traditional pattern of behaviour. The worker and the client were not able to radically change the value-system but when the members of the family, specially the mother-in-law, became aware that this system would make inroads on the joint family system and break it up, she agreed to check her son and allow her daughter-in-law to lead a peaceful life in the house. The encouraging sign was that the old lady had begun to see the new emerging trends and wanted to adjust gradually. The husband also saw the point of the client and began to react favourably towards her and her value-system.

Worker's Responsibilily: The problem in such cases before the worker is not to adjust the client to the environment, but to help the client to stand up against the value system which is not acceptable to her. The social worker also attempts to change the environment and does not act like an onlooker. The worker may have to disregard the old institutions and develop new institutions to help the people who have acquired new values as a result of education and urbanization. In our anxiety to glorify our past, we over-emphasize our social institutions unduly. No doubt the study of social institutions and other aspects of culture are very important to understand the problem of a client. But if these institutions and values have outlived their purposes they should be modified or changed or new institutions should be developed. In such instances the worker has to work not with the client alone but with others who are affecting the value system of the client and in the process help them to see the changing value pattern in the society and to adjust to the new demand.

In our work we come across a number of women who took decisions contrary to the established traditional practices and either set up an independent nuclear family or moved along with their husbands to live in the city. This change in the traditional values may be attributed to the fact that this particular village is a village on the urban fringe and a large number of people are employed in a nearby city where they earn their daily living and thus constantly exposing the village to values of the larger society.

CASE NO. 2

Social history of the client: She was 32 years old and belonged to a traders family in the village. She was married at the age of eleven and came to live with her husband two years later. In the nineteen years of her married life, she produced nine children—seven daughters and two sons. Both the sons died in their infancy. The family was worried about the continuity of the generation and inheritance of the property in the absence of any male child. The in-laws were eager to see a son born to their only son. This resulted in unwanted pregnancies by the client. The woman was tired of producing the children, which had ruined her health. She had reached a stage where she herself did not want any male child and was willing to adopt one if that could satisfy other members of the family. The mother-in-law however believed that one day she (client) might get a son. The husband was a considerate person and had sympathies with his wife but he was dominated by the parents. He was often forced to sleep with his wife to bring another child into the world. Not only this, but he was often laughed at by relatives and friends for not having vitality enough to produce a male child. The client, fed up with this state of affairs, approached the social worker to get some help so that she could stop conceiving.

The worker listened to her sympathetically and various methods of family planning were discussed. Also discussed was the insertion of a loop. The client, however, felt that she would prefer to use some other method since to get the loop inserted she would have to go outside the village and then everybody would come to know of it. After much discussion, the client decided to use a diaphram and jelly and the process was explained to her thoroughly.

The client started using the diaphram with the knowledge of her husband but kept it a secret from others. All was going well but one day, one of her younger daughters who was nearly five years old, got hold of the diaphram and started playing with it in the street. The equipment was seen by one of the ladies of the neighbourhood, who took it from the child and brought it to the mother-in-law. This occurred in the afternoon when a few other women were also there and it soon became clear to the mother-in-law that this was something meant to prevent any pregnancy. This infuriated the old woman beyond limits and the daughter-in-law was summoned from inside the house. The client had to admit that it was meant to prevent conception and that she had obtained it from the village social worker. The anger of the mother-in-law and others immediately shifted to the worker. They decided that she was a really harmful person introducing such unconventional things into the village. The client also had her share of rebuke and abuse and escaped from it by going to the fields. She had a talk there with her husband. In the evening the atmosphere in the house was tense and the husband dare not support his wife as he was afraid of his parents' wrath. The client waited patiently for the night to pass so that she could discuss the happening with the worker in the morning.

There were others besides the client who wanted to see the worker but for a different reason. The news had spread rapidly in the village and the majority of the villagers were against the worker for carrying on this type of activity. Everybody had his own version of the incident but most of them believed it was something wrong.

The news also reached the house of the Sanitary Inspector who was living near the road, on entrance to the village. He and his wife were greatly respected by the villagers. They had three healthy children and sent them to school. He was a Brahmin and was criticised by the villagers when he first took the job of a sanitary inspector in the city but gradually, due to his good behaviour, his sociability and his interest in the good of the village and its people, he won back the admiration of the villagers. He was also on very good terms with the social worker and always tried to cooperate in the programme she introduced. The worker has also taken his help in organizing sanitary drives and cleanliness campaigns in the village. When the sanitary inspector and his wife learnt of the villagers' designs, they planned to warn the worker and to help her as far as possible.

They were on the look out the next day and as soon as they saw the worker getting off the bus, they invited her to their house and told her about the previous day's incident and the villagers' reaction. The worker felt a little nervous. The sanitary inspector and his wife decided to accompany the worker to the centre to prevent any untoward thing happening.

The mother-in-law of the client and certain other people were on the look out for the worker and the moment she reached the centre they came and, headed by the mother-in-law started passing insulting remarks. They said that they had enough of the worker and she should leave the village for good. They did not approve of her methods of work. She was spreading all sorts of non-sense ideas in the village and was exciting the daughters-in-law to disregard the wishes of the elders. The worker realised that it was best to keep quiet and let the group pour out its anger. When the group started abusing the worker, the sanitary inspector's wife came to her rescue and tried to control their anger. She told them that they should not decide against the worker because of one incident and she made them recall the good things they had learnt from her and the things she had done to improve the condition of the village. This quietened the villagers somewhat and most of them felt that they had been rather rash in their decision. A few of them even left the centre to go to their work. The client's mother-in-law however was not pacified and she raised the incident of the diaphram. Here again, the sanitary inspector and his wife intervened and said that it was not a bad thing in itself. It had helped them in limiting their family and they were all the happier for it. The mother-in-law agreed that their children were perhaps the show pieces of the village. The crowd had quite thinned by then and only a few ladies and children remained. The sanitary inspector also left but his wife stayed back. The mother-in-law was still not completely pacified. The mother-in-law, the worker, the client, the sanitary inspector's wife and one or two other ladies then had a thorough discussion about the incidence and family planning in general. Since the atmosphere had somewhat cleared, everybody listened to the other's point of view patiently. The mother-in-law began to feel ashamed of her behaviour because of the worker's calm and dignified handling of the situation. The worker agreed that she should have consulted the old woman before giving the contraceptive to the daughter-in-law and then went on to explain the problem of population in the country and benefits of having a small family. The mother-in-law did not dispute these points but was still unable to give up the desire of a male grandchild.

Analysis: The case illustrates a conflict in the traditional and modern values. The influence of tradition is so great that it is very difficult to introduce new innovations in the village society. The ignorance and lack of awareness on the part of the villagers is responsible for many of the ills of the rural society.

The case shows that two forces are operating in the village. One may be called the innovative change and the other restorative. The innovative change is generally accepted by young people of the villages who are exposed to education and a modern way of living. The youth who were working in the city were not opposed to the ideas of family planning. Similarly, the acceptance of the family planning methods by the Brahmin couple also had "demonstrative effect" on the villagers. But it was not contagious enough to be accepted in practice by all the villagers. The restorative force involved opposition to innovations and attempts to re-establish or strengthen the tradition. This is evident from the reaction of the old ladies of the village towards the worker, who was an agent of bringing about change in their lives.

The role of authority is also very important in bringing about change to the traditional society. In this case, the client and her husband had no option but to yield to the wishes of the parents. The authority in such cases is the influence of somebody, whose position in a hierarchy, or whose structural and strategic superiority over others has not been freely chosen nor voluntarily accepted by those whom he influences, but who nevertheless yields a degree of compulsion on them. The means of exercising influence in this instance are formal or structural, i.e. the authority, power, status and office of the influences and the involuntary dependence of the influenced.

In real life, however, society is in the process of continuous change. The leadership and authority emerge not as consequences of traditions but as means of changing tradition or of evolving new ones. Change, it may be noted, is also implied when traditional institutions struggle to maintain themselves. When forces of change emerge in a society, even the means of retaining and restoring former customs and institutions are instruments of change.

From the *case* it appears that the worker was at ease while working with her peer group but failed to invoke the older generation. The link between the old and the new was missing and resulted in the general conflict between the old and the young.

The case also illustrates that there may be two ways of changing values in the village. The first is to convince those who already wield influence either of traditional or modern kind of the need and necessity of adopting family planning. This will require an improvement in communication between the worker and the influential villagers. The second method is to select individuals who show enthusiasm for acceptance of new practices as also leadership qualities and make them influential. In this case, the role of the Brahmin couple proved very effective and significant in keeping under control the otherwise explosive situation. It may be possible and worthwhile to create at village level some voluntary groups which have some position and office within them and whose members, particularly the office holders, may be able to resist the tradition-bound influential elements and lend support to others for innovative change.

Radiation Effect

A follow up study and work shows that the case had a radiation effect in the village. Most of the newly married couples in the reproductive age group took to conventional methods of contraceptives and those having four children to permanent devices. The client when turned into a mother-in-law encouraged—her daughters and daughters-in-law to restrict the size of their respective families after two or three children. The children of the third generation when became parents were satisfied to have one boy and one girl. They took to third chance, if the first two arrivals were girls. Thus, the value got crystallised by the third generation.

Conclusions

Social workers must make a good study of family in the Indian social structure. The support system available through it, in the absence of any agency, will provide the much needed anchor and an effective alternative to deal with the problems of the people. There is considerable difference between the individual Indian and his counterpart in the Western society. We can safely say that the atomised individual found in the West is absent in India. All the studies in modernisation or Westernisation indicate that the process of atomisation of the individual in India has hardly begun. It has not made much headway and because of the powerful hold of old traditions as well as because of the prevailing social customs, and norms, it is unlikely to proceed very far.

The doyen of Indian Sociological Thought late Prof. Radhakamal Mukherjee, in his eloquent and perceptive first convocation address on 'Social Disorganisation in India' at the Tata Institute of Social Sciences in 1938 (reproduced in the *Indian Journal of Social Work,* Vol. XLVI, No. I, April 1985), said that the essence of Social Work is to fight anti-social attitudes and behaviour through the re-establishment of stable community organisation, which may re-define the social situation, and gradually re-build the life organisation for persons who have suffered loss of status.... The way of recovery lies in each case through the re-establishment of stable social contacts with adequate social rules and definitions, which may give the heartening support for a satisfactory reorientation on the person's life organisation.

Gandhi had said: India's "soul" lives in villages. He, therefore, in his Constructive Work Programme gave information to rural work. He wanted workers to go to villages and to work with people. His special emphasis was to improve the status of village women. He felt once women get active, right place in Indian society and India's social, economic and political development will be very fast.

In my view, key to become developed nation is to raise the status of women.

REFERENCES

Dimensions of Social Work in India, Marwah Publications, New Delhi, 1976.

Gangrade, K.D., *Crisis of Values: A Study in Generation Gap,* Chetna Publications. New Delhi, 1975.

Mukherjee, Radhakamal, *Social Disorganisation in India* (First convocation address delivered at the Tata Institute of Social Sciences, 1938), reprodueed in *Indian Journal of Social Work,* Golden Jubilee, Vol. XLV, No. I, April, 1985, p. 39.

Social Networks and Social Work Crisis Management in Indian Families, Northern Book Centre, New Delhi, 1985.

Veeraraghavan, Vimla, *A Textbook of Psychotherapy,* Storing Publishers, Pvt. Ltd., New Delhi, 1985.

❑❑❑

Bibliography

A New Social Order, The Gandhian Alternative, Sarva Kalelkar Kaka, Seva Sangh Prakashan, Varanasi, 1991.

Ackerman, Peter and Duvall, *A Force More Powerful*, Palgrave, New York, 2001.

Ahmed, Feroz (ed) *Atom and Self-Collection of Lectures Delivered* by D.S. Kothari, New Age, International Publishers, Mumbai, 2002.

Ahmed, Feroz (ed) *Science and Humanism*, Collection of Articles, Addresses and Speeches delivered by D.S. Kothari, Galgotia Publications, Pvt. Ltd., 2004.

Ahmed, Feroz (ed), *Knowledge and Wisdom*, Collection of Lectures and Addresses Delivered by D.S. Kothari, New Age International [P] Publishers, New Delhi, 2003.

Ahmed, Feroz (ed) *Education and Character Building*, Collection of Convocation Addresses (1962-1983) delivered by Prof D.S. Kothari, National Institute of Science Communication, Council of Scientific & Industrial Research, New Delhi, 2000.

Bakshi, S.R., (ed.), *Gandhi and Status of Women,* Critarion Publication, New Delhi, 1987, pp. 145.

Begum Janatun, *Poverty Alleviation and Rural Development,* Rajesh Publication, New Delhi, 1997.

Berger, Brigitte and Berger, Peter, *The War over the Family Capturing the Middle Ground,* Anchor Press/Double day Garden City, New York, 1983.

Betai, Ramesh, *Gita and Gandiji,* National Gandhi Museum, New Delhi and Gyan Publishing House, New Delhi, second revised edition, 2002.

Bhole, L. M., *Essays on Gandhian Socio-economic Thought*, Shipra Publications, Delhi, 2000.

Bourai, Himanshu, *Gandhi and Modern Indian Liberals*, Abhijeet Publications, Delhi, 2004.

Chandhuri, E.R., *Planning with the Poor,* Gandhi Peace Foundation, New Delhi, 1998.

Chauhan, Sandeep, *GATT to WTO, Gandhian Alternative to NIEO,* Deep and Deep Publication, New Delhi, 2001.

Chavan, Sheshrao, (ed.), *Mahatma Gandhi Man of the Millennium,* Bharatiya Vidya Bhawan, Authors Press, New Delhi, 2001, pp. 354.

Choudhary, G.P., (ed.), *Relevance of Gandhism,* Capital Publishing House, Delhi, 1985, pp. 136.

Dalton, Dennis, *Gandhi's Power, Non-violence in Action,* Oxford University Press, Delhi, 1998, pp. 279.

Das Gupta, A.K., *Gandhi's Economic Thought,* Routledge, London, 1996.

Dasgupta, Sugata, *Social Work and Social Change - A case study in Indian Village Development*, Porter Sargent Publishers, Boston, 1978.

Dunham, Arthur, *Community Welfare Organization Principles and Practice*, Thomas Y. Crowwell Company, New York, 1958.

Dwivedy, S.N., *Thoughts on Gandhi and Social Change,* Gandhi Smriti and Darshan Samiti, 1995.

Gandhi, Jagdish P., *Globalised Indian Economy, Contemporary Issues and Perspectives*, Deep and Deep Publications (P) Ltd., New Delhi, 2003.

Gandhi, M. K.,*Thought For the Day* [specially written for Anand T. Hingorani, translated in English by Anand T. Hingorani], Publication Division, Ministry of Information & Broadcasting,

Government of India, New Delhi, fifth edition, 2000.

Gandhi, M. K., *Fellowship of Faiths and Unity of Religions*, Gandhi Book House, New Delhi, 1990.

Gandhi, P. K. (ed) *Social Action Through Law--Partnership for Social Justice*, Concept Publishing Company, New Delhi, 1985, pp. 19-32.

Gangadhar (ed), *Change and Development,* Viking, New Delhi, 2002.

Gangrade, K.D., *Moral Lessons From Gandhi's autobiography and other Essays*, Gandhi Smriti and Darshan Smriti and Concept Publishing Company, New Delhi, 2004.

Gangrade, K.D., *Social Work and Development - Role of Religion, Caste in Three Delhi Villages*, Northern Book Centre, New Delhi, 1986.

Gangrade, K. D., *Gandhi since 50 years of Azadi*, Gandhi Smriti and Darshan Samiti, New Delhi, 1999.

Gangrade, K.D., *Constructive Programmes,* Gandhi Smriti and Darshan Samiti, New Delhi, 2001.

Gangrade, K.D., *Gandhian Path to Development,* Gandhi Smriti and Darshan Samiti, 1997.

Gangrade, K.D., *Working with Community at the Grassroot Level—Strategies and Programmes*, Radha Publications, New Delhi, 2001.

Gangrade, K.D. and Sooryamoorthy, *NGOs in India—A Cross-Sectional Study*. Greenwood Press, Westport, Connecticut, London, 2001.

Gangrade, K.D. and Radhakrishnan (eds), *Gandhi and the Changing Facets of India*, Gandhi Smriti and Darshan Samiti, New Delhi, 1998.

Ganguli, B.N., *Gandhi's Social Philosophy—Perspective and Relevance*, National Gandhi Museum and Radha Publications, 2000.

Ganguli, B.N., (ed.), *Gandhi's Social Philosophy: Perspective and Relevance,* Vikas Publishing House Pvt. Ltd., Delhi, 1973, pp. 453.

Gedam, Ratnakar, *Socio-economic Development in India,* Anmol Publication, New Delhi, 1991.

Gedam, Ratnakar, *Economic Growth in India,* Anmol Publication, New Delhi, 1991.

Gore, M.S., *Social Development: Challenges faced in and Unequal and Plural Society*, Rawat Publications, Jaipur, 2003.

Gore, M.S., *Unity in Diversity: The Indian Experience in nation-building*, Rawat Publications, Jaipur and New Delhi, 2002.

Guha, B.P., *Economic Development,* B.R. Publication, New Delhi, 1998.

Gupta, R.K., *Social Action and Non-violence,* ICPR, New Delhi, 1995.

Gupta, Shyam Ratna and Schottli, (eds), *Good Citizenship Rights, Duties, Responsibilities*, Citizens Development Society, New Delhi, in association with Friedrich Nauman Stiftung, Kings Winter, West Germany, Roli Books International, 1987.

Halmos, Paul, *The Personal and the Political-Social Work and Political Action*, Hutchinson of London, 1978.

Hussain, Abid S., *Gandhiji and Communal Unity*, Orient Longmans, New Delhi, on behalf of Gandhi Peace Foundation, New Delhi, 1969.

Iyer, Raghavan, (ed.), *The Essential Writings of Mahatma Gandhi,* Oxford University Press, Delhi, 1991, pp. 441.

Iyer, Raghavan, (ed.), *The Moral and Political wirings of Mahatma Gandhi,* Volume III, Clarendon Press, Oxford, 1987, pp. 641.

Jack, Homer A., (ed.), *The Gandhian Reader—A Source of his Life and Writings,* Samta Book, Madras, 1983, pp. 532.

Jain, R. B., *Environmental Stewardship and Sustainable Development*, Friedrich Ebert Stiftung, New Delhi, 1997.

Jain, R. B. (ed) *Environmental Security in South Asia*, published by the International Institute for Environmental Strategies and Security, Canada, 2002.

James, Mac Gregor Burns, *Leadership*, Harper Books, New York, 1978.

John, Bondurant, Satyagraha *versus* Duragraha, in *Gandhi, His Relevance For Our Times* (ed) G. Ramchandra, Bharatiya Vidya Bhawan, 1964.

Joshi, Kireet, *Philosophy of Value-Oriented Education: Theory and Practice*. Indian Council of Philosophical Research, New Delhi. 2002.

Joshi, Y. G., and Verma, (ed) *Social Environment for Sustainable Development*, Rawat Publications, Jaipur and New Delhi, 1998.

Kher, V.B., (ed.), *Social Service Work and Reform*, Vol. I, Navjeevan Publishing House, Ahmedabad, 1976, pp. 412.

Kher, V.B., (ed.), *Social Service Work and Reform*, Vol. II, Navjeevan Publishing House, Ahmedabad, 1976, pp. 376.

Kher, V.B., (ed.), *Social Service Work and Reform*, Vol. III, Navjeevan Publishing House, Ahmedabad, 1976, pp. 467.

Kothari, D. S., *Some thoughts on Science and Religion*, Shri Raj Kishen Jain Charitable Trust, New Delhi, 1977.

Kumar, Mahendra and Low, Peter (eds) *Legacy and Future of Non-violence*, Gandhi Peace Foundation, 1996.

Lal, A.K. (ed) *Social Exclusion Essays in Honour of Dr. Bindheswar Pathak* (Vol. 1), Concept Publishing Company, New Delhi, 2003.

Lindley, Mark, *Gandhi and the World Today (1998)—An American View*, Centre for Gandhian Studies University of Kerala, Trivandrum, 1999.

Mahapatra, L.K., *Tribal Development in India*, Vikas Publishing House, New Delhi, 1984.

Maharajan, M., (ed.), *Gandhian Thought—A Study of Tradition and Modernity*, Sterling Publishers Pvt. Ltd., New Delhi, 1996, pp. 164.

Maharishi, Anuradha and Dhillon, *A Common Cause, NGOs & Civil Society*, National Foundation for India, 2002.

Majumdar, A.K., *Panchayat Politics and Community Development*, Radha Publication, New Delhi, 1996.

Majumdar, A.K., *Historical and Conceptual Development of Panchayati Raj*, Radha Publication, New Delhi, 1996.

Majumdar, Annu Menon, (ed.), *Social Welfare in India, Mahatma Gandhi's Contributions*, Asia Publishing House, New Delhi, 1964, pp. 179.

Malagatti, Aravinda and Malagatti, Dharani Devi, *What Gandhi says about Ambedkar*, University of Mysore, 2000.

Mamali, Catalinn S., *The Gandhian Mode of Economics*, Gujarat Vidyapith, Ahmedabad, 1998.

Marulasiddaiah, H. M. (ed), *Dimension of Bhakti Movement in India*, Akhil Bharatha Sharana Sahitya Parishat, Mysore, 1998.

Marulasiddaiah, H. M., *The Elephant in the Mirror*, Indian Academy of Social Sciences, Karnataka Chaper, Bangalore, 2000.

Mehrotra, Santosh, *Development with a Human Face*, Oxford University Press, New York, 1997.

Mehta, Prof. J.K., *Gandhian Thought*, Ashish Publishing House, New Delhi, 1995, pp. 243.

Mehta, Usha, *Mahatma Gandhi and Humanism*, Bharatiya Vidya Bhawan, Mumbai, Mani Bhawan Gandhi Sangrahalaya, Mumbai and Gandhi Smriti and Darshan Samiti, New Delhi, 2000.

Mishra, Anil Dutta (ed) *Perspectives on Human Rights*, Radha Publications, New Delhi, 2002.

Mishra, Anil Dutta, (ed) *Gandhism after Gandhi*, Mittal Publications, New Delhi, 1999.

Mishra, G.P., (ed.), *Gandhi To-day's India*, Ashish Publishing House, New Delhi, 1979, pp. 233.

Mishra, S. N., Mishra, Anil D. and Mishra, Sweta (eds), *Public Governance and Decentralisation* (Essays in Honour of T.N. Chaturvedi), Mittal Publications, New Delhi, 2003.

Moddie, A. D. (ed) *The Concept of work in Indian Society*, Indian Institute of Advanced Study, Shimla in association with Manohar Publications, New Delhi, 1990.

Mohan, Surendra and Tripathi, Chandrabhal (eds), *Regeneration of India—Its Imperatives*, Society for Communal Harmony, New Delhi, 2001.

Mukherjee, K. K., *Emerging Societal Changes and Voluntary Organisations. Challenges and Responses*, Gram Niyojan Kendra, Ghaziabad, 1994.

Mukhopadhyay, Marmar, (ed) *Education for a Global Society Interfaith-dimensions*, Shipra Publication, New Delhi, 2003.

Nanda, B.R., *Gandhi and His Critics*, Oxford University Press, Bombay, Calcutta, Madras, Delhi, 1985, pp. 178.

Owens, Edgar and Shaw, Robert, *Development Reconsidered Bridging the Gap Between Government and People*, Oxford, New Delhi, 1972.

Oza, D.K., *Voluntary Action and Gandhian Approach*, National Book Trust, New Delhi, 1991.

Paige, Glenn D., *Non-killing - Global Practical Science*, Gandhi Media Centre, New Delhi, 2002.

Parel, Anthony (ed) *Gandhi, Freedom and Self Rule*, Vistaar Publications, New Delhi, 2002.

Parel, Anthony J., *Hind Swaraj and Other Writings*, Cambridge University Press, 1997, pp. 208.

Pasricha, Ashu, *Gandhian Approach to Integrated Rural Development*, Shipra Publication, Delhi, 2000.

Patel Chaya (ed) *Social Work Practice*, Religio-Philosophical Foundations, Essay in honour of Prof. Indira Patel, Rawat Publications, Jaipur and Delhi, 1999.

Prasad, Bimal, *Gandhi, Nehru and JP - Studies in Leadership*, Chanakya Publications, Delhi, 1985.

Prasad, Nageshwar, *Gandhi Historical and Contemporary Perspectives*, Segment Book Distributors, New Delhi, 1990, pp. 175.

Radhakrishnan, N., and Vasudevan N., (eds) *Gandhi in the Global Village*, Gandhi Media Centre, New Delhi, & Centre for Global Nonviolence, Hawaii, 1998.

Radhakrishnan, S., *The Bhagvadgita*, Blackkie & Son India Ltd., Mumbai ninth impression, 1970.

Raghavan, N. Iyer, *The Moral and Political thought of Mahatma Gandhi*, Oxford University Press, New York, 1973.

Ranade, R. D., *Spiritual Awakening in Gandhi and other Indian Saints*, Sarva Seva Sangh Prakashan, Varanasi, 2003.

Ranganathananda, Swami, *Science and Religion*, Advaita Ashram, Kolkata, 1976.

Rani, Asha, (ed.), *Gandhian Non-violence and India's Freedom Struggle*, Shree Publishing House, Delhi, 1981, pp. 348.

Ray, Biswanath. *Socio-economic Transformation in India*, Kanishka Publication, New Delhi, 1996.

Reddy, Sanjeev, P. L., Singh, Jaideep and Tiwari, R.K., *Pursuit of Institutional Excellence*, (Essays in Honour of V.K.N. Menon). Indian Institute of Public Administration, New Delhi, 2004.

Reddy, Sanjeev, P. L. Singh and Mishra, S. N., *Sardar Vallabhbhai Patel - The Nation Builder*, Indian Institute of Public Administration, New Delhi, 2004.

Risher, William, *Towards Sustainable Development*, Rawat Publications, New Delhi, 1997.

Rosenblatt, Aaron, Welter, Marianne Wojciechowski, *The Adelphi Experiment - Accelerating Social Work Education*, Council of Social Work Education, New York, 1976.

Sankhdher, M.M., (ed.), *Understanding Gandhi Today*, Deep & Deep Publications, New Delhi, 1996, pp. 191.

Saxena, D. N. (ed) *Citizenship Development and Fundamental Duties*, Abhinav Publications, 1988.

Seitz, John L. *The Politics of Development - An Introduction to Global Issues*, Popular Prakashan, Mumbai, 1990.

Sen, Amartya, *Choice Welfare and Development*, Oxford University Press, Delhi, 1995.

Sen, Amartya, *Commodities and Capabilities*, Oxford University Press, New Delhi, 1999.

Sen, Amartya, *Development as Freedom*, Oxford University Press, New York, 1999.

Sen, Amartya, *Hunger and Public Action*, Oxford University Press, New Delhi, 1993.

Sen, Amartya, *Indian Development*, Oxford University Press New Delhi, 1996.

Sen, Amartya, *Indian Economic Development*, Oxford University Press, New Delhi, 1995.

Sen, Amartya, *Poverty and Famines*, Oxford University Press, New Delhi, 1999.

सेन, अमर्त्य, *भारत विकास की दिशाएं,* राजपाल एन्ड सन्स, नई दिल्ली, 2000.

सेन, अमर्त्य, *भारतीय राज्यों का विकास,* राजपाल एण्ड सन्स, नई दिल्ली, 2000.

Sethi, J.D., *International Economic Disorder and a Gandhian Solution,* Vikas Publishing House, New Delhi, 1990.

Setty, E.D., *Janmabhoomi-Rural Development,* HRD Institute of Hyderabad, Andhra Pradesh, 2001.

Shah, A.M. Baviskar and Ramaswamy, E. A. (eds), *Social Structure and Change,* Vol. 5, Religion and Kinship, Sage Publications, New Delhi, 1998.

Sharma, D.N., *Dilemmas of Development,* Vikas Publishing House, New Delhi, 1993.

Sharma, D.N., *Economic Development and Environment,* Roy, Kartik, Oxford University Press, Kolkata, 1995.

Sharma, K.D., *Impact of Gandhi on Rural Development and Social Change,* Mohit Publication, New Delhi, 1997.

Sharp, Gene, *Gandhi as Political Strategist, with Essays on Ethics and Politics,* Gandhi Media Centre, New Delhi, Indian Edition, 1999.

Singh, J.K., *Dynamics of Rural Development,* Janaki Prakashan Patna, 1996.

Singh, L.R., *National Building and Development Process,* Rawat Publications, Jaipur, 1994.

Singh, Narendra, *Peace and Development,* Lancer Publication, New Delhi, 1996.

Singh, Ramjee, *Gandhi and the Twenty First Century,* Peace Publication, New Delhi, 1993.

Singh, Ramjee (ed), *Gandhi and the Future of Humanity,* Manak Publication, New Delhi, 1997.

Singh, Ramjee (ed), *Gandhian Perspective on Population and Development,* Concept Publication, New Delhi, 1996.

Singh, Ramjee (ed.), *The Relevance of Gandhian Thought,* Classical Publishing Company, New Delhi, pp. 295.

Singh, Savita (ed) *Empowerment of Women—Miles to Go,* International Centre of Gandhian Studies & Research, Gandhi Smriti and Darshan Samiti, New Delhi. 2001.

Sinha, B. P. (ed) *Points of View, Essays in Memory of Shri Ranchor* Prasad, Published by Ranchor Prasad Commemoration Committee, Patna, 2000.

Siwach, Rajkumar, *Voluntary Organisations and Social Welfare*, Shankar Publication, Delhi, 2004.

Srinivas, M. N., *Religion and Society among the Gorgs of South India*, Oxford University Press, New Delhi, 2003.

Stiglitz Joseph E., *Globalization and its Discontents*, Allen Lane [an imprint of] Penguin Books, 2002.

Swami, Ranjeet, *Gandhi--Appropriate Technology and Rural Development*, Gandhi Smriti and Darshan Samiti, 1995.

Swaminathan, K., C.N. Patel (ed.), *A Gandhi Reader*, Orient Longman, Madras, 1988, pp. 172.

Thomas, Mark, (ed.), *Gandhi and His Ashrams*, Popular Prakashan, Bombay, 1993, pp. 279.

Tilak, Bal Gangadhar, *Srimad Bhagvadgita-Rahasya*, (eightieth edition) publishers Tilak, D.J. and Tilak, S.S., Pune, 1995.

Tisdell Clem and Sen Raj Kumar, (eds) *Economic Globalisation, Social Conflicts, Labour and Environment Issues*, Enward Elgan Cheltenham, U.K. Northampton, M.A. USA.

Unithan, T. K. N., *Gandhi & Social Change*, Rawat Publications, Jaipur, 1979, pp. 266.

Upadhyaya, H.C., *Modernisation and Rural Development*, Anmol Publication, New Delhi, 1991.

Varma, Ravindra, *The Spiritual Basis of Satyagraha*, Navajivan Publishing House, Ahmedabad, 2001.

Vasudevan, K., *Gandhian Economics*, Bharatiya Vidya Bhawan, Bombay, 1967.

Visvesvaran, P. K., (ed) *Social Work Today, Present Realities and Future Prospects*, The Madras School of Social Work, Golden Jubilee Commomorative Volume, 2002.

□□□

Index

□□□